Cybercrime: An Introduction to an Emerging Phenomenon

George E. Higgins, Ph.D.
University of Louisville

D1511832

Mc Graw Hill **Higher Education**

Boston   Burr Ridge, IL   Dubuque, IA   New York   San Francisco   St. Louis
Bangkok   Bogotá   Caracas   Kuala Lumpur   Lisbon   London   Madrid   Mexico City
Milan   Montreal   New Delhi   Santiago   Seoul   Singapore   Sydney   Taipei   Toronto

The McGraw-Hill Companies

Higher Education

This book is printed on acid-free paper.

1 2 3 4 5 6 7 8 9 0 DOC/DOC 0 9

ISBN: 978-0-07-340155-3
MHID: 0-07-340155-2

Editor in Chief: *Michael Ryan*
Editorial Director: *Beth Mejia*
Publisher: *Frank Mortimer*
Executive Editor: *Katie Stevens*
Editorial Coordinator: *Teresa Treacy*
Executive Marketing Manager: *Leslie Oberhuber*
Media Project Manager: *Ron Nelms*
Production Editor: *Alison Meier*
Production Service: *Jill Eccher*
Design Coordinator: *Margarite Reynolds*
Cover Design: *Kay Lieberherr*
Photo Credit: *Chad Baker/Getty Images*
Production Supervisor: *Louis Swaim*
Composition: *10/12 Palatino by Aptara®, Inc.*
Printing: *45# New Era Matte Plus, R. R. Donnelley & Sons*

Credits: A credits section for this book begins on page 181 and is considered an extension of the copyright page.

Library of Congress Cataloging-in-Publication Data

Cybercrime : an introduction to an emerging phenomenon/edited by George E. Higgins. — 1st ed.
   p. cm.
Includes index.
ISBN-13: 978-0-07-340155-3 (alk. paper)
ISBN-10: 0-07-340155-2 (alk. paper)
1. Computer crimes.   I. Higgins, George E.
HV6773.C918 2010
364.16′8—dc22

2009022638

The Internet addresses listed in the text were accurate at the time of publication. The inclusion of a Web site does not indicate an endorsement by the authors or McGraw-Hill, and McGraw-Hill does not guarantee the accuracy of the information presented at these sites.

Table of Contents

1   Introduction to Cybercrime   1

2   Cyberharassment/Cyberstalking   5

Sexual harassment on the Internet   5

*Online aggressor/targets, aggressors, and targets: A comparison of associated
    youth characteristics   24*

3   Cyberpornography   40

*Demographic characteristics of persons using pornography in three
    technological contexts   40*

Adult social bonds and use of Internet pornography   55

4   Cyberfraud/Identity Theft   67

Who are you? How to protect against identity theft   67

A contextual framework for combating identity theft   74

5   Intellectual Property Theft   88

Causes and Prevention of Intellectual Property Crime   88

*Digital piracy: Assessing the contributions of an integrated self-control theory
    and social learning theory   109*

6   Hackers, Crackers, and Phone Phreaks   129

Hackers   129

7   Criminal Justice and Cyberspace   133

*Perceptions of local and state law enforcement concerning the role of computer
    crime investigative teams   133*

An ad hoc review of digital forensic models   151

8   Future Issues   159

Theory and policy in online privacy   159

Index   183

Preface

Cybercrime can no longer be trivialized as merely "street-oriented crime" perpetrated in a cyber environment. Rather, this emerging area of criminal justice and criminology is comprised of many sophisticated forms of violation such as cyberharassment, cyberstalking, identity theft, and intellectual property theft. The goal of this text is to provide students, instructors, and scholars with the basic framework for understanding, discussing, and critically analyzing this timely issue

I hope that in reading this text, others will recognize the significance and relevance of cybercrime in their own lives. If this is achieved, this book will have been a success.

George E. Higgins

1

Introduction

In the United States, two revolutions have taken place. At the turn of the 20th century, an industrial revolution took place where technology changed. For instance, electricity was harnessed and used in innovative ways. Toward the end of the 20th century, a second revolution took place. This revolution also centered around technology. Unlike the first revolution, the second revolution was more about the development of technology. The development of high technology has led to several different forms of criminal behavior. According to Moore (2004), crimes using this technology may be considered high-technology crimes.

Technology, Computer Crimes, and Cybercrimes

Technology crimes generally involve the use of any high-technology device, such as computers, telephones, check-reading machines, and credit-card machines. An example of a technology crime involving computers is identity theft through spam e-mail (i.e., unsolicited and unwanted e-mail). An individual who receives an unsolicited e-mail that asks for personal identifying information under the guise of some other form of activity is a spam e-mail that is likely sent from an identity thief.

A number of activities may be considered technology crimes. However, two forms of technology crimes are of interest in this book—computer crimes and cybercrimes. Computer crimes are generally activities that involve a computer but are made illegal by statute. In general, computer crimes may be classified in three genres. First, the computer may be used as an instrument. For instance, a computer may be the instrument that an individual uses to perpetrate a crime. That is, individuals may choose to illegally download music, movies, or software using a computer.

Second, the computer may be the object of the criminal activity. Some are interested in the structure of the computer making the computer the object of the criminal activity. For instance, some individuals (hackers) may wish to intrude upon the connection of an individual's computer. That is, hackers are likely to use various means to infiltrate another's computer.

Third, the computer may be the repository of criminal activity. Some may use the computer to maintain the "spoils" of criminal activity. For instance, some may use their computer to house their illegal downloads or to maintain different forms of pornography that is shared over the Internet.

Technology crimes may also be crimes that make use of computers over a network. A network links multiple computers in some way (through wires or wireless connections). These types of crimes are generally considered cybercrimes. The main network that is generally associated with cybercrimes is the Internet.

The Internet is the discovery of J. C. R. Licklider (Licklider & Clark, 1962). Licklider had developed an idea for connecting a set of computers that would allow for the easy accessibility of information—the "Galactic Network." The Galactic Network, now known as the Internet, creates an information highway that enables people of all ages, races, and sexes to expand their social circles and improve their ability to communicate (Roberts, Foehr, Rideout, & Brodie, 1999; Rosenbaum, Altman, Brodie, Flournoy, Blendon, & Benson, 2000). The empirical literature has shown that adolescents and adults use the Internet frequently (Beebe, Asche, Harrison, & Quinlan, 2004; Lenhart, Rainie, & Lewis, 2001; Mitchell, Finkelhor, & Wolak, 2003; United States Department of Commerce, 2002).

The Internet does not provide much security. That is, the Internet is an open system that allows anyone with a computer and a phone connection to participate. With the openness of the Internet, crime (an act of force or fraud) and deviance (an act that goes against societal norms) are easy to perpetrate. In addition to the perpetration, the Internet makes victimization an issue. The Internet brings about special legal issues that are important for understanding the difference between crime, deviance, and criminal justice responses. The legal issues that are important for criminologists include cyberharassment/cyberstalking, cyberpornography, identity theft, intellectual property theft, and hackers. These forms of cybercrimes may be perpetrated in several different ways over the Internet.

One will notice that computer crimes and cybercrimes are very much the same. A computer crime cannot be perpetrated without a computer. A cybercrime cannot be performed without a computer and a network. Thus, the differences between a computer crime and cybercrime are trivial. An individual cannot illegally download music, movies, or software without the use of technology that include computers. Therefore, the closeness of the two views suggests that computer crimes can be considered cybercrimes.

Extent of Cybercrimes

The true extent of cybercrimes is unknown. Some evidence indicates that some forms of cybercrimes are growing. For instance, the Business Software Alliance indicates that incidences of illegal downloading of software fluctuate. The Motion Picture Association of America (MPAA) indicates that illegal downloading of music continues to grow. The United States Federal Trade Commission indicates that identity theft and fraud cases that involve computers are continuing to grow as well. So too are different forms of pornography. These examples indicate that cybercrimes are increasing.

The perpetration and the continuation of cybercrimes create issues concerning the location of the act. For instance, an individual making pornography of children may be in Russia while distributing the pornography in Spain. This suggests that cybercrime is a fluid activity that takes place worldwide. The worldwide nature of cybercrime makes law enforcement, prosecution, and defense of the behavior difficult because no clear jurisdiction is evident in many forms of the behavior.

Purpose of the Book

The purpose of this book is to provide readers (private citizens, investigators, academics, and students) with an introduction to cybercrime as an emerging issue. As mentioned earlier, cybercrime is increasing along with the advent of new technologies. These new technologies and the changing environment of criminal activity mean that both private citizens and those interested in criminal justice need to be aware of different forms of cybercrimes. The reality is that private citizens and those in the criminal justice system, including academics, will encounter cybercrimes. That said, this book is not able to account for all forms of cybercrimes; it will not make an individual an expert in the area of cybercrime. But it will provide an introductory orientation to these emerging criminal behaviors and an introduction to their major forms. This introduction begins with the following themes.

Chapter 2—Cyberharassment

The issue of harassment (an intentional act of aggression of an individual or group toward another individual or group) is a major issue offline as well online in the cyber environment. Some researchers have found harassment to be one of the more pervasive forms of behavior in society. The cyber environment is not any different. This chapter orients the reader to the issues that surround cyberharassment. Further, it introduces the reader to a typology of cyberharassment. Then, it provides the reader with an example of an important form of cyberharassment—cyberbullying.

Chapter 3—Cyberpornography

This chapter introduces the reader to cyberpornography, which refers to explicit sexual material that is available over the Internet. The use of sexually explicit material is not a new crime, the modern use of underage individuals is new. Further, the reader is introduced to issues surrounding the distribution and production of pornography using the Internet. This chapter also includes information showing the impact that different forms of technology have on using pornography. The chapter also includes information about who is likely to use pornography over the Internet and why these individuals are likely to do so.

Chapter 4—Identity Theft

In this chapter, the reader is introduced to issues of identity theft. Identity theft involves financial or other personal information stolen with the intent of establishing another person's identity as the thief's own. In this chapter, the definition of identity theft is broadened along with the definition of an identity thief. It emphasizes tactics that are available to reduce instances or the likelihood of becoming an identity theft victim.

Chapter 5—Intellectual Property Theft

This chapter introduces the reader to intellectual property and defines and describes intellectual property theft. The theoretical issues or reasons why individuals may produce this type of behavior are presented. Next, the broad topic of intellectual property theft is narrowed to focus on digital piracy. The causes of digital piracy are explored.

Chapter 6—Hackers

In this chapter, the reader is introduced to hackers. Issues surrounding hackers are defined and described. Hackers are described in the context of a subculture (a culture within a culture).

Chapter 7—Criminal Justice and Cyberspace

In this chapter, the reader is introduced to the technological needs of criminal justice (law enforcement). The chapter illuminates the key issues that surround the development of law enforcement training. The chapter also defines and describes several models of an emerging field—digital forensics.

Chapter 8—Future Issues

This chapter, introduces the reader to new issues that will be emerging as cybercrimes continue to change and grow in number and magnitude. For instance, the chapter presents issues of privacy and the conflicts that arise in this area.

Discussion Questions

1. What is a technology crime?
2. What is a computer crime? What is a cybercrime?
3. Discuss the similarities of computer crimes.

2

Cyberharassment

Harassment is an intentional act of aggression of an individual or group toward another individual or group. This definition of harassment includes several different forms of behavior; however, sexual harassment and bullying behaviors are probably the best-known anecdotal forms of the behavior.

Sexual harassment is a pervasive behavior in society. The behavior occurs in multiple settings including work, school, military installations, and social gatherings. The cyber environment is not immune to sexual harassment. This form of behavior is increasing and important.

The first paper in this chapter, written by Azy Barak, defines sexual harassment offline. Barak then outlines different forms of sexual harassment that occur online. This outline is then used to develop a typology of online sexual harassment. Barak next delves into some of the cases of online sexual harassment, a discussion that leads naturally into the dynamics of online sexual harassment. Barak then presents the potential effects of online sexual harassment and proposes some strategies for reducing instances of online sexual harassment.

The second paper in this chapter, written by Ybarra and Mitchell, seeks to explore issues surrounding perpetration of online harassment and the victimization that results. Ybarra and Mitchell define Internet harassment (cyberharassment) and move into issues that surround cyberbullying. They use national data to identify and examine the characteristics of perpetrators (aggressors) and victims.

SEXUAL HARASSMENT ON THE INTERNET

AZY BARAK   *University of Haifa*

Sexual harassment (SH) is a well-known social problem that affects people at work, school, military installations, and social gatherings (for a comprehensive review, see Paludi & Paludi, 2003; Sbraga & O'Donohue, 2000). A worldwide phenomenon (Barak, 1997), it has been thoroughly investigated in recent decades in terms of prevalence, correlates, individual and organizational outcomes, and prevention; the range of studies provides an interdisciplinary perspective covering psychological, sociological, medical, legal, and educational aspects of the phenomenon. SH potentially relates to any human being; however, in fact, most victims are women (Gruber, 1997; Paludi & Paludi, 2003); other target populations—men, homosexuals, and children—are sexually harassed, too, although to a lesser degree. Similarly, most victims of SH on the Internet are women, though other populations have been targeted as well (Barnes, 2001). The purpose of the current article is to review the limited existing professional literature that refers to SH in cyberspace, to propose a typology—equivalent to that offline—of types of SH on the Internet, to analyze the dynamics of online SH, to review what is known about the effects of SH on the Internet, and to propose a comprehensive approach for preventing SH on the Internet.

The Internet provides an environment in which healthy and pathological behaviors may be pursued (Suler, 1999). Indeed, the Internet is known to possess the two contradictory aspects, as it is exploited for good or for evil purposes (Barak & King, 2000). Joinson (2003), in a thoughtful review, explored how new technological tools have constructive, positive aspects for people's advancement and joy, as well as destructive, negative aspects that humiliate, terrorize, and block social progress. Similarly, specifically in the context of women using the Internet, Morahan-Martin (2000) noted the "promise and perils" facing female Net users. SH and offense on the Internet is considered a major obstacle to the free, legitimate, functional, and joyful use of the Net, as these acts drive away Net users as well as cause significant emotional harm and actual damage to those who remain users, whether by choice or by duty. The objective of this article is to act as a catalyst for needed research and absent theoretical analysis (cf. Adam, 2002) in this important area and to provide a framework for prevention so that, eventually, the positive face of the Internet will prevail.

Offline Sexual Harassment

SH is a prevalent phenomenon in face-to-face, social environments (Gutek & Done, 2001; Paludi & Paludi, 2003; Sbraga & O'Donohue, 2000). It is widespread at work (e.g., Petrocelli & Repa, 1998; Richman et al., 1999), schools of all levels (Matchen & DeSouza, 2000; McMaster, Connolly, Pepler, & Craig, 2002; Timmerman, 2003), and the military (Fitzgerald, Drasgow, & Magley, 1999; Fitzgerald, Magley, Drasgow, & Waldo, 1999). SH is not a local phenomenon but exists in all countries and cultures, although its perceptions and judgment, and consequently definitions, significantly differ from one culture to another (Barak, 1997). Originally, Till (1980) classified SH behaviors into five categories, which were used for intensive assessment and research attempts to describe the behaviors and understand their causes, correlates, impact on victims, personal coping with occurrences, and more. Later, following a series of studies, suggestion was made to change the classification of types of SH into three distinct categories: gender harassment, unwanted sexual attention, and sexual coercion (Fitzgerald, Gelfand, & Drasgow, 1995).

Gender harassment involves unwelcome verbal and visual comments and remarks that insult individuals because of their gender or that use stimuli known or intended to provoke negative emotions. These include behaviors such as posting pornographic pictures in public or in places where they deliberately insult, telling chauvinistic jokes, and making gender-related degrading remarks. *Unwanted sexual attention* refers to uninvited behaviors that explicitly communicate sexual desires or intensions toward another individual. This category includes overt behaviors and comments, such as staring at a woman's breasts or making verbal statements that explicitly or implicitly propose or insinuate sexual activities. *Sexual coercion* involves putting physical or psychological pressure on a person to elicit sexual cooperation. This category includes actual, undesired physical touching, offers of a bribe for sexual favors, or making threats to receive sexual cooperation. Empirical research has found the three types of sexually harassing behaviors to be distinctive from one another, to be reliably and validly measurable in terms of perceptions and ratings of actual behaviors, and to correlate with various relevant personal, situational, and social factors (cf. Fitzgerald et al., 1995; Paludi & Paludi, 2003).

Sexual Harassment in Cyberspace

All three types of SH that exist offline also exist on the Internet. However, because of the virtual nature of cyberspace, most expressions of SH that prevail on the Net appear in the form of gender harassment and unwanted sexual attention. Nevertheless, as sexual coercion is the type that occurs the least often offline, too, it is impossible to conclude whether its relatively low prevalence in cyberspace is a result of the medium or its very nature. In terms of virtual imposition and assault, sexual coercion does exist nonetheless on the Net, though without, of course, the physical contact.

Gender harassment in cyberspace is very common. It is portrayed in several typical forms that Internet users encounter very often, whether communicated in verbal or in graphical formats and through either active or passive manners of online delivery. *Active verbal SH* mainly appears in the form of offensive sexual messages, actively initiated by a harasser toward a victim. These include gender-humiliating comments (e.g., "Leave the forum! Go to your natural place, the kitchen"), sexual remarks (e.g., "Nipples make this chat room more interesting"), so-called dirty jokes, and the like. All these are considered harassing and offending when they are neither invited or consented to nor welcomed by the recipient. This type of gender harassment is usually practiced in chat rooms and forums; however, it may also appear in private online communication channels, such as the commercial distribution through e-mail (a kind of spamming) of pornographic sites, sex-shop accessories, sex-related medical matters (such as drugs such as Viagra and operations similar to penis enlargement). Mitchell, Finkelhor, and Wolak (2003) reported that 62% of the adolescents in their survey received unwanted sex-related e-mails to their personal address, 92% from unknown senders. Of the 73% of respondents who unintentionally entered sex sites, most did so as a result of automatic linking, pop-up windows and unintended results while using a search engine.

Passive verbal SH, on the other hand, is less intrusive, as it does not refer to one user communicating messages to another. In this category, the harasser does not target harassing messages directly to a particular person or persons but, rather, to potential receivers. For instance, this type of harassment refers to nicknames and terms attached to a user's online identification or to personal details that are clearly considered offensive (e.g., CockSucker, WetPussy, XLargeTool, or GreatFuck for nicknames; "want a fuck?" in Internet relay chat (IRC) user's details, for offensive message). This category also includes explicit sex messages attached to one's personal details in communication software (e.g., "The best clit licker in Germany" in a personal info section of an ICQ User Details) or on a personal web page. Scott, Semmens, and Willoughby (2001) pointed out how flaming—a common, online, aggressive verbal behavior that typically and frequently appears in online communities—particularly creates a hostile environment for women. Although flaming is not necessarily aimed at women, it is considered, in many instances, to be a form of gender harassment because flaming is frequently, typically, and almost exclusively initiated by men. The common result of flaming in online communities is that women depart from that environment or depart the Internet in general—what has been termed *flamed out.* "Flamed out highlights the fact that the use of male violence to victimize women and children, to control women's behaviour, or to exclude women from public spaces entirely, can be extended into the new public spaces of the Internet" (Scott et al., 2001, p. 11). A constructive solution has been the design of women-only sanctuaries that offer communities where flaming is rare and obviously not identified with men.

Similar to verbal gender harassment, graphic-based harassment can be active and passive, too. *Active graphic gender harassment* mainly involves the intentional sending of erotic and pornographic still pictures or digital videos through individual online communication channels, such as e-mail, or posting them in an online environment. Pictures (and videos) might be judged as less or more offensive as a result of personal sensitivities, on one hand, and the explicitness and nature of their content, on the other. For instance, it could be expected that the picture of an innocent nude will be perceived as less offensive than the close-up picture of a vagina or the animation of a penis when ejaculating. *Passive graphic gender harassment* mainly includes pictures and movies published on web sites (Carnes, 2003; Gossett & Byrne, 2002). Contrary to materials published in designated pornography sites or online sex shops, where surfers usually deliberately choose to enter and know what materials to expect, SH comes into effect when web users do not know in advance and have no prior clue concerning what might later prove offensive to them. The massive use of forced pop-up windows and redirected links to porno sites makes this type of gender harassment highly prevalent.

The degree to which each of the four possibilities of gender harassment actually becomes subjectively experienced personal harassment is dependent on two major factors, one objective and one subjective: (a) the nature of the verbal or graphic stimulus in terms of explicitness, blatancy, or clamorousness, in addition to its continuity and repetition and (b) the personal attitudes, sensitivities, and preferences of the recipient. The combination of these factors determines the degree of subjective experience of offense.

Unwanted sexual attention in cyberspace usually necessitates direct personal verbal communication between a harasser and a victim. This may appear in personal communication, with messages directly relating to sex and sexuality. In this category are messages that refer to or ask about a victim's sex organs ("how large are your boobs?"), sex life ("when did you fuck last time?"), or intimate subjects ("do you have your period now?"); invite, insinuate, or offer sex-related activities ("I'd like to show you my super tool"); or impose sex-related sounds or images on a message. In contrast to gender harassment, unwanted sexual attention is specifically intended to solicit sexual cooperation of some sort, either virtual or in face-to-face contact. Obviously, for sexual attention or invitation to become harassing, it must be uninvited and unwelcome on the part of the victim. Therefore, a person who deliberately enters a chat room that clearly exists for the sake of finding partners, all the more so sex partners, is implicitly consenting, even inviting, sexual suggestions; hence, a message of sexual attention cannot be regularly considered harassing in this context. Unwanted sexual attention on the Internet may take place in public forums or chat rooms as well as in private communications. It may be communicated through synchronous or asynchronous channels. It may be verbal or nonverbal (i.e., via images and/or sounds) in nature. It may be explicit and direct or implicit and indirect. It may be as aggressive as suggesting sexual acts or more moderate in offering a massage or in asking a sex-related intruding question. Perpetrators of these types of behavior look for sex contact; however, their basic motive might be to cause emotional harm and to abuse victims, not necessarily to gain sexual cooperation.

Sexual coercion on the Internet is essentially different from gender harassment and unwanted sexual attention. Online sexual coercion entails the use of various means, available or possible online, to elicit sexual cooperation by putting some kind of pressure on a victim. Although the use of physical force is impossible online, victims might perceive threats to use physical force realistic on the Internet as in face-to-face situations. Likewise, explicit threats of some kind of harm to an Internet user or to his or her relatives or friends or threats of damage to a users' property might be a source of great anxiety. Even following a person's virtual tracks—by trailing his or her visits in chat rooms and forums—might cause panic. Thus, online stalking (also termed *cyberstalking*), if it involves sexual insinuations and hints, should be considered a form of psychological pressure to achieve sexual gains—that is, a form of sexual coercion (Adam, 2001; Deirmenjian, 1999; Griffith, Rogers, & Sparrow, 1998; Spitzberg & Hoobler, 2002).

However, online sexual coercion might be manifested by activities that more closely parallel offline situations. Experienced perpetrators, for example, might use their technical knowledge to break into a victim's personal computer and cause damage or threaten to do so. Sending frightening e-mails, sending viruses, and flooding an e-mail inbox are just a few examples of actual—as opposed to virtual—online sexual coercion (e.g., Dibbell, 1998).

Online sexual coercion might also be expressed in the form of bribes and seductions to achieve sexual gains. The online environment is an easy and convenient way to not only convey these types of messages, and perhaps especially effective for those perpetrators who have high writing skills, but also readily allows impersonation and cheating of innocent people. Thus, the use of incentives—baits—to encourage sexual cooperation is rather common. In this regard, one should note the well-documented phenomenon of pedophiles that operate online and seduce young children through the effective use of luring correspondence and the offer of various attractive baits (Durkin, 1997; Durkin & Bryant, 1999; Fontana-Rosa, 2001; Fulda, 2002; Quayle, Holland, Linehan, & Taylor, 2000; Quayle & Taylor, 2002, 2003). Likewise, the illegal practice of child pornography—in exploiting nude pictures of innocent children—makes use of baits and pressures to achieve children's cooperation to satisfy the needs of Internet-based pedophiles (Jenkins, 2001).

Cases and Prevalence of SH on the Internet

Various authors refer to SH in cyberspace and describe it as prevalent and risky. Unfortunately, no empirical survey on the extent and prevalence of SH in cyberspace has been carried out to date; thus, writers refer to general impressions and sporadic reports. For instance, Cooper, McLoughlin, Reich, and Kent-Ferraro (2002) referred to SH by e-mail as a common abuse of women in workplaces. Leiblum and Döring (2002) argued that the Internet provides a convenient vehicle, commonly used, to force sexuality on women through nonsocial (logging into web pages) and social (interpersonal communication) uses of the Net. McCormick and Leonard (1996) contended that because of the Net's so-called boys club atmosphere (apparently more relevant up to the mid-1990s than today), this environment is typically characterized by antiwomen attitudes and behaviors, including SH. Employing the same conception, Döring (2000) stated that men's created sexualized online atmosphere, mainly through pornographic materials, make unwanted sexual advances more likely. Adam (2001) argued that the phenomenon of SH on the Internet downplays the positive process of empowerment that women gain from egalitarian use of the Internet. McGarth and Casey (2002) saw cyberspace as an ideal environment for sex offenders to commit SH and imposition because of its unique characteristics (see below). Cooper, Golden, and Kent-Ferraro (2002) described the case of a man with a paraphilia-related disorder who obsessively used chat and e-mails to communicate his sexual thoughts to women. Cunneen and Stubbs (2000) reported a phenomenon in which Australian men solicited sex among Filipino women through the Internet in return for economic privileges. Barak and Fisher (2002) even predicted—in regard to the Internet's special characteristics—that the scope of sex offenses on the Internet would grow in the future. Several specific and restricted research studies provide some indication of the scope of SH behavior on the Internet. Griffiths (2000) reported the finding of a British survey that 41% of regular Internet female users had been sent unsolicited pornographic materials or been harassed or stalked on the Internet. Mitchell et al. (2001), in a survey of American teenagers, found that 19% of these youths—mostly older girls—had experienced at least one sexual solicitation while online in the past year (3% had received so-called aggressive solicitations). Goodson, McCormick, and Evans (2001) found that 24% of the female and 8% of the male college students who accessed online sexually explicit materials had experienced SH.

The Dynamics of SH on the Internet

A leading model pertaining to the causes and dynamics of SH was conceptualized by Pryor and colleagues (Pryor, Giedd, & Williams, 1995; Pryor, LaVite, & Stoller, 1993; Pryor & Whalen, 1997); it argues that SH behavior is determined by the interaction of a person's and a situation's characteristics. Consistent evidence supports this general equation (e.g., O'Hare & O'Donohue, 1998). There is no reason to believe that this process is different in the online environment: quite the contrary, because of the special characteristics informing online communication and online behavior. Specifically, it may be argued that the online disinhibition effect (Joinson, 1998, 1999, 2001; Suler, 2004) that promotes exposure of the so-called true self (McKenna & Seidman, in press), on one hand, and the special features of computer-mediated communication, on the other, produce human behaviors that more closely reflect authentic inner personal needs and desires. In reference to the personal factor in the equation, it has been well established that SH is not about sex, but about power (Barak, Pitterman, & Yitzhaki, 1995; Bargh, Raymond, Pryor, & Strack, 1995; Hoffspiegel, 2002; Wayne, 2000; Zurbriggen, 2000); that is, contrary to what seems to be an obvious reason for imposed sexual or sexually related activities—satisfaction of a perpetrator's sex drive—it has repeatedly been argued, and empirically supported, that sex is only a means of satisfying the perpetrator's need for power and domination. In cyberspace, the online disinhibition effect causes Internet users to behave less defensively and more naturally; that is, powerful factors that exist in and are typical of cyberspace, such as anonymity, invisibility, lack of eye contact, easy escape, and neutralizing of status, influence people to remove facades and masks when online to employ much fewer games and tricks and to reduce the use of existing social (or specific environmental) norms and behavioral standards in determining their behavior. Rather, when affected by the online disinhibition effect, users behave more consistently with their basic personality characteristics. At the same time, Internet communication, in general, is heavily affected by what has been termed "the Penta-A Engine" (Barak & Fisher, 2002), composed of anonymity, availability, affordability, acceptability, and aloneness. This engine is powerful enough to influence surfers' behaviors in a way that they become more daring, open, and ready to take risks in getting involved with sex-related activities than would otherwise be the case, or certainly to a much lesser extent, in the offline environment (Cooper, McLoughlin, & Campbell, 2000; Cooper, Scherer, Boies, & Gordon, 1999; Cooper & Sportolari, 1997).

Associating these factors—online disinhibition, together with elevated openness, venture, and bravado—with an atmosphere characterized by typical masculine attitudes (e.g., Kendall, 2000; Scott et al., 2001) produces a high probability of SH behaviors, especially by men against women. In masculine-dominated environments, the users' personal needs, values, desires, habits, and expectations become more transparent and blatant. Moreover, these personal proclivities apparently are accelerated by the effects of increased salience of social identities in online environments (e.g., Douglas & McGarty, 2001, 2002; Postmes, Spears, & Lea, 2002; Spears, Postmes, Lea, & Wolbert, 2002). According to this viewpoint (commonly referred to as SIDE, or Social Identity explanation of Deindividuation Effects), people in cyberspace may incline under certain circumstances to follow group standards of behavior rather than using their own standards; in other words, a social or a group identity (and expressed norms of behavior) may replace an individual identity (Reicher, 1987). These two explanatory models of the nature of online behavior, which imply that it is affected by disinhibition, by SIDE, or their combination, lay the grounds for the dynamic of online SH. The effects of online disinhibition might reinforce exposure of a person's true self or inner self (Barak, 2004; Bargh, McKenna, & Fitzsimons, 2002; McKenna & Seidman, in press); thus, people who possess personality traits engendering a proclivity to sexually harass (Barak & Kaplan, 1996; Pryor et al., 1993; Pryor & Stoller, 1994; Sheskin & Barak, 1997) might tend to behave according to their inner urge while online. Similarly, people who are affected by the SIDE process while in cyberspace might follow typical male-dominating, power-based, masculine attitudes and behaviors toward women.

The situational component of the equation is highly significant in cyberspace. Several of the unique characteristics of this environment not only encourage and reinforce harassment behaviors but also actually elicit them by providing an atmosphere in which harassers receive reinforcement to behave consistently with their SH proclivities. First, there are technical and practical features of the Internet that make antisocial behaviors more common. Thus, a harasser can take advantage of being unidentifiable, anonymous, and invisible, in addition to having immediate, easy-to-execute, almost untraceable escape route mechanisms (Postmes, Spears, Sakhel, & De Groot, 2001; Sassenberg & Kreutz, 2002; Suler & Phillips, 2000). In addition, the highly interactive nature of cyberspace allows reinforcement contingency, which apparently contributes to the maintenance and escalation of behaviors (cf. Rafaeli & Sudweeks, 1997). By the same token, one should keep in mind that the virtual environment enables people to provide themselves with relative protection from SH and other aggressions. Ben-Ze'ev (2003, 2004) has thoroughly discussed and analyzed the effects of emotional closeness and openness in cyberspace as a function of the relative privacy and the individually selective exposure experienced in this environment. Because surfers can increase their privacy (for instance, by using nicknames), in his view the potential harm from SH in cyberspace is reduced relative to offline encounters.

Second, the problematic legal status of the Internet, in addition to serious difficulties in enforcing laws and regulations pertaining to it, creates an environment in which breaking a law is common (e.g., Hiller & Cohen, 2002; Lessig, 1999). The (near) lack of clear legal boundaries, the absence of visible authorities and enforcement vehicles, and the absence of significant sanctions encourage people with criminal intentions to do what they would have been restrained from doing in offline situations. Related to this is the fact that the Internet has provided availability and easy access to public records, which include a great amount of private information that can be (and are) abused by cyberharassers and cyberstalkers (Tavani & Grodzinsky, 2002). The third and perhaps most critical ingredient that causes the online environment to be risky, particularly in regard to being victimized by SH, pertains to its culture and social norms. Cyberspace is a culture that is characterized by dominant masculine values and aggressive communications, one that perhaps also delivers a message that antiminority behaviors are welcome and even praised. Specifically in regard to women, quite a few online environments—practiced in chat rooms or in forums—are characterized by an antiwomen spirit, the attitude communicated by verbal messages, by providing links to selective sites, and by displaying obscene pictures. Research of offline environments have consistently shown the relationship between social norms and the phenomenon of SH, so that the degree of tolerance positively correlates with the extent and severity of harassment (e.g., Ellis, Barak, & Pinto, 1991; Folgero & Fjeldstad, 1995; Pryor et al., 1995; Williams, Fitzgerald, & Drasgow, 1999).

The interaction between a proclivity to sexually harass by people who possess problematic attitudes and are searching for an opportunity to execute behaviors to satisfy their needs and desires, which are magnified in cyberspace, and an environment that enables and often reinforces such behaviors clearly produces the dynamics of SH on the Internet; that is, a person who tends to sexually harass would not have behaved this way without the situational opportunities provided by the Net; SH would not be taking place in cyberspace without people whose needs and intentions are to sexually offend. The combination of an environment in which SH is invited by virtue of its special characteristics and people who possess a particular pattern of personality characteristics makes online SH almost inevitable. For this reason, as argued by Finn and Banach (2000), women who innocently use the Net for legitimate causes, such as seeking health information, may encounter dangerous situations. Similarly, women who seek online friendly connections often encounter harassment and "virtual rape" (Döring, 2000). Power-driven men express their attitudes on the Internet—even when gender differences are supposedly minimized (Sussman & Tyson, 2000). Women find it difficult to hide—their writings can be validly identified in most cases, despite invisibility, anonymity, and even the lack of personal handwriting (Koppel, Argamon, & Shimoni, 2002). Furthermore, gender inequality, as expressed by gender-stereotypic behaviors, has been found not to be reduced by online anonymity (Postmes & Spears, 2002). Apparently, different populations behave differently online, according to their culture and indigenous social norms—toward children (Calvert, 1999; Griffiths, 1997), women (Boneva & Kraut, 2002; Morahan-Martin, 1998) or ethnic groups (Back, 2002; Matei & Ball-Rokeach, 2002)—a fact that might trigger stereotypic, sometimes hostile, behaviors by other groups. In analyzing web pages and the self-expressions of men and women on the Net through their web presence, Miller and Arnold (2001) came to the conclusion that

> Internet provides new ways of being in the World, but not in a way which is intrinsically mysterious or different from other aspects of being. . . . The frames for action in cyberspace are not necessarily less (or more) problematical than in real life—because they are part of real life. (p. 92)

It is important to note, however, that perceptions of SH behaviors might be reinforced or, in contrast, lessened online. This was found by Biber, Doverspike, Baznik, Cober, and Ritter (2002), who compared in-person and online communication discourse media. They revealed that misogynist comments, nicknames, and comments about dress (all considered gender harassment) were rated more harassing when they appeared online than offline. Ben-Ze'ev (2003) explained the difference in judgmental standards by the difference between text-based and face-to-face communication. Requests for company, considered unwanted sexual attention, however, was rated more harassing offline than online. For this reason—perhaps consistent with the online disinhibition effect—it might be advisable to refer to hard evidence and professional judgment (though not perfect, too) in regard to evidence of SH in cases in which a law suit is threatened (McGarth & Casey, 2002).

Effects of SH on the Internet

Offline SH has a severe impact on its victims. Dansky and Kilpatrick (1997) reviewed a variety of empirical studies on the effects of SH and pointed to severe work-related and school-related effects (reduced performance and satisfaction, decreased motivation and morale, lower productivity, and the like), as well as psychological effects, reflected in psychological disorders, negative emotions, and related behavioral consequences. Similarly, O'Donohue, Downs, and Yeater (1998), in a broad review of the literature, found consistent negative psychological, occupational, and economic consequences for victims. In the same vein, Schneider, Swan, and Fitzgerald (1997) and Glomb et al. (1997) found a series of psychological and job-related negative effects of SH of working women in several different types of organizations. Munson, Hulin, and Drasgow (2000) found that experiences of SH by university employees yielded severe outcomes, independent of dispositional influences or response biases, van Roosmalen and McDaniel (1998) found that SH had direct effects on women's physical (e.g., nausea, sleeplessness) and mental health (e.g., loss of self-esteem, feelings of helplessness and isolation, depression). Furthermore, Harned and Fitzgerald (2002) found a link in three independent samples between SH and eating disorders, psychological distress, self-esteem, and self-blame—for women but not for men. Wonderlich et al. (2001), too, found a significant link between sexual assault and severe eating behaviors, sometimes many years after the abuse had taken place. Krakow et al. (2000) found sleeping disorders that consequently affected depression and suicidal proclivities. Pathe and Mullen (1997) reported that severe emotional (e.g., increased anxiety) and behavioral (nightmares, appetite disturbances) effects characterized most female victims of stalking. Stein and Barrett-Connor (2000) found significant effects of sexual assault on victims' health. Redfearn and Laner (2000) showed that women who were victims of sexual abuse had problematic effects in regard to their sexual attitudes and behaviors. Avina and O'Donohue (2002) reviewed the relevant literature and showed that the effects of SH on victims consistently met the criteria of post-traumatic stress disorder (PTSD). Davis, Coker, and Sanderson (2002) and McGuire and Wraith (2000), who reviewed the effects of stalking on victims, described the immense disruption to their lives, as well as increased physical injuries, health problems, PTSD, substance abuse, and contemplation of suicide.

In contrast to the above review, little is as yet empirically known about the effects of SH that is experienced on the Internet. In 1998, Morahan-Martin noted the domination of the Internet by male users, its aggressive language, and limited attention to ethics and netiquette, on one hand, and the avoidance by women of the free use of the Internet, on the other. Although much has changed in terms of women's presence on the Internet (Pew Internet Project, 2003; UCLA Center for Communication Policy, 2003), it seems that the social norms in relation to the status of women versus men, as well as of other minority groups (e.g., homosexuals, children), have a spillover effect, and they penetrate the Internet. Therefore, it is common to find reports, usually based on impressions and informal complaints, about the negative impact of SH of women on the Net (e.g., Döring, 2000; Finn & Banach, 2000). More specifically, Gáti, Tényi, Túry, and Wildmann (2002) reported a case describing a causal connection between the online SH of a 16-year-old girl and her developing of anorexia nervosa. Although a clear-cut, causal connection between traumatic life events and the development of eating disorders has not been established, this case clearly resembles descriptions reported by Harned and Fitzgerald (2002) in regard to offline SH effects.

Prevention of SH on the Internet

Generally, three parallel ways of preventing offline SH have been advised and executed: legislation and law enforcement, changing of the organizational-social culture, and education and training of potential victims as well as of potential harassers (cf. Paludi & Paludi, 2003; Sbraga & O'Donohue, 2000).

Legislation seems to be necessary to erect strict, well-defined boundaries for interpersonal sex-related behaviors and to define the sanctions attached to unlawful conduct (Gutek, 1997; Riger, 1991). Legislation also plays an important social role in communicating the social context of what is accepted and what is not in a given society and, thus, serves as a clear sign of values and morals. Law enforcement is necessary for implementing laws, so that they do not just remain theoretical declarations. Although legislation and law enforcement are of top priority offline and take place in all societies, their usefulness in cyberspace is only partial for a number of well-known reasons. For example, the owner of a computer server, the owner of a web site, and different web surfers might be located in different locations, including different countries, and therefore subject to different legal systems. In addition, there is the physical location of the server itself. Thus, a server may physically be located in Aruba and owned by a Brazilian who happens to reside in Morocco; a web site accessed by that server offers a chat room hosted by an Israeli who resides in France; in the chat room, an Australian man sexually harasses, by means of unwanted verbal sexual attention, a Danish female surfer who entered the site. In addition, because of anonymity, high-level privacy, invisibility, and the often lack of individual traces that characterize the Internet environment, the efficiency of enforcing the law is at best very partial.

As noted above, legal guidelines and procedures are desirable and highly important, but only secondary in combating SH. As Barak (1992) argued and as has been consistently found in places where prevention attempts were implemented and followed up (e.g., Bell, Quick, & Cycyota, 2002; O'Hare-Grundmann, O'Donohue, & Peterson, 1997), effective means of combating SH should include two major aspects: changing the culture and norms in which SH might take place, and educating potential victims and harassers. By focusing on these two independent factors—referring as they do to the situation and to the personal components of the SH equation reviewed above—the behavioral product, it is believed, will be changed (Pryor et al., 1993, 1995). In a way, this approach parallels Joinson's (2003), which employs the strategic and motivated user and expected and emergent effects (SMEE); he argued that a surfer's behavioral and psychological outcomes are a function of the effects of the media (i.e., situation) and of user aspects (i.e., person).

Attempts at changing the culture in regard to SH should include the delivery of clear, consistent messages of zero tolerance for SH and the rejection of any leniency, in addition to stances that are antimisogyny, proegalitarian, advocating interpersonal sensitivity and acceptance, respecting minorities, and the like (Bell et al., 2002; Fitzgerald, Drasgow, et al., 1999; Glomb et al., 1997). Educational interventions may include awareness and training workshops for potential victims (e.g., Barak, 1994; Paludi & Barickman, 1998) as well as for potential harassers (e.g., Paludi & Barickman, 1998; Robb & Doverspike, 2001).

Although the targeting of specific populations offline, especially in local organizations, is doable and desirable, it is impractical in cyberspace; that is, it is practically impossible to change the culture of the Internet because of its limitless space and multicultural users. However, much can be done in local online communities through the exercise of responsible, dedicated leadership endorsing a firm anti-SH policy. Such an approach can be implemented through continuous messages, verbal messages and attractive banners, as well as by transparent sanctioning against any deviation from these standards. Obviously, this step will not prevent SH on the Internet as a whole; however, it will create safe havens for surfers who want to take advantage of online communities while avoiding ridicule and emotional harm. In Ben-Ze'ev's (2003) terms, this means that two unique personal values of online communication—privacy and openness—should be overtly and explicitly negotiated and settled between users to avoid unwanted, unwelcome behaviors.

In regard to educating potential victims and harassers, this can be carried out in various forms. For instance, the subject of SH on the Internet can be taught in schools in the framework of programs devoted to smart and safe Internet use (Dombrowski, LeMasney, Ahia, & Dickson, 2004; Oravec, 2000; Teicher, 1999). Such an educational intervention—offered to children, as well as to any vulnerable population—may review standards of netiquette behavior, together with tips on identifying hostile and malicious communications and impingement of privacy and boundaries (Plaut, 1997). Furthermore, online guides that contain explanations, recommendations, tips, and instructions can be posted on numerous sites to complement previous training and to highlight important issues. It is apparent that educational attempts will not prevent people with high proclivities to sexually harass resulting from their personal needs and dispositions; however, these will perhaps make them aware of possible negative outcomes, to themselves and to victims. It is hoped that for some of these people, educational intervention might change perceptions, attitudes, and values. At the very least, make them aware of considerations new to them and, thus, contribute to changing their potential problematic behaviors.

Conclusion

The Internet has a great potential to empower minorities and people who feel oppressed, weak, disadvantaged, or discriminated against. The empowerment process refers to a variety of groups, among them women (e.g., Döring, 2000; Harcourt, 1999, 2000), children (e.g., D'Alessandro & Dosa, 2001), the old (e.g., McMellon & Schiffman, 2002), ethnic minorities (Matei & Ball-Rokeach, 2002), and people who are disabled (Bowker & Tuffin, 2002). At the same time, however, cyberspace might be a dangerous, even degrading environment for these very same populations, thus functioning in an opposite direction from empowerment; namely, further weakening, humiliation, and alienation. SH exists on the Internet as much as it exists off the Internet; indeed, SH behaviors parallel those offline. The special characteristics of the Internet, such as anonymity, make this medium more prone to provide the means needed for unlawful and unethical behaviors, despite the ability of surfers to mask their identifying features as well as their ability to abruptly disconnect contact at will.

Although implementation of legal procedures and their enforcement on the Internet are practically impossible, steps could be taken to reduce the prevalence of SH on the Net. Attempts should be made at changing the violent, threatening, dominant, domineering, hostile, and malicious facets of the Internet culture by a consistent, comprehensive, and determined delivery of messages, as well as by setting leadership examples, using every means of communication available in cyberspace. Changing social norms and behavioral standards regarding the acceptance of and lenient attitudes toward SH will eventually influence many users and, consequently, affect the scope of SH.

Concomitant with attempts at modifying Internet culture, at least in indigenous communities, and notwithstanding the expected difficulties in executing this change, much effort should be made in designing and implementing educational interventions. These programs should focus on developing awareness and influencing values and attitude sets toward specific populations and on modifying specific, relevant target behaviors. The initiative to develop and operate such programs could be by governmental or public offices and interested associations. The social benefit and, consequently, the free effective use of the Net make such initiatives worthwhile, to say the least.

References

Adam, A. (2001). Cyberstalking: Gender and computer ethics. In E. Green & A. Adam (Eds.), *Virtual gender: Technology, consumption and identity* (pp. 209–224). London: Routledge.

Adam, A. (2002). Cyberstalking and Internet pornography: Gender and the gaze. *Ethics and Information Technology, 4,* 133–142.

Avina, C., & O'Donohue, W. (2002). Sexual harassment and PTSD: Is sexual harassment diagnosable trauma? *Journal of Traumatic Stress, 15,* 69–75.

Back, L. (2002). Aryans reading Adorno: Cyber-culture and twenty-first century racism. *Ethnic and Racial Studies, 25,* 628–651.

Barak, A. (1992). Combating sexual harassment. *American Psychologist, 47,* 818–819.

Barak, A. (1994). A cognitive-behavioral educational workshop to combat sexual harassment in the workplace. *Journal of Counseling and Development, 72,* 595–602.

Barak, A. (1997). Cross-cultural perspectives on sexual harassment. In W. O'Donohue (Ed.), *Sexual harassment: Theory, research, and treatment* (pp. 263–300). Boston: Allyn & Bacon.

Barak, A. (2004). Internet counseling. In C. D. Spielberger (Ed.), *Encyclopedia of applied psychology* (pp. 369–378). San Diego, CA: Academic Press.

Barak, A., & Fisher, W. A. (2002). The future of Internet sexuality. In A. Cooper (Ed.), *Sex and the Internet: A guidebook for clinicians* (pp. 267–280). New York: Brunner-Routledge.

Barak, A., & Kaplan, N. (1996). Relationships between personal characteristics and sexual harassment behaviours in male university professors. In *NATCON papers 1996* (pp. 261–273). Toronto, Canada: National Consultation on Career Development.

Barak, A., & King, S. A. (2000). The two faces of the Internet: Introduction to the special issue on the Internet and sexuality. *CyberPsychology and Behavior, 3,* 517–520.

Barak, A., Pitterman, Y., & Yitzhaki, R. (1995). An empirical test of the role of power differential in originating sexual harassment. *Basic and Applied Social Psychology, 17,* 497–517.

Bargh, J. A., McKenna, K. Y. A., & Fitzsimons, G. M. (2002). Can you see the real me? Activation and expression of the "true self" on the Internet. *Journal of Social Issues, 58,* 33–48.

Bargh, J. A., Raymond, P., Pryor, J. B., & Strack, F. (1995). Attractiveness of the underling: An automatic power? Sex association and its consequences for sexual harassment and aggression. *Journal of Personality and Social Psychology, 68,* 768–781.

Barnes, S. B. (2001). *Online connections: Internet interpersonal relationships.* Cresskill, NJ: Hampton.

Bell, M. P., Quick, J. C, & Cycyota, C. S. (2002). Assessment and prevention of sexual harassment of employees: An applied guide to creating healthy organizations. *International Journal of Selection and Assessment, 10,* 160–167.

Ben-Ze'ev, A. (2003). Privacy, emotional closeness, and openness in cyberspace. *Computers in Human Behavior, 19,* 451–467.

Ben-Ze'ev, A. (2004). *Love online: Emotions on the Internet.* Cambridge, UK: Cambridge University Press.

Biber, J. K., Doverspike, D., Baznik, D., Cober, A., & Ritter, B. A. (2002). Sexual harassment in online communications: Effects of gender and discourse medium. *CyberPsychology and Behavior, 5,* 33–42.

Boneva, B., & Kraut, R. (2002). Email, gender, and personal relationships. In B. Wellman & C. Haythornthwaite (Eds.), *The Internet in everyday life* (pp. 372–403). Malden, MA: Blackwell.

Bowker, N., & Tuffin, K. (2002). Disability discourses for online identities. *Disability and Society, 17,* 327–344.

Calvert, S. L. (1999). *Children's journeys through the information age.* New York: McGraw-Hill.

Carnes, P. J. (2003). The anatomy of arousal: Three Internet portals. *Sexual and Relationship Therapy, 18,* 309–328.

Cooper, A., Golden, G., & Kent-Ferraro, J. (2002). Online sexual behaviors in the workplace: How can human resource departments and employee assistance programs respond effectively? *Sexual Addiction and Compulsivity, 9,* 149–165.

Cooper, A., McLoughlin, I., Reich, P., & Kent-Ferraro, J. (2002). Virtual sexuality in the workplace: A wake-up call for clinicians, employers and employees. In A. Cooper (Ed.), *Sex and the Internet: A guidebook for clinicians* (pp. 109–128). New York: Brunner-Routledge.

Cooper, A., McLoughlin, I. P., & Campbell, K. M. (2000). Sexuality in cyberspace: Update for the 21st century. *CyberPsychology and Behavior, 3,* 521–536.

Cooper, A., Scherer, C. R., Boies, S. C., & Gordon, B. L. (1999). Sexuality on the Internet: From sexual exploration to pathological expression. *Professional Psychology: Research and Practice, 30,* 154–164.

Cooper, A., & Sportolari, L. (1997). Romance and cyberspace: Understanding online attraction. *Journal of Sex Education and Therapy, 22,* 7–14.

Cunneen, C., & Stubbs, J. (2000). Male violence, male fantasy and the commodification of women through the Internet. *Interactive Review of Victimology, 7,* 5–28.

D'Alessandro, D. M., & Dosa, N. P. (2001). Empowering children and families with information technology. *Archives of Pediatrics and Adolescent Medicine, 155,* 1131–1136.

Dansky, B. S., & Kilpatrick, D. G. (1997). Effects of sexual harassment. In W. O'Donohue (Ed.), *Sexual harassment: Theory, research, and treatment* (pp. 152–174). Needham Heights, MA: Allyn & Bacon.

Davis, K. E., Coker, A. L., & Sanderson, M. (2002). Physical and mental health effects of being stalked for men and women. *Violence and Victims, 17,* 429–443.

Deirmenjian, J. M. (1999). Stalking in cyberspace. *Journal of American Academic Psychiatry Law, 27,* 407–413.

Dibbell, J. (1998). *A rape in cyberspace.* Retrieved September 15, 2004, from www.juliandibbell.com/texts/bungle.html

Dombrowski, S. C., LeMasney, J. W., Ahia, C. E., & Dickson, S. A. (2004). Protecting children from online sexual predators: Technological, psychoeducational, and legal considerations. *Professional Psychology: Research and Practice, 35,* 65–73.

Döring, N. (2000). Feminist views of cybersex: Victimization, liberation and empowerment. *CyberPsychology and Behavior, 3,* 863–884.

Douglas, K. M., & McGarty, C. (2001). Identifiability and self-presentation: Computer-mediated communication and intergroup interaction. *British Journal of Social Psychology, 40,* 399–416.

Douglas, K. M., & McGarty, C. (2002). Internet identifiability and beyond: A model of the effects of identifiability on communicative behavior. *Group Dynamics, 6,* 17–26.

Durkin, K. F. (1997). Misuse of the Internet by pedophiles: Implications for law enforcement and probation practice. *Federal Probation, 61*(3), 14–18.

Durkin, K. F., & Bryant, C. D. (1999). Propagandizing pederasty: A thematic analysis of the on-line exculpatory accounts of unrepentant pedophiles. *Deviant Behavior, 20,* 103–127.

Ellis, S., Barak, A., & Pinto, A. (1991). Moderating effects of personal cognitions on experienced and perceived sexual harassment of women at the workplace. *Journal of Applied Social Psychology, 21,* 1320–1337.

Finn, J., & Banach, M. (2000). Victimization online: The downside of seeking human services for women on the Internet. *CyberPsychology and Behavior, 3,* 785–796.

Fitzgerald, L. F., Drasgow, F., & Magley, V. J. (1999). Sexual harassment in the armed forces: A test of an integrated model. *Military Psychology, 11,* 329–343.

Fitzgerald, L. F., Gelfand, M., & Drasgow, F. (1995). Measuring sexual harassment: Theoretical and psychometric advances. *Basic and Applied Social Psychology, 17,* 425–445.

Fitzgerald, L. F., Magley, V. J., Drasgow, F., & Waldo, C. R. (1999). Measuring sexual harassment in the military: The Sexual Experiences Questionnaire (SEQ–DoD). *Military Psychology, 11,* 243–263.

Folgero, I. S., & Fjeldstad, I. H. (1995). On duty—off guard: Cultural norms and sexual harassment in service organizations. *Organization Studies, 16,* 299–313.

Fontana-Rosa, J. (2001). Legal competency in a case study of pedophilia: Advertising on the Internet. *International Journal of Offender Therapy & Comparative Criminology, 45,* 118–128.

Fulda, J. S. (2002). Do Internet stings directed at pedophiles capture offenders or create offenders? And allied questions. *Sexuality and Culture, 6*(4), 73–100.

Gáti, Á., Tényi, T., Túry, F., & Wildmann, M. (2002). Anorexia nervosa following sexual harassment on the Internet: A case report. *International Journal of Eating Disorders, 31,* 474–477.

Glomb, T. M., Richman, W. L., Hulin, C. L., Drasgow, F., Schneider, K. T., & Fitzgerald, L. F. (1997). Ambient sexual harassment: An integrated model of antecedents and consequences. *Organizational Behavior and Human Decision Processes, 71,* 309–328.

Goodson, P., McCormick, D., & Evans, A. (2001). Searching for sexually explicit materials on the Internet: An exploratory study of college students' behavior and attitudes. *Archives of Sexual Behavior, 30,* 101–118.

Gossett, J. L., & Byrne, L. (2002). "CLICK HERE": A content analysis of Internet rape sites. *Gender & Society, 16,* 689–709.

Griffiths, M. (2000). Excessive Internet use: Implications for sexual behavior. *CyberPsychology and Behavior, 3,* 537–552.

Griffiths, M. D. (1997). Friendship and social development in children and adolescents: The impact of electronic technology. *Educational and Child Psychology, 14*(3), 25–37.

Griffith, M. D., Rogers, M. E., & Sparrow, P. (1998). Crime and IT (part II): "Stalking the net." *Probation Journal, 45,* 138–141.

Gruber, J. E. (1997). An epidemiology of sexual harassment: Evidence from North America and Europe. In W. O'Donohue (Ed.), *Sexual harassment: Theory, research, and treatment* (pp. 84–98). Boston: Allyn & Bacon.

Gutek, B. A. (1997). Sexual harassment policy initiatives. In W. O'Donohue (Ed.), *Sexual harassment: Theory, research, and treatment* (pp. 185–198). Boston: Allyn & Bacon.

Gutek, B. A., & Done, R. S. (2001). Sexual harassment. In R. K. Unger (Ed.), *Handbook of the psychology of women and gender* (pp. 367–387). New York: John Wiley.

Harcourt, W. (Ed.). (1999). *Women@Internet: Creating new cultures in cyberspace.* London: Zed Books.

Harcourt, W. (2000). The personal and the political: Women using the Internet. *CyberPsychology and Behavior, 3,* 693–697.

Harned, M. S., & Fitzgerald, L. F. (2002). Understanding a link between sexual harassment and eating disorder symptoms: A mediational analysis. *Journal of Consulting and Clinical Psychology, 70,* 1170–1181.

Hiller, J., & Cohen, R. (2002). *Internet law and policy.* Upper Saddle River, NJ: Prentice Hall.

Hoffspiegel, L. (2002). Abuse of power: Sexual misconduct in the legal workplace. *Sexual Addiction and Compulsivity, 9,* 113–126.

Jenkins, P. (2001). *Beyond tolerance: Child pornography on the Internet.* New York: New York University Press.

Joinson, A. N. (1998). Causes and implication of disinhibited behavior on the Internet. In J. Gackenbach (Ed.), *Psychology and the Internet: Intrapersonal, interpersonal, and transpersonal implications* (pp. 43–60). San Diego, CA: Academic Press.

Joinson, A. N. (1999). Social desirability, anonymity, and Internet-based questionnaires. *Behavior and Research Methods, Instruments, and Computers, 31,* 433–438.

Joinson, A. N. (2001). Self-disclosure in computer-mediated communication: The role of self-awareness and visual anonymity. *European Journal of Social Psychology, 31,* 177–192.

Joinson, A. (2003). *Understanding the psychology of Internet behaviour.* Basingstoke, UK: Palgrave Macmillan.

Kendall, L. (2000). "Oh no! I'm a nerd!" Hegemonic masculinity on an online forum. *Gender & Society, 14,* 256–274.

Koppel, M., Argamon, S., & Shimoni, A. R. (2002). Automatically categorizing written texts by author gender. *Literary and Linguistic Computing, 17,* 401–412.

Krakow, B., Artar, A., Warner, T. D., Melendrez, D., Johnston, L., Hollifield, M., et al. (2000). Sleep disorder, depression and suicidality in female sexual assault survivors. *Crisis, 21,* 163–170.

Leiblum, S., & Döring, N. (2002). Internet sexuality: Known risks and fresh chances for women. In A. Cooper (Ed.), *Sex and the Internet: A guidebook for clinicians* (pp. 19–45). New York: Brunner-Routledge.

Lessig, L. (1999). *Code and other laws of cyberspace.* New York: Basic Books.

Matchen, J., & DeSouza, E. (2000). The sexual harassment of faculty members by students. *SexRoles, 41,* 295–306.

Matei, S., & Ball-Rokeach, S. J. (2002). Belonging in geographic, ethnic, and Internet spaces. In B. Wellman & C. Haythomthwaite (Eds.), *The Internet in everyday life* (pp. 404–427). Malden, MA: Blackwell.

McCormick, N., & Leonard, J. (1996). Gender and sexuality in the cyberspace frontier. *Women and Therapy, 19*(4), 109–119.

McGarth, M. G., & Casey, E. (2002). Forensic psychiatry and the Internet: Practical perspectives on sexual predators and obsessional harassers in cyberspace. *Journal of the American Academy of Psychiatry and the Law, 30,* 81–94.

McGuire, B., & Wraith, A. (2000). Legal and psychological aspects of stalking: A review. *Journal of Forensic Psychiatry, 11,* 316–327.

McKenna, K. Y. A., & Seidman, G. (in press). You, me, and we: Self, identity, and interpersonal processes in electronic groups. In Y. Amichai-Hamburger (Ed.), *The social net: Human behavior in cyberspace.* New York: Oxford University Press.

McMaster, L. E., Connolly, J., Pepler, D., & Craig, W. M. (2002). Peer to peer sexual harassment in early adolescence: A developmental perspective. *Development and Psychopathology, 14,* 91–105.

McMellon, C. A., & Schiffman, L. G. (2002). Cybersenior empowerment: How some older individuals are taking control of their lives. *Journal of Applied Gerontology, 21,* 157–175.

Miller, H., & Arnold, J. (2001). Self in Web home pages: Gender, identity and power in cyberspace. In G. Riva & C. Galimberti (Eds.), *Towards cyberpsychology: Mind, cognition and society in the Internet age* (pp. 73–94). Amsterdam: IOS Press.

Mitchell, K. J., Finkelhor, D., & Wolak, J. (2001). Risk factors for and impact of online sexual solicitation of youth. *Journal of the American Medical Association, 285,* 3011–3014.

Mitchell, K. J., Finkelhor, D., & Wolak, J. (2003). The exposure of youth to unwanted sexual material on the Internet: A national survey of risk, impact, and prevention. *Youth & Society, 34,* 330–358.

Morahan-Martin, J. (1998). Males, females, and the Internet. In J. Gackenbach (Ed), *Psychology and the Internet: Interpersonal, and transpersonal implications* (pp. 169–197). San Diego, CA: Academic Press.

Morahan-Martin, J. (2000). Women and the Internet: Promise and perils. *CyberPsychology and Behavior, 3,* 683–691.

Munson, L. J., Hulin, C., & Drasgow, F. (2000). Longitudinal analysis of dispositional influences and sexual harassment: Effects on job and psychological outcomes. *Personnel Psychology, 53,* 21–46.

O'Donohue, W., Downs, K., & Yeater, E. A. (1998). Sexual harassment: A review of the literature. *Aggression and Violent Behavior, 3,* 111–128.

O'Hare, E. A., & O'Donohue, W. (1998). Sexual harassment: Identifying risk factors. *Archives of Sexual Behavior, 27,* 561–580.

O'Hare-Grundmann, E., O'Donohue, W., & Peterson, S. H. (1997). The prevention of sexual harassment. In W. O'Donohue (Ed.), *Sexual harassment: Theory, research, and treatment* (pp. 175–184). Needham Heights, MA: Allyn & Bacon.

Oravec, J. A. (2000). Countering violent and hate-related materials on the Internet: Strategies for classrooms and communities. *Teacher Educator, 35*(3), 34–45.

Paludi, M., & Paludi, C. (2003). *Academic and workplace sexual harassment: A handbook of social science, legal, cultural, and management perspectives.* Westport, CT: Praeger.

Paludi, M. A., & Barickman, R. B. (1998). *Sexual harassment, work, and education: A resource manual for prevention* (2nd ed.). Albany: State University of New York Press.

Pathe, M., & Mullen, P. E. (1997). The impact of stalkers on their victims. *British Journal of Psychiatry, 170,* 12–17.

Petrocelli, W., & Repa, B. K. (1998). *Sexual harassment on the job: What is it and how to stop it* (4th ed.). Berkeley, CA: Nolo.

Pew Internet Project. (2003). *America's online pursuits: The changing picture of who's online and what they do.* Retrieved September 15, 2004, from www.pewinternet.org/reports/toc.asp?Report=106

Plaut, S. M. (1997). Online ethics: Social contracts in the virtual community. *Journal of Sex Education and Therapy, 22,* 79–83.

Postmes, T., & Spears, R. (2002). Behavior online: Does anonymous computer communication reduce gender inequality? *Personality and Social Psychology Bulletin, 28,* 1073–1083.

Postmes, T., Spears, R., & Lea, M. (2002). Intergroup differentiation in computer-mediated communication: Effects of depersonalization. *Group Dynamics, 6,* 3–16.

Postmes, T., Spears, R., Sakhel, K., & De Groot, D. (2001). Social influence in computer-mediated communication: The effects of anonymity on group behavior. *Personality and Social Psychology Bulletin, 27,* 1243–1254.

Pryor, J. B., Giedd, J. L., & Williams, K. B. (1995). A social psychological model for predicting sexual harassment. *Journal of Social Issues, 51,* 69–84.

Pryor, J. B., LaVite, C. M., & Stoller, L. M. (1993). A social psychological analysis of sexual harassment: The person/situation interaction. *Journal of Vocational Behavior, 42,* 68–83.

Pryor, J. B., & Stoller, L. M. (1994). Sexual cognition processes in men high in the likelihood to sexually harass. *Personality and Social Psychology Bulletin, 20,* 163–169.

Pryor, J. B., & Whalen, N. J. (1997). A typology of sexual harassment: Characteristics of harassers and the social circumstances under which sexual harassment occurs. In W. O'Donohue (Ed.), *Sexual harassment: Theory, research, and treatment* (pp. 129–151). Boston: Allyn & Bacon.

Quayle, E., Holland, G., Linehan, C., & Taylor, M. (2000). The Internet and offending behavior: A case study. *Journal of Sexual Aggression, 6,* 78–96.

Quayle, E., & Taylor, M. (2002). Child pornography and the Internet: Perpetuating a cycle of abuse. *Deviant Behavior, 23,* 331–362.

Quayle, E., & Taylor, M. (2003). Model of problematic Internet use in people with a sexual interest in children. *CyberPsychology and Behavior, 6,* 93–106.

Rafaeli, S., & Sudweeks, F. (1997). Networked interactivity. *Journal of Computer-Mediated Communication, 2.* Retrieved September 15, 2004, from www.ascusc.org/jcmc/vol2/issue4/rafaeli.sudweeks.html

Redfearn, A. A., & Laner, M. R. (2000). The effects of sexual assault on sexual attitudes. *Marriage and Family Review, 30,* 109–125.

Reicher, S. D. (1987). Crowd behaviour as social action. In J. C. Turner, M. A. Hogg, P. J. Oakes, S. D. Reicher, & M. S. Wetherell (Eds.), *Rediscovering the social group: A self-categorization theory* (pp. 171–202). Oxford, UK: Basil Blackwell.

Richman, J. A., Rospenda, K. M., Nawyn, S. J., Flasherty, J. A., Fendrich, M., Drum, M. L., et al. (1999). Sexual harassment and generalized workplace abuse among university employees: Prevalence and mental health correlates. *American Journal of Public Health, 89,* 358–363.

Riger, S. (1991). Gender dilemmas in sexual harassment policies and procedures. *American Psychologist, 46,* 497–505.

Robb, L. A., & Doverspike, D. (2001). Self-reported proclivity to harass as a moderator of the effectiveness of sexual harassment-prevention training. *Psychological Reports, 88,* 85–88.

Sassenberg, K., & Kreutz, S. (2002). Online research and anonymity. In B. Batinic, U. D. Reips, & M. Bosnjak (Eds.), *Online social sciences* (pp. 213–227). Seattle, WA: Hogrefe & Huber.

Sbraga, T. P., & O'Donohue, W. (2000). Sexual harassment. *Annual Review of Sex Research, 11,* 258–285.

Schneider, K. T., Swan, S., & Fitzgerald, L. F. (1997). Job-related and psychological effects of sexual harassment in the workplace: Empirical evidence from two organizations. *Journal of Applied Psychology, 82,* 401–415.

Scott, A., Semmens, L., & Willoughby, L. (2001). Women and the Internet: The natural history of a research project. In E. Green & A. Adam (Ed.), *Virtual gender: Technology, consumption and identity* (pp. 3–27). London: Routledge.

Sheskin, R., & Barak, A. (1997, June). *Sexual harassment proclivities and vocational preferences.* Paper presented in the Annual Conference of the Canadian Psychological Association, Toronto, Ontario, Canada.

Spears, R., Postmes, T., Lea, M., & Wolbert, A. (2002). When are net effects gross products? The power of influence and influence of power in computer-mediated communication. *Journal of Social Issues, 58,* 91–107.

Spitzberg, B. H., & Hoobler, G. (2002). Cyberstalking and the technologies of interpersonal terrorism. *New Media and Society, 4,* 71–92.

Stein, M. B., & Barrett-Connor, E. (2000). Sexual assault and physical health: Findings from a population-based study of older adults. *Psychosomatic Medicine, 62,* 838–843.

Suler, J. (2004). The online disinhibition effect. *CyberPsychology and Behavior, 7,* 321–326.

Suler, J. R. (1999). To get what you need: Healthy and pathological Internet use. *CyberPsychology and Behavior, 2,* 385–393.

Suler, J. R., & Phillips, W. L. (2000). The bad boys of cyberspace: Deviant behavior in a multimedia chat community. *CyberPsychology and Behavior, 1,* 275–294.

Sussman, N. M., & Tyson, D. H. (2000). Sex and power: Gender differences in computer-mediated interactions. *Computers in Human Behavior, 16,* 381–394.

Tavani, H. T., & Grodzinsky, F. S. (2002). Cyberstalking, personal privacy, and moral responsibility. *Ethics and Information Technology, 4,* 123–132.

Teicher, J. (1999). An action plan for smart Internet use. *Educational Leadership, 56,* 70–74.

Till, F. J. (1980). *Sexual harassment: A report on the sexual harassment of students.* Washington, DC: National Advisory Council on Women's Educational Programs.

Timmerman, G. (2003). Sexual harassment of adolescents perpetrated by teachers and by peers: An exploration of the dynamics of power, culture, and gender in secondary schools. *Sex Roles, 48,* 231–244.

UCLA Center for Communication Policy. (2003). *The UCLA Internet report: Surveying the digital future—Year three.* Retrieved September 15, 2004, from http://ccp.ucla.edu/pdf/UCLA-Internet-Report-Year-Three.pdf

van Roosmalen, E., & McDaniel, S. A. (1998). Sexual harassment in academia: A hazard to women's health. *Women and Health, 28*(2), 33–54.

Wayne, J. H. (2000). Disentangling the power bases of sexual harassment: Comparing gender, age, and position power. *Journal of Vocational Behavior, 57,* 301–325.

Williams, J. H., Fitzgerald, L. F., & Drasgow, F. (1999). The effects of organizational practices on sexual harassment and individual outcomes in the military. *Military Psychology, 11,* 303–328.

Wonderlich, S. A., Crosby, R. D., Mitchell, J. E., Thompson, K. M., Redlin, J., Demuth, G., et al. (2001). Eating disturbance and sexual trauma in childhood and adulthood. *International Journal of Eating Disorders, 30,* 401–412.

Zurbriggen, E. L. (2000). Social motives and cognitive power-sex associations: Predictors of aggressive sexual behavior. *Journal of Personality and Social Psychology, 78,* 559–581.

ONLINE AGGRESSOR/TARGETS, AGGRESSORS, AND TARGETS: A COMPARISON OF ASSOCIATED YOUTH CHARACTERISTICS

MICHELE L. YBARRA   *Johns Hopkins Bloomberg School of Public Health*
KIMBERLY J. MITCHELL   *Crimes Against Children Research Center, University of New Hampshire*

Internet access and use continues to increase among American youth (National Public Radio/Kaiser Family Foundation/Kennedy School of Government, 2000; UCLA Center for Communication Policy, 2001). Many young users view the Internet as a powerful tool that increases connectivity and communication with others (Kaiser Family Foundation, 2001), as well as provides access to valuable information such as somatic and mental health advice (Borzekowski & Rickert, 2001). While most youth report positive experiences and activities online (Kaiser Family Foundation, 2001; Borzekowski & Rickert, 2001; Finkelhor, Mitchell, & Wolak, 2000b), the need to identify subpopulations potentially vulnerable to negative Internet experiences is necessary for effective intervention and prevention programs. Internet harassment is one such experience that may have deleterious consequences for youth.

Internet Harassment

Internet harassment is an overt, intentional act of aggression towards another person online. Actions can take the form of purposeful harassment or embarrassment of someone else, or making rude or nasty comments towards someone else while online. For example, youth describe instances where they were threatened with physical harm: *"Someone was threatening to kill me and my girlfriend,"* while other examples focus on embarrassing and humiliating the youth: *"They were mad at me and they made a hate page about me."* (Finkelhor, Mitchell, & Wolak, 2000a).

Internet aggression is sparsely documented, although research indicates an estimated 4% of youth have been the target of email harassment (British Broadcasting Corporation, 2002) and 6% have been the target of more general Internet harassment (Finkelhor et al., 2000b). Fifteen percent of young people have been an online aggressor (Ybarra & Mitchell, in press) at least once in the previous year. While the majority of youth targets of aggression report being relatively unaffected, a notable one-third of youth harassed online indicate feeling very or extremely upset, and one-third feel at least one symptom of stress following the incident (Finkelhor et al., 2000b).

Youth Involved in Conventional Bullying

25

*Online Aggressor/
Targets, Aggressors,
and Targets: A
Comparison of
Associated Youth
Characteristics*

Studies detailing conventional bullying behavior can be used as a reference point for investigating Internet harassment. Estimates of bullying involvement, either as a bully, victim, or both, among American youth are about 30% (Nansel et al., 2001; Haynie et al., 2001). Bullies are generally aggressive, not only with their peers but also with adults (Olweus, 1994). They tend to have more positive views of violence compared to other children (Bowers, Smith, & Binney, 1994), are impulsive, and tend to lack empathy (Olweus, 1994). Youth who bully are typically stronger and bigger than their peers (Olweus, 1994). They are more likely to spend time with friends frequently compared to non-bully involved peers in the younger grades (Forero, McLellan, Rissel, & Bauman, 1999), though their popularity tends to wane in high school (Olweus, 1994). Victims of bullying, on the other hand, are much more introverted and have lower self-esteem (Olweus, 1993). These youth typically are anxious, sensitive, cautious, and react to aggression by withdrawing from the situation. They are more likely to report feelings of being ostracized and of loneliness (Forero et al., 1999). Boys are more likely to be both targets and perpetrators of bullying, especially direct (i.e., physical) bullying, but also indirect (e.g., slandering, manipulation of friendships) bullying (Forero et al., 1999; Olweus, 1993). Similarly poor ratings of school commitment are offered for bullies and targets (Forero et al., 1999). Long-term effects seen into adulthood include delinquency, crime, and alcohol abuse for bullies (Loeber & Disheon, 1984; Magnusson, Stattin, & Duner, 1983), and depression and lower self-esteem for victims (Magnusson Olweus, 1993).

In general, characteristics of bully/victims, youth who are both bullied and bully others, tend to be more aligned with bullies than targets. For example, they are more likely to be male (Nansel et al., 2001; Haynie et al., 2001; Forero et al., 1999), to report poor academic achievement, and to engage in cigarette smoking (Nansel et al., 2001). On the other hand, they report many of the social challenges victims do, including poor relationships with peers and heightened feelings of loneliness (Nansel et al., 2001). Studies indicate, however, that bully/victims may be a distinct subgroup among those involved in bullying as they likely are manifesting the greatest psycho-social challenge (Olweus, 1993, 1994; Nansel et al., 2001; Austin & Joseph, 1996; Haynie et al., 2001; Forero et al., 1999; Kumpulainen, Rasanen, Henttonen et al., 1998; Kaltiala-Heino, Rimpela, Rantenen, & Rimpela, 2000). A number of studies have reported that bully/victims have higher rates of depression (Kaltiala-Heino et al., 2000), anhedonia (Kumpulainen et al., 1998), somatization (Forero et al., 1999), co-occurring disorders (Kaltiala-Heino et al., 2000), and psychiatric referral (Kumpulainen et al., 1998) compared to bullies only, targets only, and youth not involved in bullying. Bully/victims also have been noted to have the highest rates of behavior problems compared to all other groups (Austin et al., 1996;

Wolke, Woods, Bloomfield, & Karstadt, 2000). Additional psychosocial challenges have been noted to be extremely severe, including interpersonal problems (Nansel et al., 2001; Haynie et al., 2001; Kumpulainen et al., 1998; Forero et al., 1999), and overall levels of functioning (Austin et al., 1997; Haynie et al., 2001; Kumpulainen et al., 1998; Forero et al., 1999) compared to their bully and non-bully involved peers. Finally, in addition to findings suggesting poor caregiver-child relationships associated with child aggression (Barnow, Lucht, & Freyberger, 2001), bully/victims are most likely to report their parents' discipline and monitoring practices as erratic and emotional warmth to be lacking compared to both bullies only and targets only (Bowers et al., 1994).

It is possible that, similar to conventional bullying, a similar subset of "bully-victim" youth can be identified among those involved in Internet harassment. Using data from the Youth Internet Safety Survey, the most detailed survey of young Internet users to date (Finkelhor et al., 2000b), the current investigation aims to expand upon the traditional bully/victim literature by examining Internet aggressor/targets and identifying their potentially unique characteristics and challenges.

Methods

Data Source Sampling Method

The Youth Internet Safety Survey (YISS) was based on a two-stage probability sample, resulting in a nationally representative group of young regular Internet users ($N = 1,501$) (Finkelhor et al., 2000b). The research was approved and supervised by the University of New Hampshire's Human Subjects Committee and conformed to the rules mandated by research projects funded by the Department of Justice.

Phone numbers were derived from the Second National Incidence Study of Missing, Abducted, Runaway, and Thrownaway Children (NISMART 2). NISMART 2 was a nationally representative telephone survey, conducted by the Institute for Survey Research at Temple University (Hammer, Finkelhor, & Sedlak, 2002). Households that were identified as having at least one child between 9 and 17 years of age during the NISMART 2 adult screening process were flagged for possible YISS selection. In total, 6,594 phone numbers were forwarded to YISS investigators.

All phone numbers received by YISS from NISMART 2 were dialed and successful contact was made with 3,446 households by the end of the survey period. Seventy-five percent of those households contacted completed the eligibility screen, 72% of which were identified as eligible for YISS participation. Finally, 82% ($N = 1,501$) of eligible households completed both the adult and youth surveys (Finkelhor et al., 2000b) when the desired sample size was reached. Unfortunately, characteristics of eligible, nonparticipants were not available for comparison.

Methods in YISS Data Collection

Schulman, Ronca, and Bucuvals, Inc. (SRBI), a national survey research firm, conducted interviews via telephone. Upon reaching a household, interviewers requested to speak with an adult and the presence of a child in the household meeting inclusion criteria was confirmed. The adult who was most familiar with the child's Internet use was then interviewed after providing informed consent. At the close of the parent survey, the interviewer asked if the child could also participate; confidentiality was assured, and the adult was informed that questions would be asked about "sexual material your child may have seen," and would receive $10 for his or her time. In households where there were more than one youth in the appropriate age range who used the Internet, the one who used the Internet the most often was chosen to participate in the study. The youth interview was scheduled at the convenience of the child, when he or she felt able to talk freely and confidentially. Confidentiality was assured, and young people were told that they could skip any question if desired. Youth participants were mailed Internet safety-related brochures and $10 upon completion of the survey. Verbal consent from both adult and child were required for the youth interviews. The average youth interview lasted between 15 and 20 minutes. The adult survey lasted an average of ten minutes.

27

*Online Aggressor/
Targets, Aggressors,
and Targets: A
Comparison of
Associated Youth
Characteristics*

Study Population

The YISS was conducted between the fall of 1999 and the spring of 2000 in an effort to quantify and detail youth experiences on the Internet, specifically reporting online harassment, unwanted sexual solicitation, and unwanted exposure to sexual material (Finkelhor et al., 2000b). Participants were regular Internet users who had used the Internet at least once a month for the past 6 months from any location, and one caregiver in the household self-identified as the one most knowledgeable about the youth's Internet practices (69.1% female). This broad definition of 'regular Internet use' was used to ensure a wide range of Internet use behaviors, from relatively low use to high use. Location of Internet access was similarly wide-ranging, and included home, school, library, another person's house, or any other point of access.

Youth participants ranged between the ages of 10 and 17 ($M = 14.14$, $SD = 1.96$). Forty-eight percent of respondents were female, and more than three-quarters (76%) self-identified as non-Hispanic White. Highly educated, highly prosperous families and White individuals were over-represented in the YISS sample compared to the national average (U.S. Census Bureau, 2002), but they were reflective of the typical Internet household at the time of data collection (National Public Radio et al., 2000; UCLA Center for Communication Policy, 2001).

Measures

Online Aggression. Online aggression was conceptualized as similar to conventional bullying behavior. For example, both bullying and Internet harassment were behaviors intended to psychologically agitate another person (Olweus, 1993; Nansel et al., 2001). And, as revealed by the youth testimonials above, a real or perceived imbalance of power was achieved by the aggressor regardless of whether the action was online or in-person. Internet harassment research was still in its infancy, so standardized and accepted measures were yet to be developed when YISS data collection commenced. Questions used in the study aimed to identify episodes where one person tried to emotionally disturb another person either by things "said" or actions taken.

Youth *targets of online aggression* were identified based upon two questions: (1) whether anyone had used the Internet in the previous year to threaten or embarrass the respondent by posting or sending messages about him or her for other people to see; and (2) whether the respondent ever felt worried or threatened because someone was bothering or harassing him or her while online. Being a target of aggression was dichotomized (yes/no), with youth responding positively to at least one of the two items compared to youth responding negatively to both items.

Youth *engaging in online aggression* were identified based upon two questions: (1) making rude or nasty comments to someone on the Internet; and (2) using the Internet to harass or embarrass someone with whom the youth was mad. The measure of aggression was dichotomized to reflect youth responding positively to at least one of the two items compared to youth responding negatively to each question.

Youth online aggressor/targets were defined as responding positively to at least one item for each of the above aggression measures. Nonharassment involvement was defined as those that responded negatively to all target and aggressor items.

Psychosocial Challenge. Current symptoms (i.e., within the previous month) of depression were queried (yes/no) based upon the nine items outlined in the *Diagnostic Statistical Manual-IV* (American Psychological Association, 1999). Acceptable inter-item correlation was observed (KR-20 = .81). Based upon the DSM-IV definition of major depressive disorder, youth were defined as reporting major depressive-like symptomatology if: (1) at least five of the nine symptoms were endorsed, one of which was either anhedonia or dysphoria, and additionally (2) functional challenge was reported in at least one of three areas: self-efficacy, personal hygiene, or school work.

The number of times in the previous year youth engaged in drinking and smoking behavior was also assessed (0–5+, with an artificial ceiling at 5). Two dichotomous variables were created, to compare high users (i.e., those engaging in the behavior four or more times) versus all other. Four questions were asked to reflect behavior problems: (1) purposefully damaging property; (2) police contact; (3) physically assaulting a non-family member; and (4) taking something that did not belong to the respondent within the previous year. The measure was reduced to a dichotomous indicator of those indicating at least one of the four behaviors in the previous year versus none. Youth were asked to rate how well they liked school (referred to in the current analyses as 'school commitment') on a Likert scale of 1 to 5 (1 being 'the worst thing one could think of', 5 being 'love every minute of it'). Respondents scoring one or two (i.e., disliking school) were compared to all others. Finally, the report of *offline* bullying victimization was indicated for youth reporting having been either hit or picked on by another child in the previous year.

Caregiver-Child Relationships. Youth respondents were asked to rate their daily interactions with their caregiver based upon nine questions. Each

29

*Online Aggressor/
Targets, Aggressors,
and Targets: A
Comparison of
Associated Youth
Characteristics*

response was measured on a 4-point Likert scale ranging from very badly, to very well on emotional indicators, and never/rarely to all of the time for monitoring and discipline indicators. Exploratory factor analysis suggested three factors (all eigenvalues $> = 1$): (1) emotional closeness (i.e., how well caregiver and child get along, caregiver trust of child, discussing problems with caregiver when feeling sad or in trouble, and frequency of having fun together), (2) general monitoring (i.e., frequency with which caregiver knows where child is, and with whom child is spending time), and (3) discipline (i.e., frequency of "nagging" child, taking away privileges, and yelling). One variable was created for each of the above three aspects of the caregiver-child relationship by reverse scoring the items to make a higher score reflect a poorer rating, and then summing the scores of the associated variables (Ranges: emotional closeness: 4–16; parental monitoring: 2–8; harsh discipline: 3–12). Finally, because of indications of nonlinearity, each was dichotomized at one standard deviation above the mean.

Internet Use. Several Internet usage characteristics were included in the analyses. Average frequency and duration of Internet use were gathered via youth report. Based upon indications of nonlinearity, each was categorized at one standard deviation above the mean (6 days per week/3 hours per day, respectively). Youth were also asked for what activities they use the Internet most often and four categories were created to reflect communication-related activities: (1) chat rooms, (2) email, (3) Instant Messaging, and (4) all other activities (e.g., playing games, school assignments, downloading software). Location of Internet access was reported by youth and entered as using the Internet most often from home versus all other places. Additionally, youth were asked to rate the importance of the Internet to them based upon a 5-point Likert scale (not at all important–very important). This was dichotomized into two categories: not at all to average importance (reference group) versus very or extremely important. Respondents were also asked to rate their expertise on the Internet from 1 to 5, ranging from novice to expert. A dichotomous variable was created to compare almost expert/expert users versus less learned (reference group).

Internet Controls. Two indications of restrictions of Internet use were included in the analyses. Caregivers were asked whether blocking software was used on the home computer (yes/no), as well as whether there were household rules about acceptable Internet practice (yes/no).

Demographics. Youth-reported age was dichotomized at 15 years and older versus younger. Self-reported race was dichotomized as White versus all other. Caregivers reported youth gender and 1998 household income. Income was categorized at one standard deviation above the mean ($75,000 and higher) versus lower.

Statistical Methods

Stata 7.0 (StataCorp, 2000) was used for all analyses. Cases were required to have valid data for the majority of variables analyzed. Specifically, cases missing more than two data points in a subcategory of child characteristics (i.e., online aggression behaviors, Internet use, psychosocial characteristics, or demographics) were excluded. Three cases were thus dropped, resulting in a final sample of 1,498. "Do not know" answers were categorized as "symptom absent" ($<1\%$ in each variable affected). Missing values were imputed based upon best-set regression (StataCorp, 2000). Most affected variables had less than 1% imputed, except for household income (7.28% of values), average number of days Internet is used (1.13% values), and the frequency of caregiver 'nagging' (1.13% of values).

Following exploratory data analysis, χ^2 tests were used to identify significant differences in the data distribution between each of the four groups of youth based upon each specific characteristic examined. Next, in order to quantify specific differences between aggressor/target and other Internet harassment-involved youth, two parsimonious models of significant characteristics were created using backward stepwise deletion ($p > .05$). The first model compared aggressor/targets to victim-only youth, while the second compared aggressor/targets to aggressor-only youth.

Results

Descriptive Results

Almost one in five (19%), young regular Internet users in the sample were involved in online harassment in some capacity within the previous year. Three percent were aggressor/targets. An additional 4% reported being targets of aggression, and 12% reported aggressive behavior towards others online. The data indicated that aggressor youth frequently targeted people they knew in conventional environments. Youth who reported they had harassed or embarrassed someone online were asked to report whether they knew the target in person; 84% ($N = 16$) said they did. In contrast, few youth who reported being a target of Internet aggression reported knowing the harasser in person (31%, $N = 30$). In general, Internet aggression was similar to traditional bullying in its repetitive nature; 55% of Internet targets of aggression indicated they were harassed more than once by the same individual, with 16% harassed four or more times in the previous year.

The prevalence of most youth characteristics assessed was higher for aggressor/target youth compared to nonharassment involved youth (see Table 1). In general, psychosocial and caregiver–child relationship characteristics were similar for youth who reported aggressor/target behavior and aggressor-only behavior. For example, about half of youth in each group reported being the target of offline bullying, around 20–25% indicated cigarette or alcohol use, and more than 50% reported poor parental monitoring. Over 50% of aggressor/victim youth and aggressor-only youth similarly rated themselves as being almost or expert online. Further, about 30% of caregivers of these two groups of youth indicated using blocking software on their home computers. Several Internet usage characteristics of aggressor/targets, however, were more similar to target-only youth. About 35% of youth in each group reported using the Internet most frequently for Instant Messaging, and around 30% use the Internet for 3 hours or more per day.

TABLE 1. Characteristics of Young Regular Internet Users by the Report of Internet Harassment Involvement (N = 1,498)

Youth Characteristics	Aggressor/ Victim (N = 43) (% N)	Aggressor-only (N = 176) (% N)	Victim-only (N = 55) (% N)	Nonharassment involved (N = 1,224) (% N)
Psychosocial characteristics				
Target of offline bullying[c,e]	55.8% (24)	49.4% (87)	43.6% (24)	29.2% (357)
Problem behavior[b,c,d,e]	44.2% (19)	34.7% (61)	14.6% (8)	12.5% (153)
Low school commitment[e]	27.9% (12)	27.8% (49)	12.7% (7)	14.1% (172)
Alcohol use[c,d,e]	25.6% (11)	28.4% (50)	10.9% (6)	8.7% (107)
Cigarette use[c,e]	23.3% (10)	17.6% (31)	7.3% (4)	6.8% (83)
Major depressive like symptomatology[c]	16.3% (7)	10.2% (18)	9.1% (5)	3.8% (47)
Parent–child relationship				
Infrequent parental monitoring[c,d,e]	51.2% (22)	54.0% (95)	29.1% (16)	30.2% (370)
Poor emotional bond[c,e]	37.2% (16)	46.0% (81)	27.3% (15)	18.7% (229)
Frequent discipline	27.9% (12)	33.5% (59)	20.0% (11)	16.0% (196)
Internet characteristics				
Use Internet most often at home[c,e]	81.4% (35)	73.9% (130)	72.7% (40)	62.2% (761)
Almost expert/expert Internet user[c,d,e]	58.1% (25)	52.8% (93)	32.7% (18)	28.9% (354)
6+ days per week[b,c,e]	44.2% (19)	29.0% (51)	20.0% (11)	17.5% (214)
Importance of Internet to self (very or extremely)[c,e]	37.2% (16)	30.1% (53)	32.7% (18)	17.7% (216)
3+ hours per day[c]	34.9% (15)	17.6% (31)	29.1% (16)	11.1% (136)
Most frequent Internet activity[c,e]				
Instant Messaging	34.9% (15)	27.8% (49)	36.4% (20)	24.4% (299)
Chat room	25.6% (11)	18.8% (33)	16.4% (9)	8.2% (100)
Email	23.3% (10)	36.9% (65)	36.4% (20)	59.6% (730)
All else	16.3% (7)	16.5% (29)	10.9% (6)	7.8% (95)
Internet controls				
Parent has rules about Internet use	76.7% (33)	83.5% (147)	85.5% (47)	81.1% (993)
Use of blocking software	30.2% (13)	27.3% (48)	20.0% (11)	22.1% (270)
Demographic characteristics				
White race	83.7% (36)	80.1% (141)	80.0% (44)	74.0% (906)
15 years old and higher[d,e]	55.8% (24)	67.1% (118)	47.3% (26)	44.0% (538)
Male	53.5% (23)	52.8% (93)	47.3% (26)	53.0% (649)
High income ($75,000+)	32.6% (14)	28.4% (50)	20.0% (11)	22.2% (272)

Statistically significant ($p < .01$) based upon χ^2 tests: a: Aggressor/victim vs. Aggressor-only; b: Aggressor/target vs. Victim-only; c: Aggressor/victim vs. nonharassment involved; d: Aggressor-only vs. Victim-only; e: Aggressor-only vs. Nonharassment involved.

A Profile of Aggressor/Targets Youth

A cross-sectional profile of aggressor/target youth was identified using logistic regression to estimate the odds of being an aggressor/target versus victim-only youth, as well as aggressor-only youth, respectively. Two parsimonious models of characteristics necessary to explain the observed differences between youth were created using backward stepwise deletion (variables with $p < .05$ were retained). The resulting adjusted odds ratios estimated the odds of being an aggressor/target versus being a victim-only or aggressor-only youth, respectively.

Aggressor/target youth differed significantly from victim-only youth in terms of Internet use, parent–child relationships, and psychosocial challenge ($N = 97$). Youth engaging in problem behavior were almost four times as likely (AOR: 3.90, 95% CI: 1.37, 11.09) to also report being an Internet aggressor/target versus victim-only youth after adjusting for all other significant characteristics. Infrequent parental monitoring was additionally significant in the odds of reporting aggressor/target behavior, with a threefold increase in likelihood (AOR: 2.76, 95% CI: 1.05, 7.26) for youth indicating poor parental monitoring. Confidence in Internet use also discriminated youth behaviors, with those rating themselves as having almost expert or expert knowledge of the Internet 2.5 times more likely (AOR: 2.61, 95% CI: 1.03, 6.64) to also report being an aggressor/target versus victim-only youth. Compared to otherwise similar youth, those who reported Internet usage six or more days a week were more than three times as likely (AOR: 3.18, CI: 1.15, 8.77) to also indicate being an aggressor/target.

The parsimonious logistic regression model comparing aggressor/target and aggressor-only youth revealed that they share many similarities ($N = 219$). Only one characteristic was retained in the parsimonious logistic regression model and was able to significantly discriminate between the two groups of youth. Those who reported using the Internet three hours a day or more versus fewer were 2.5 times as likely (OR: 2.51, 95% CI: 1.20, 5.23) to also report engaging in aggressor/target behavior compared to aggressor-only behavior.

Consequences of Internet Harassment

As reported previously, one-third of youth harassed online reported feeling emotionally distressed as a direct result (Finkelhor et al., 2000b). The odds of distress appeared to be related to status of harassment involvement. Subsequent analyses in the current investigation revealed that aggressor/targets of online harassment were almost six times as likely (OR: 5.94, 95% CI: 3.06, 11.51) to report emotional distress as a result of being the target of Internet harassment compared to victim-only youth.

Discussion

Overlap of Participation in Conventional and Internet Bullying

Many youth involved in Internet harassment are also targets of conventional bullying. Over half of aggressor/targets (56%) report being the target of offline bullying, while 49% of aggressor-only and 44% of victim-only youth

33

*Online Aggressor/
Targets, Aggressors,
and Targets: A
Comparison of
Associated Youth
Characteristics*

report similar experiences. These data also suggest however, that some youth are exclusively involved in harassment online. Thus, for some youth who are bullied, the Internet may simply be an extension of the schoolyard, with victimization continuing after the bell and on into the night. For other youth victims of conventional bullying, the Internet may be a place to assert dominance over others as compensation for being bullied in person. And for youth who are not involved in conventional bullying, the Internet may be a place where they take on a persona that is more aggressive than their in-person personality.

Internet harassment and conventional bullying differ in one important aspect of asymmetrical power; one's ability to keep his or her identity unknown is a unique method of asserting dominance online that conventional bullying disallows. This important difference may help explain the incomplete overlap in participation of both conventional and online harassment. In fact, it is interesting to note that the majority of aggressors (84%) indicate knowing who their target is, whereas most targets (69%) indicate the aggressor is unknown to them. It could also be, however, that aggressors say they "know" the victim, but are reacting to an online persona one has created for online interaction.

Comparisons of Characteristics to Conventional Bully/Victims

As with bully/victims (Kaltiala-Heino et al., 2000; Haynie et al., 2001), aggressor/targets share more characteristics with aggressor-only than victim-only youth. Additionally, similar to previous reports of bully/victims (Haynie et al., 2001; Forero et al., 1999), psychosocial challenge is most frequently endorsed by aggressor/targets compared to all other youth. Two in five (44%) report problem behaviors (Austin et al., 1996; Wolke et al., 2000), and one-quarter has engaged in drinking (26%) and smoking (23%) on multiple occasions (Nansel et al., 2001; Kaltiala-Heino et al., 2000). They also have the highest rate of current depressive symptomatology (16%) (Kaltiala-Heino et al., 2000). These findings suggest that like conventional bully/victims (Haynie et al., 2001), aggressor/targets indicate the poorest psychosocial functioning and are likely in need of intervention and services.

In contrast to youth involved in conventional bullying (Nansel et al., 2001; Olweus, 1994), aggressor-only youth and aggressor/targets are more likely to be high school rather than middle school age. SES and race/ethnicity demonstrate similarly weak associations with both Internet aggressor/target and offline bully/victim status (Nansel et al., 2001; Wolke et al., 2000).

Unique Internet Characteristics

Identifying unique Internet characteristics is an integral component of understanding youth Internet aggressor/targets. These youth are intense Internet users who are confident of their abilities. Compared to victim-only youth, aggressor/targets are three times as likely to report using the Internet for 6 days or more, and 2.5 times as likely to rate themselves almost or an expert at Internet navigation after adjusting for other significant characteristics. Further, while aggressor/targets and aggressor-only youth are comparable in terms of most characteristics, the odds of reporting aggressor/target behavior are 2.5 fold higher for youth who use the Internet three hours a day or longer versus fewer. Notably, average daily usage is similar for aggressor/targets and targets-only, indicating that the "time at risk" may be intense daily use instead of frequent weekly usage.

Measuring Internet Harassment

The study of Internet harassment is still in its relative infancy and standardized methods for measuring the behavior have not yet been developed. Experts in adolescent health crafted the questions in the current study, however, and they were then pilot tested with youth to ensure applicability and understandability. An ever/never approach was taken to indicate Internet harassment in the current study. This does not take into account that some youth are harassed only once, while others are repeatedly targeted. This measurement is therefore a more inclusive definition of Internet harassment. It is possible that repetitive harassment is associated with different youth correlates; this is certainly an area for future research.

Another challenge in measuring Internet harassment is the inherently sensitive nature of the subject. As with all surveys, the method of data collection chosen has both positive and negative consequences. Telephone surveys are superior to school surveys in terms of economy (i.e., they are less expensive to carry out) and generalizability (i.e., not just public-schooled youth, etc.). Further, studies indicate that a high level of self-disclosure of sensitive information is achieved via telephone interviews (Ellen et al., 2002). On the other hand, privacy is more of an issue for telephone surveys because it is completed in the home. Young people might underplay their role in some online interactions while overplaying that of others if they believe their caregiver is privy to the information. YISS surveyors were mindful of scheduling the interview at a time when the youth felt he or she could talk in confidence, thus ensuring more accurate answers. Future studies should look at the differential rates of disclosure using telephone versus Internet-based collection methods.

Limitations

This study represents the first of its kind to rigorously examine characteristics of Internet aggressor/targets, but it is not without limitations. First, although the four categories of harassment involvement are exclusive, it cannot be determined whether aggressor/targets were both the target and the instigator during one encapsulated encounter, or as different interactions. Second, the measures for aggression and victimization may be less than symmetrical; for example, it is not a requirement for aggressors that the rude or nasty comment is posted where others can read it. This may lead to a lower threshold of aggression/bad temper for aggression than victimization. Third, the definition of Internet harassment does not take into account severity or frequency. Future studies should take into account these potentially important nuances. Fourth, the data were collected in 1999/2000 and thus cannot be said to represent the trends and patterns of Internet usage today. More youth are connected today and they have a greater level of Internet savvy. Many behaviors have stayed the same, however; for example, email remains the most commonly cited reason youth use the Internet (Turow & Nir, 2000; Lenhart, Rainie, & Lewis, 2001; U.S. Department of Commerce, 2002). Given the wide prevalence of conventional bullying, this may mean that more youth are involved in Internet harassment today (i.e., it is more than a growing pain for new users, but rather just as pervasive as conventional bullying); certainly further research is needed. Finally, it is possible that characteristics in the current model may modify one another. Due to necessary cell stability restrictions, however, such exploration was not conducted.

Implications

Despite limitations, the current study adds an important first look at the characteristics associated with youth Internet aggressor/targets. Several important implications arise from the findings.

Psychosocial Challenge

Youth who report aggressor/target behavior are especially likely to also reveal serious psychosocial challenges, including problem behavior, substance use, depressive symptomatology, and low school commitment. The findings make clear that those involved in Internet aggression are likely facing challenges on multiple fronts. Mental health, school, social work, and other professionals interfacing with youth should be knowledgeable about the Internet, and specifically about experiences young people are having and engaging in online. Conceptualizations of traditional exposure settings for bullying such as school and the community should now be expanded to include the Internet. Questions about Internet experiences should be included in routine well-being checks as well as more intensive therapeutic conversations and risk assessments. Psychological challenges such as depressive symptomatology may confer risk for negative experiences online in a similar fashion to the way they are related to victims of conventional bullying (Kaltiala-Heino et al., 2000). Alternatively, Internet harassment may be related to the onset of mental health challenge just as negative experiences often precede the onset of major depressive disorder for youth (Kazdin & Marciano, 1998). Given that one-third of youth harassed online reported feeling distressed by the incident, and the deleterious effects associated with conventional bullying (Olweus, 1993), the current findings are enough to indicate that professionals working with youth need to, first, recognize that Internet victimization includes more than sexual exploitation (Finkelhor et al., 2000b), and second, address the seriousness of Internet harassment issues just as they would conventional bullying involvement. Further research is needed to better understand the temporality and relationship between psychosocial challenges and online negative experiences.

The Caregiver's Role

The majority of current Internet safety guidelines (e.g., American Academy of Pediatrics, 2001; Magid, 1998) recommend parental involvement and monitoring of their children's Internet use to ensure safe and appropriate online navigation. These are certainly worthy recommendations. Results of this study indicate, however, that additional measures are necessary. In fact, neither caregiver report of the use of blocking software nor their indication of household rules about Internet use was related to a significant difference in the likelihood of being involved in Internet harassment. Further, youth report accessing the Internet from many places other than the home, including school, the library, and other people's homes; 27% of victim-only youth said they log on to the Internet most frequently from somewhere other than their own home, as do 20% of aggressor/targets and 25% of aggressor-only youth. Thirdly, older youth, who tend to be more independent and demand more privacy, are more likely to be involved in Internet harassment. Professionals working with youth who are asked by caregivers what methods promote safe Internet use for their children should emphasize general positive parenting styles. Indeed, general monitoring and positive caregiver–child relationships may be more important factors in Internet safety as global parental monitoring is significantly related to a decrease in the likelihood of being an online aggressor. As with conventional victims of bullying, however (Nansel et al., 2001), parental monitoring is generally high among harassment victims. While the underlying reason is not clear, this indicates that alternative interventions may be necessary.

Recommendations for Interventions

Clearly, not only parents but also youth should be empowered and responsible for their own online safety. Youth-oriented healthcare professionals should be as aware of the resource as youth are themselves in terms of generating Internet safety techniques. For example, as suggested by Finkelhor et al. (2000b), youth should be included in advocacy and educational campaigns about standard and healthy Internet behavior, and encouraged to take responsibility for youth-oriented aspects of the Internet. Young people should be viewed as resources for crafting intervention messages that are well received by youth and take into account realistic expectations of behavior change and Internet behavior.

Messages about modifying Internet usage by suggesting youth spend less time online, or staying away from specific types of sites, is not wholly sufficient in addressing the problem of Internet harassment, given the preponderance and degree of non-Internet related characteristics such as problem behavior. Interventions aimed at conventional psychosocial issues need to integrate an Internet component. For example, currently implemented bullying prevention programs should reflect youth interactions of today and recognize that the Internet represents a new mode by which aggression and bullying behavior is expressed. Additional modules speaking specifically about Internet harassment issues should be added, including behaviors that constitute harassment, and the associated psychological distress experienced by some youth who are targeted. Discussion points should integrate Internet harassment into the conversation of bullying, recognizing that many youth are involved in both types of aggression.

Conclusions

The current study is an important first step in illuminating the characteristics of youth aggressor/targets on the Internet. Many parallels between online aggressor/targets and offline bully/victims were identified, including behavior problems and depressive symptomatology. Yet, a number of important differences were also identified. There is a notable lack of significant differences between male and female youth and an increased risk among older teens rather than younger. Future studies are necessary to determine how psychosocial challenge as well as mental illness may increase the likelihood of negative experiences online, as they have been noted offline. And as with research aimed at in-person psychosocial challenges youth are facing, future Internet-related research may do well to focus on the protective factors of safe Internet navigation.

37

*Online Aggressor/
Targets, Aggressors,
and Targets: A
Comparison of
Associated Youth
Characteristics*

Acknowledgement

This research was commissioned by the National Center for Missing and Exploited Children, and supported by the Office of Juvenile Justice and Delinquency Prevention, the Association of Schools of Public Health, and the Centers for Disease Control, Prevention Research Centers, Grant #U48/CCU309670.

Correspondence To

Kimberly Mitchell, Crimes against Children Research Center—West Edge, University of New Hampshire, 7 Leavitt Lane, Durham, NH 03824, USA; Tel: 603-682-1888; Fax: 603-862-2899; Email: Kimberly.Mitchell@unh.edu

References

American Academy of Pediatrics. (2001). *Media matters.* Retrieved July, 2003, from http://www.aap.org/advocacy/mmcamp.htm

American Psychological Association. (1999). *Diagnostic and statistical manual of mental disorders (DSM-IV).* Washington, DC: American Psychiatric Association.

Austin, S., & Joseph, S. (1996). Assessment of bully/victim problems in 8 to 11 year olds. *British Journal of Educational Psychology, 66,* 447–456.

Barnow, S., Lucht, M., & Freyberger, H. J. (2001). Influence of punishment, emotional rejection, child abuse, and broken home on aggression in adolescence: An examination of aggressive adolescents in Germany. *Psychopathology, 34,* 167–173.

BBC News. (April 15, 2002). *Youngsters targeted by digital bullies.* Commissioned by Children's charity NCH. Retrieved January, 2004, from http://news.bbc.co.uk/1/hi/uk/1929944.stm.

Borzekowski, D., & Rickert, V. (2001). Adolescent cybersurfing for health information: A new resource that crosses barriers. *Archives in Pediatric Adolescent Medicine, 155,* 813–817.

Bowers, L., Smith, P. K., & Binney, V. (1994). Perceived family relationships of bullies, targets and bully/victims in middle childhood. *Journal of Social and Personal Relationships, 11,* 215–232.

Ellen, J. M., Gurvey, J. E., Pasch, L., Tschann, J., Nanda, J. P., & Catania, J. (2002). A randomized comparison of A-CASI and phone interviews to assess STD/HIV-related risk behaviors in teens. *Journal of Adolescent Health, 31,* 26–30.

Finkelhor, D., Mitchell, K., & Wolak, J. (2000a). *General description of incident.* Unpublished raw data.

Finkelhor, D., Mitchell, K., & Wolak, J. (2000b). *Online victimization: A report on the nation's youth.* National Center for Missing & Exploited Children. Retrieved July, 2003, from http://www.unh.edu/ccrc/Youth_Internet_info_page.html.

Forero, R., McLellan, L., Rissel, C., & Bauman, A. (1999). Bullying behavior and psychosocial health among school students in New South Wales, Australia: Cross sectional survey. *British Medical Journal, 319,* 344–334.

Hammer, H., Finkelhor, D., & Sedlak, A. J. (2002). *NISMART-2 Household Survey Methodology Technical Report.* Washington, DC: U.S. Department of Justice, Office of Justice Programs, Office of Juvenile Justice and Delinquency Prevention.

Haynie, D. L., Nansel, T. R., Eitel, P., Davis Crump, A., Saylor, K., Yu, K., & Simons-Morton, B. (2001). Bullies, targets, and bully/victims: Distinct groups of youth at-risk. *Journal of Early Adolescence, 21,* 29–50.

Kaiser Family Foundation. (2001). *Generation Rx.com.* Retrieved July, 2003, from http://www.kff.org.

Kaltiala-Heino, R., Rimpela, M., Rantenen, P., & Rimpela, A. (2000). Aggression at school—an indicator of adolescents at risk for mental disorders. *Journal of Adolescence, 23,* 661–674.

Kazdin, A. E., & Marciano, P. L. (1998). Childhood and adolescent depression. In E. J. Mash & R. A. Barkley (Eds.), *Treatment of childhood disorders* (2nd ed). New York: The Guilford Press.

Kumpulainen, K., Rasanen, E., Henttonen, I., Almqvist, F., Kresanov, K., Linna, S., Moilanen, I., Piha, J., Puura, K., & Tamminen, T. (1998). Bullying and psychiatric symptoms among elementary school-age children. *Child Abuse and Neglect, 22,* 705–717.

Lenhart, A., Rainie, L., & Lewis, O. (2001). *Teenage life online: The rise of the instant-message generation and the Internet's impact on friendships and family relations.* Retrieved January, 2004, from http://www.pewinternet.org/reports/pdfs/PIP_Teens_Report.pdf.

Loeber, R., & Disheon, T. J. (1984). Early predictors of male delinquency: A review. *Psychological Bulletin, 94,* 68–99.

Magid, L. (1998). *Teen safety on the information highway.* National Center for Missing and Exploited Children. Retrieved July, 2003, from http://www.safeteens.com.

Magnusson, D., Statten, H., & Duner, A. (1983). Aggression and criminality in a longitudinal perspective. In K. T. Van Dusen & S. A. Mednick (Eds.), *Prospective studies of crime and delinquency* (pp. 277–301). Netherlands: Kluwer Nijoff.

Nansel, T. R., Overpeck, M., Pilla, R. S., Ruan, W. J., Simons-Morton, B., & Scheidt, P. (2001). Aggression behaviors among U.S. youth: Prevalence and association with psychosocial adjustment. *Journal of the American Medical Association, 285,* 2094–2100.

National Public Radio/Kaiser Family Foundation/Kennedy School of Government. (2000). *NPR/Kaiser/Kennedy School Kids & Technology Survey.* Retrieved January, 2004, from http://www.npr.org/programs/specials/poll/technology/technology.kids.html.

Olweus, D. (1993). *Bullying at school.* Oxford: Blackwell.

Olweus, D. (1994). Bullying at school: Basic facts and effects of a school based intervention program. *Journal of Child Psychology and Psychiatry, 35,* 1171–1190.

StataCorp. (2000). *Stata Statistical Software: Release 7.0.* College Station, TX: Stata Corporation.

Turow, J., & Nir, L. (2000). *The Internet and the Family 2000.* Retrieved January, 2004, from http://www.appcpenn.org/04_info_society/family/finalrepor_fam.pdf.

UCLA Center for Communication Policy. (2001). *The UCLA Internet Report 2001: Surveying the digital future, year two.* Retrieved January, 2004, from http://www.ccp.ucla.edu/pages/internet-report.asp.

U.S. Census Bureau. (2002). *United States Census 2000.* Retrieved July, 2003, from http://www.census.gov/main/www/cen2000.html.

U.S. Department of Commerce. (2002). *A nation online: How Americans are expanding their use of the Internet.* Retrieved July, 2003, from http://www.ntia.doc.gov/ ntiahome/dn/.

Wolke, D., Woods, S., Bloomfield, L., & Karstadt, L. (2000). The association between direct and relational bullying and behavior problems among primary school children. *Journal of Child Psychology and Psychiatry, 41,* 989–1002

Ybarra, M. L., & Mitchell, K. J. (2004). Youth engaging in online aggression: Associations with caregiver–child relationships, Internet use, and personal characteristics. *Journal of Adolescence.*

Conclusion

The studies in this chapter provide an overview of the most common forms of harassment that take place over the Internet. These behaviors are important social problems offline as well as online. Thus, the importance of these social problems cannot be overstated.

These studies indicate that sexual harassment continues as a potential pathology online that may be presented as a typology. The typology indicates that the behavior needs oversight and important regulation. However, the problem that occurs is that oversight is difficult on the Internet. These studies also indicate the individuals that are likely to be perpetrators of cyberbullying behaviors.

Discussion Questions

1. Define and describe the different forms of online sexual harassment.
2. Define and describe the similarities between the offline and online forms of sexual harassment.
3. List and describe the different types of individuals who are likely to be aggressors of cyberbullying.
4. What are the different correlates of aggressors of cyberbullying?

3

Cyberpornography

Pornography is explicit sexual material, and cyberpornography is explicit sexual material that is available over the Internet. While pornography may not be criminal for those of age, the Internet does not discriminate based on age. That is, teenagers' fantasies about nudity are replaced by hardcore pornographic images of every conceivable sexual activity. Thus, some forms of cyberpornography may fit as a deviant behavior, but when the subject of the pornography is underage, the pornography becomes criminal.

The first paper in this chapter, written by Timothy Buzzell, examines the influence of technology on the distribution and psychological implications of pornography. Buzzell's paper is an empirical study that uses national level data from the General Social Survey. The results suggest that most users of pornography were male, young, and lived in urban areas. Importantly, Buzzell shows that technology does matter in the use of pornography.

The second paper in this chapter, written by Steven Stack, Ira Wasserman, and Roger Kern, examines the theoretical rationale why individuals use pornography over the Internet. Stack et al. investigate Hirschi's (1969) social control theory to understand this issue, using national random sample data for their study. Their study shows that individuals' weak ties with religion, lack of a happy marriage, and previous sexual deviance were important influences for why individuals use pornography over the Internet.

DEMOGRAPHIC CHARACTERISTICS OF PERSONS USING PORNOGRAPHY IN THREE TECHNOLOGICAL CONTEXTS

TIMOTHY BUZZELL *Baker University*

As the history of pornography shows, technology has typically been the spark in public debates about the control of the distribution of sexually explicit material. Hawkins and Zimring (1988) noted the role of technology in instigating political reaction to pornography use in the 1970s and 1980s, when film and videotape technology changed the pornography industry. In each of these decades, social reactions were captured in the work of commissions on the "pornography problem" (1970, 1986) brought on by technological advances. The growth of personal computing and the Internet has renewed public concerns about pornography. Pornography use is feared to be on the rise, and feared to be more accessible to segments of the population that should not have access to sexually explicit material (National Research Council, 2001; Mitchell, Finkelhor, & Wolak, 2003). Stern and Handel (2001) astutely recognized the sociohistorical context of technological development and pornography and have challenged current research, especially to address the question: Does technology matter to the access to and use of pornography? Using descriptive analysis of items from the General Social Survey (GSS) since 1973, this analysis attempts to answer that question.

Technology and Pornography since 1970

Few studies have explored the significance of technology to making pornography more accessible, and thus the use of pornography. This is disappointing given the political and legal significance often attributed to the role technology plays in the distribution and use of pornography. The research that does exist tends to address two rather limited themes: (1) the impact of technology on the pornography industry in general, and (2) the impact of the technology on the qualitative forms of pornography.

The Attorney General's Commission on Pornography in 1986 (referred to as the Meese Commission) gave attention to the fact that technology was changing the pornography industry and the availability of pornography as a result of new communication systems. This commission especially noted at the time the growing availability of the videocassette recorder/player (VCR). Based on surveys of pornography outlets in selected large cities, the commission found that the emerging VCR technology was having an impact on the number of adult theaters, which had grown in the late 1960s and early 1970s (Attorney General's Commission on Pornography 1986). In their study of the work of this commission and others, Hawkins and Zimring (1988) noted that the adult bookstores and theaters of the prior decade were dwindling in number as the new technologies of pornography emerged in the 1980s. They also noted that little data was available on just what impact these technologies were having on the use of pornography at the societal level, Lane (2000) assigned greater significance to the role of technology in the expanded distribution of pornography throughout American society by the end of the 20th century. According to his history, the invention of the Internet has been especially important. This technology has fostered the growth in varieties of sexually explicit materials (Holmes, Tewksbury, & Holmes, 1998) and changed access to sites that distribute images and sexual interactions (Waskul, 2002)—in some cases without cost.

Other research has focused on the role of technology in the creation of different pornographic content, finding that different pornographic forms emerge often facilitated by the medium being used. For example, Williams (1999) suggested that video and more recently the Internet have played a significant role in the emergence of specific "genres" of pornography. She concluded that these technologies have transformed the imagery of sexually explicit material from "soft-core" to more prevalent "hardcore" forms. Barron and Kimmel (2000) studied the imagery of sexual violence in different media. Their research suggests there are differences in male experiences with pornography in different technological media, describing the Internet as a virtual "locker room" which could not exist in other technological forms. Thus, some argue that the "genres" of pornography change as a result of technology.

The analyses by Williams and Lane identified three technological innovations in particular that are worthy of examination given their contribution to the expansion of pornography in the last 30 years: (1) films in the 1970s, (2) videotapes in the 1980s, and (3) the Internet in the 1990s. As Williams noted, the films of the 1960s and 1970s were important alternative forms to the printed pornography of the day. The technology of film offered pornography to persons willing to visit theaters where these films were being shown, typically by a retail (for profit) outlet. Others could use film but this required that viewers have access to the appropriate sources for purchase of a pornographic film, and owned or perhaps borrowed film projection equipment. With the invention of the videocassette recorder (VCR) in the late 1970s and widespread marketing of the technology, die context shifted once again. As Lane points out, the pornography industry was quick to adapt films to videotapes, which resulted in an expanded market that shifted the accessibility of pornography from films (8mm or 35mm formats) to videotapes (VHS or Beta formats). The technology of the VCR required patrons to rent or purchase videotapes, in some cases made available in mainstream video rental outlets. A third technology emerged with growing use of the personal computer and the growth of home based computing and Internet access in the 1990s. This technology eliminated the need for users of pornography to go to a retail outlet to purchase a film or rent a videotape. Instead, the Internet brought access to pornography to the privacy of the home. Interactions needed for accessing pornography were limited to those between the user and the computer system. This technology offered access to sites that required no corporal disclosure, or perhaps at most, a credit card. Again, the change of context altered not only ease of access to pornography, but also access to multiple forms of pornography.

Research on the Pornography–Technology Nexus

What is missing from the literature is a societal level survey of pornography access and use, one that examines the long-term changes in technology and the shifts in the social organization of pornography as a form of sexual expression broadly defined (Laumann, Gagnon, Michael, & Michaels, 1994). This gap is notable given Gagnon and Simon's observation in 1970 that "technological" and "scientific" changes in society would result in a restructuring of sexual practices.

There have been a few attempts to assess the role technology has played in the quantitative aspects of pornography (distribution, use). In 1986, the Meese Commission collected survey data from selected cities in order to make some preliminary conclusions about the use of pornography. One significant conclusion from these collected studies was that pornography was shifting from an urban milieu of adult bookstores and theaters to home-based viewing, thanks to the technology of the videotape. This report provided some early clues about what direction future research might take. However, the conclusions were based on a few limited urban samples, and no subsequent national sample was ever designed or initiated.

Current research is focused on the role of Internet technology in the distribution of pornography and the psychological impact of the relationship between individuals and the technology itself (Cooper, Scherer, Boies, & Gordon, 1999). Unfortunately, many of these efforts suffer from a number of limitations. For example, research on Internet pornography tends to give attention to understanding the content of images (Rimm, 1995; Mehta & Plaza, 1997; Mehta, 2001) or the "pathological" use of pornography (Delmonico & Miller, 2003). Few national, cross-sectional survey designs have been used to develop an accurate picture of the nature of online pornography use. The units of analysis for much of this research are pictures or messages taken from pornographic websites identified by the researchers (Rimm, 1995; Durkin & Bryant, 1995). Generally, these studies fail to use true random sampling techniques of cyberspace because of the difficulty in establishing a frame for Internet pornography websites. This was the principle criticism leveled at Rimm's study (Mehta & Plaza, 1997; Mehta, 2001), which ironically had significant impact on Congressional attention given to policies related to pornography on the Internet. As a result, selection bias taints conclusions about the nature and characteristics of users of online sexual materials. One of the most prominent large-sample cross sectional surveys of online "cybersex" (Cooper, Scherer, Boies, & Gordon, 1999) relied upon responses from self-presenting subjects to the MSN corporation website. Use of this methodology raises questions about self-selection bias in the subjects studied. The research also failed to use cross-sectional samples. As prior research on Internet use in general demonstrates, white persons with higher SES tend to use the Internet, although this may be changing (Norris, 2001).

No national cross-sectional random sample survey of pornography use in America exists. There is, however, a useful alternative—the General Social Survey (GSS). The GSS does offer a valuable cross-sectional analysis of opinions and behaviors related to pornography and to some extent technology. This paper utilizes items from the GSS to construct an empirical assessment of whether technology matters to the use of pornography. Since 1973, questions from the GSS have asked respondents if they have "seen an X-rated movie" and since 2000, has asked respondents if they have "used a sexually explicit website" on the Internet. Specifically, this study draws upon this national cross-sectional survey to empirically advance current discussions about the societal impact of technology on the use of pornography. Using three separate items from the GSS at three separate points in time, a descriptive analysis is constructed which evaluates access to pornography since 1973, and reports demographic characteristics of people who access pornography in different technological contexts found in the years 1973, 1994, and 2002.

Methodology

The General Social Survey (GSS) is a project of the National Opinion Research Center. Since 1972, the survey has studied public opinion and behaviors on a variety of topics related to sexuality (Smith, 2003; Smith, 1990). The cross-sectional survey design includes interviews from about 1,200 randomly selected individuals. Surveys conducted to date have included a number of measures useful in evaluating the use of pornography in different technological contexts across time. For purposes of this study, responses to questions from the 1973, 1994, and 2002 surveys were analyzed. Each of the years represents a different technological context for use of pornography: films, films in theaters or on a VCR, and websites.

For the first time in 1973, respondents to the GSS were asked "have you seen an X-rated movie in the past year?" In 1973 the principal technology available for viewing an X-rated film was a movie projection system (e.g., an 8 mm or 35mm projector) either at home, in a theater, or in an adult bookstore. Citing their own research as well as that of the U.S. Department of Justice, Hawkins and Zimring (1988) explained that "videocassette recorders (VCR's) were first introduced into the American market in 1975 . . . Sexually explicit films were first put on videotape around 1977" (38). Thus, by using the 1973 item, the analysis is able to operationalize use of pornography in a pre-VCR and pre-Internet technological context. Respondents answered "yes" or "no" to this question.

In 1994, GSS respondents were asked if they had in the last year viewed an "X-rated film in a theater or on a VCR" (this particular question appeared only in 1994, making the distinction in the technology between theater and VCR). Because this item referred specifically to VCRs it is used here to operationalize a second technological context for the use of pornography. The Meese Commission (1986) reported that as early as 1984, videotape "adult films" made up 13% of the video market. The Commission predicted that 85% of the nation's households with a TV would have a VCR by 1995. Lane (2001; 33) confirmed this prediction and reported that by 1998, 87% of all households with a TV owned a VCR. Thus, this particular item from the 1994 GSS asks respondents to think back on their viewing of pornography in the prior year, using a different form of technological access to pornography than that found in 1973. Subjects answered "yes" or "no."

A third technology for pornography use is differentiated, namely that created by "websites." Beginning with the 2000 GSS, respondents were asked a series of questions about their computer use at home, at work, and in other settings. In the combined 2000 and 2002 surveys, 63% of the respondents report that they use a computer, 83% have a computer at home, and 88% can use the World Wide Web from home. Clearly, the availability of the personal computer for home use (beginning in 1982–1985), and the subsequent role of this technology in accessing an increasingly market-oriented Internet (1995), marked yet another change in the technological context for pornography. Results from the most recent GSS (2002) are included in this analysis as the third technological context. Participants were asked to indicate how often in the last 30 days they had "visited a sexually explicit website" (coded here so that having visited one or more times is "yes").

The analysis examined the percentage of survey respondents who report yes and no to these three items in the GSS (1973, 1994, 2002). The analysis looked at the distribution of percentages across eight demographic characteristics: sex, age, race, education, income, employment status, marital status, and population setting. Chi squared was reported to test the null hypothesis that there is no difference in reported use of pornography by demographic characteristics for each particular technological context.

Findings and Discussion

Consistently since 1973, approximately one-fourth of the sample each year in the GSS reported having seen an X-rated movie in the prior year (22.6% for all years combined, $N = 43,698$). Figure 1 plots for the 30-year period the percentage of persons answering, "yes," that they had seen an X-rated movie in the last year. Figure 1 illustrates that reported use of X-rated movies has varied over the decades. For example, the percentage that reported use was at an all time low in 1980 with only 16% having seen an X-rated movie. Throughout the 1980s, however, that proportion increased steadily to reach an all-time high in 1987, with 29.9% of those surveyed having seen an X-rated movie. Since 1990, the proportion of the respondents that have reported use has been fairly consistent, around 20–25% of those participating in the GSS.

Also consistent across the years is the fact that more men than women have reported seeing an X-rated movie in the previous year. Overall, a greater proportion of persons who were male, young, nonwhite, completed high school, and reported higher income, had seen an X-rated movie in the previous year. On average, 25–35% of the males, and in contrast, only 15–20% of the females answered this question in the affirmative. A greater share of younger persons (18 to 35) reported having seen an X-rated movie whereas

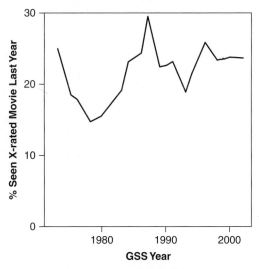

FIGURE 1. Trend in Percent of GSS Respondents Who "Have Seen an X-rated Movie" in the Past Year, 1973 through 2002

fewer older respondents reported having done so in the prior year. The results also reveal racial differences in use, as more nonwhites than whites on average reported seeing an X-rated film. More employed persons and more single persons also reported seeing an X-rated film.

Two patterns in particular are worth noting here. First, about one-fourth of the respondents reported having used pornography at least on one occasion. While the GSS does not allow for an assessment of the frequency of use of pornography, it does suggest some level of prevalence and indicates that over the 30-year period (1973 to 2002), consistency in the finding that about one-fourth of the population reports some use of pornography. Second, the patterns in the trend analysis provided some clues about what impact selected events may have had on the fluctuations in reported use. For example, the baseline year in this study—1973—was significant in that it followed the work of the 1970 Johnson Commission, and is also the year of the *Miller v. California* Supreme Court decision, which created a standard for the prosecution of obscenity. The decline in reported use between 1973 through 1979 may be related to increased efforts at governmental regulation. The subsequent increase in reported use between 1980 and 1988 may reflect the impact of VCR technology. The decline in the late 1980s (after the work of the 1986 Meese Commission) may reflect the impact of renewed governmental control, as the number of persons in the GSS having seen an X-rated movie declined through the early 1990s. Then again, in 1992 the proportion having seen an X-rated movie started to rise, perhaps in parallel with the emergence of home computing and Internet access. While it is difficult to establish causal effects in the fluctuation in the proportion of the population that had seen an X-rated movie, these results do suggest that pornography use has been affected by the introduction of new technology.

The thesis that the characteristics of persons who use pornography varies by technology are next examined for each of the three technological settings. Tables 1, 2, and 3 report the percentages of users and nonusers of pornography in three technological settings: a theater (1973), theater or VCR (1994), or websites (2002). The tables allow for a comparison of the characteristics of the persons who accessed pornography using the three different technologies. Recognizing that these items are quite different, the argument made here is that data from the nationally representative sample provides clues about who uses pornography and whether or not these patterns of use vary by technology.

The total percent of persons who reported having seen an X-rated movie in 1973 was 25.4%. In 1994 the percent of persons who reported having seen an X-rated movie in a theater or on a VCR was 22.5%. The percentage of persons who reported having used a sexually explicit website in 2002 was 14%. This would suggest that the film and videotape technologies of the 1970s and 1980s had reached a greater proportion of the population than the Internet technology of 2002. This may be a function of availability of the VCR technology, although one would predict that access to the Internet has been relatively widespread as well. The surprising result here is the lower proportion of respondents who reported access to a pornography website (14%). This suggests that the Internet has not resulted in widespread use of pornography as some would propose especially in contrast to the availability of past technologies (e.g., VCRs). Patterns related to Internet use are worth tracking in future GSS reports.

Demographic
Characteristics of
Persons Using
Pornography in
Three Technological
Contexts

TABLE 1. Characteristics of Respondents Who Have Seen an X-Rated Film in the Last Year, GSS 1973

Demographic Variable	% Who Report Not Having Seen an X-Rated Movie in the Last Year	% Who Report Having Seen an X-Rated Movie in the Last Year	X^2
Sex			
male	68	31	
female	80	20	p<.000
Age			
18 to 25	46	55	
26 to 35	67	33	
36 to 45	74	26	
46 to 55	82	28	
56 to 65	88	12	
66 and older	98	2	p<.000
Race			
white	75	25	
black	72	28	
other	68	33	p<.583
Education			
<high school	83	17	
high school	71	29	
college	64	36	p<.000
Family Income			
<$10,000	77	23	
$10–14,999	74	26	
$15–19,999	71	29	
$20–24,999	67	33	
>$25,000	73	27	p<.147
Employment			
full-time	69	31	
part-time	67	33	
not working	82	18	p<.000
Marital Status			
married	77	23	
single	70	30	p<.010
Population			
12 largest SMSA	66	34	
SMSA 13-100	75	25	
12 largest Suburbs	72	28	
Suburb 13-100	73	27	
other urban	75	25	
other rural	83	17	p<.004

Table from 1973 GSS. $N = 1,491$

TABLE 2. Characteristics of Respondents Who Have Seen an X-Rated Film in a Theater or on a VCR in the Last Year, GSS 1994

Demographic Variable	% Who Report Not Having Seen an X-Rated Movie in the Last Year	% Who Report Having Seen an X-Rated Movie in the Last Year	X^2
Sex			
male	68	32	
female	84	16	p<.000
Age			
18 to 25	70	30	
26 to 35	75	25	
36 to 45	69	31	
46 to 55	78	22	
56 to 65	91	9	
66 and older	88	12	p<.004
Race			
white	80	20	
black	63	37	
other	79	21	p<.015
Education			
<high school	76	24	
high school	77	23	
college	78	22	p<.947
Family Income			
<$10,000	80	20	
$10–14,999	66	34	
$15–19,999	80	20	
$20–24,999	79	21	
>$25,000	76	24	p<.549
Employment			
full-time	73	27	
part-time	75	25	
not working	84	16	p<.03
Marital Status			
married	82	18	
single	73	27	p<.021
Population			
12 largest SMSA	70	30	
SMSA 13-100	72	28	
12 largest Suburbs	72	28	
Suburb 13-100	75	25	
other urban	81	19	
other rural	85	15	p<.246

Table from 1994 GSS. $N = 503$

*Demographic
Characteristics of
Persons Using
Pornography in
Three Technological
Contexts*

TABLE 3. Characteristics of Respondents Visiting a Pornographic Website, GSS 2002

Demographic Variable	% Who Report Not Visiting Pornographic Site in Last 30 Days	% Who Report Visiting Pornographic Site in Last 30 Days	X^2
Sex			
male	75	25	
female	96	4	p<.000
Age			
18 to 25	82	18	
26 to 35	85	15	
36 to 45	83	17	
46 to 55	90	10	
56 to 65	93	7	
66 and older	88	12	p<.042
Race			
white	86	14	
black	91	9	
other	86	19	p<.230
Education			
<high school	89	11	
high school	82	18	
college	87	13	p<.121
Family Income			
<$10,000	72	28	
$10–14,999	83	17	
$15–19,999	87	13	
$20–24,999	84	16	
>$25,000	87	13	p<.021
Employment			
full-time	84	16	
part-time	89	11	
not working	91	9	p<.001
Marital Status			
married	91	9	
single	81	19	p<.000
Population			
12 largest SMSA	84	16	
SMSA 13-100	82	18	
12 largest Suburbs	86	14	
Suburb 13-100	88	12	
other urban	87	13	
other rural	90	10	p<.623

Table from 2002 GSS. *N* = 988

Consistent with prior research and the general patterns identified earlier in the combined GSS responses (1973–2002), a greater proportion of young males reported accessing pornography as film, in a theater or on a VCR, or on a website (Tables 1, 2, and 3). This pattern has been consistent across time and thus across technologies. The 2002 survey affirms this for pornography use on the Internet. Website access to pornography is predominately a male phenomenon (25% of males compared to only 4% of females). As age increased the proportion of persons who had reported use of pornography declined. Overall, the distribution of persons by sex and age within each of these three technological contexts is consistent with prior findings (Hawkins & Zimring, 1988).

More nonwhites than whites have seen an X-rated film in a theater or on a VCR compared to film or website access. This may be indicative of race differences in sexual scripts and practices as identified by Mahay, Laumann, and Michaels (2001) especially related to "conventional" sexual habits which might not include use of pornography. Use of website pornography follows the same pattern except that its use is less likely to be reported by nonwhite populations. Close to 20% of the nonwhite portion of the sample reports use of website pornography. As others have found, the "digital divide" in this case may also affect societal patterns of pornography use online (Norris, 2001).

The distribution of persons across educational categories having reported use of pornography yielded conflicting patterns. College educated persons constituted a larger share of persons who reported seeing an X-rated movie in 1973 (36%). By 1994, however, there was only a 1% difference in the share of respondents having reported seeing an X-rated movie in a theater or on a VCR, suggesting little difference between educational levels. One would predict that a greater share of persons with a high school or college degree would report having visited a website as opposed to a theater or VCR, to access sexually explicit material. Internet use would arguably be related to education levels. The results show that that the greatest share of persons visiting a sexually explicit website were persons with a high school education (18%) and a college education (13%).

Since access to technology usually costs, it was anticipated that persons with greater income would be more likely to access pornography across all technological settings. This was the case in 1973 as more persons in the $20–24,999 group reported seeing an X-rated movie than in the lower income categories. However, in 1994, a lower income group—$10–14,999—had the highest proportion of persons having seen an X-rated movie in this different technological context. It appears that the theater and VCR technology of the 1980s was an "equalizer" in pornography access. In other words, this technology may provide access to persons across educational and income groups, including the lower income groups. One would predict that as income rises, access to Internet technology would also increase. However, the results showed that website use of pornography declined as income increased. Employment status appears to enhance access to the Internet, although further testing of this assertion is required. The results from the 2002 GSS showed that a greater share of full-time employed persons (16%) reported visiting a pornographic website. Clearly, these patterns related to website use, income and employment are more complex and deserve further investigation.

51

*Demographic
Characteristics of
Persons Using
Pornography in
Three Technological
Contexts*

Consistently, single persons are more likely to have reported pornography use than married persons, which is consistent with prior research (Zimring & Hawkins, 1988; Laumann, Gagnon, Michael, & Michaels, 1994). On average, around 29% of the single respondents in both 1973 and 1994 reported use of pornography. In 2002, more single persons reported use of pornographic websites than married persons (19%).

The patterns of use of pornography in urban, suburban and rural settings also varied. Early research tended to link pornography distribution and access to life in urban areas (Sundholm, 1973; Karp, 1973; Potter, 1989; Tewksbury, 1990). In the 1986 Meese Commission Report, the number of these outlets was predicted to decline as the technology shifted to VCR forms. Across all three technologies studied here, more persons in urban areas reported use of pornography. Nearly twice as many in urban and suburban areas had seen an X-rated film, seen an X-rated film in a theater or VCR, and visited a pornographic website, Close to one-third of the respondents in the largest urban locations in the U.S. reported having seen an X-rated movie in a theater or on a VCR. Moreover, a larger proportion of individuals in urban areas (16% and 18%) reported visiting a pornographic website in contrast to persons in rural areas (10%). Overall, in all three technologies, fewer persons in rural areas reported having seen pornography.

Conclusions

This study is a preliminary analysis using fairly rudimentary measures of pornography access and use. There are limitations here that should be noted. The study relies on responses to a single item in the periods studied, asking subjects if they "have seen an X-rated film in the previous year." This question did not attempt to measure the frequency of X-rated film viewing. Clearly, a better measure in the study of pornography usage would focus on frequency of viewing or frequency of attending an adult theater, or frequency of renting/buying adult videotapes. The analysis is also limited by the precision of operationalizing the kinds of technology used in each context, especially in 1973 and 1994. While survey items in these years of the GSS are different and conceptually measure different things, the exactness remains undifferentiated because of the questions used. A better measure would ask respondents to report the technology or setting where the pornography use took place; film in a theater, in an adult bookstore, on a VCR, on a DVD, on cable TV, on a website, or any number of technological forms. Nonetheless, the analysis here provides results from a nationally representative survey sample that tests critical assumptions in current research about the role of technology in sexual life.

This analysis set out to briefly examine whether technological formats mattered to the use of pornography in various ways. In examining the trends since 1973, the GSS data reveal that about one-fourth of population consistently reports having seen an X-rated movie. This pattern fluctuates from year to year, and there is some evidence that these fluctuations could be attributed to periodic political and legal control efforts. The fluctuations also seem to parallel the introduction of new technological forms in society, especially the

VCR. In general, this analysis suggests that the technology does matter for fluctuations in pornography use in society.

The low percentage of persons reporting having visited a pornographic website in the last 30 days is worth noting. Popular impressions and media reports suggest that use of Internet pornography is quite high. This national survey of randomly selected participants suggests otherwise, as around 16% of the respondents reported having used pornography on the Internet. Two factors may be at work here. First, respondents may be under-reporting use, and as a result the GSS does not report realistic levels of access. Under reporting is a methodological problem for many studies of deviant behavior and sexuality in general, and may be at work in these results. A related caution involves the wording of the items used here. Note that in 1973 and 1994 respondents reported on "past year" use, whereas respondents in 2000–2002 report on use "in the last 30 days." The comparatively low proportion of website users may reflect this different time frame. Second, the results may reflect the "cultural lag" that Zimring and Hawkins noted in their 1988 analysis. We may find that in the next decade the percentage of persons reporting use will increase as Internet access increases to households and more workplaces across society.

The analysis also examined what impact different technological contexts of pornography had for different segments of the population. Clearly, technology does not seem to matter for pornography use by males, younger persons, and single persons. However, there are differences for persons of differing racial, educational, and employment statuses. The reasons for these differences should be explored. Moreover, the apparent link between technology and urban life has changed, perhaps as noted by the 1986 Meese Commission, which suggested that the urban-based adult bookstore was giving way to more home-based opportunities to use pornography. This study provides evidence that technology has mattered over time as access and use varies with the technologies used to distribute pornographic material.

Changing technological contexts raise other questions worthy of research especially related to access and use of pornography. Williams (1999) concludes that technology has played a role in redefining what is pornographic, as content and forms of pornography have shifted with the technology. Her research demonstrates for example, how the meaning of "hardcore" has shifted in part due to technological changes embraced by the pornography industry as well as shifting societal values about sexuality. Respondents to the GSS over a 30-year period may differ in the meaning they give to "hardcore" or in this case, "X-rated." As hardcore pornography becomes accessible to larger audiences, the notion of "pornographic" or "sexually explicit" may vary with individual philosophies about pornography and sex (Linz and Malmuth 1993). Changing meanings of what constitutes "X-rated" may result in under-reporting in surveys like the GSS. Today's NC-17 rating may have been judged as X-rated 30 years ago. Research on the role of technology in changing access and use of pornography will need to give greater precision to operationalizing what is meant by pornographic. The lack of research in this area is a good example of what Binik (2001) means by "lots of hypotheses—little data" in the study of pornography, technology, and a variety of issues related to sexuality.

53

*Demographic
Characteristics of
Persons Using
Pornography in
Three Technological
Contexts*

Stem and Handel (2001) recently challenged researchers by asking does technology matter to current forms of "cybersex" including use of pornography. The current emphasis on understanding the role of the Internet in a number of cybersexualities could benefit from theorizing in a number of fields. Especially important in this current effort, however, is the construction of some sense of contrast, or development of a sense of how this technology compares to others. This is noticeably absent in the current literature. Binik (2001) astutely described the study of sexuality and technology as a field characterized by "lots of hyp(otheses)—only a little data" (281). The purpose of the study presented here is to move beyond hype and use cross-sectional survey data to examine the question of whether technology matters in the use and distribution of pornography. This study has constructed a sociohistorical context of technology and pornography which others will hopefully address in critique and future research.

References

Barron, M., & M. Kimmel. (2000). Sexual violence in three pornographic media: Toward a sociological explanation. *Journal of Sex Research 37* (2).

Binik, Y. (2001). Sexuality and the Internet: Lots of Hyp(othesis)—only a little data. *Journal of Sex Research 38* (4): 281–282.

Cooper, A., C. Scherer, S. Boies, & B. Gordon. (1999). Sexuality on the Internet: From sexual exploration to pathological expression. *Professional Psychology: Research and Practice 30* (2): 154–164.

Cooper, A., & E. Griffin-Shelley. (2002). Introduction: The Internet: The next sexual revolution. Pp. 1–15 in A. Cooper (ed.), *Sex & the Internet: A guidebook for clinicians.* New York: Brunner-Routledge.

Cooper, A., J. Morahan-Martin, R. Mathy, & M. Maheu. (2002). Toward an increased understanding of user demographics in online sexual activities. *Journal of Sex and Marital Therapy 28:* 105–129.

Delmonico, D., & J. A. Miller. (2003). The Internet screening test: A comparison of sexual compulsives versus non-sexual compulsives. *Sexual and Relationship Therapy 18* (3): 261–276.

Dines, G., R. Jensen, & A. Russ. (1998). *Pornography: The production and consumption of inequality.* New York: Routledge.

Downs, D. (1989). *The new politics of pornography.* Chicago: University of Chicago Press.

Dworkin, A. (1981). *Pornography: Men possessing women.* New York: Putnam.

Durkin, K., & C. Bryant. (1995). "Log on to sex": Some notes on the carnal computer and erotic cyberspace as an emerging research frontier. *Deviant Behavior 16:* 179–200.

Gagnon, J., & W. Simon. (1973). *Sexual conduct: The social sources of sexuality.* Chicago: Aldine.

Gagnon, J., & W. Simon. (1970). Prospects for change in American sexual patterns. *Medical Aspects of Human Sexuality 4:* 100–117.

General Social Survey (1972–2002) [Cumulative data file]. Available from Survey Documentation and Analysis, SDA Archives, Berkley University, www.csa.berkley.edu:752/.

Hawkins, G., & F. Zimring. (1988). *Pornography in a free society.* New York: Cambridge University Press.

Holmes, R., R. Tewksbury, & S. Holmes. (1998). Hidden JPGs: A functional alternative to voyeurism. *Journal of Popular Culture 32* (3): 17–29.

Jenkins, P. (2001). *Beyond tolerance: Child pornography on the Internet.* New York: New York University Press.

Jones, S. (ed.). (1997). *Virtual culture: Identity and communication in cybersociety.* California: Sage Publications.

Karp, D. (1973). Hiding in pornographic bookstores: A reconsideration of the nature of urban anonymity. *Urban Life and Culture 2:* 427–451.

Lane, F. S., III. (2000). *Obscene profits: The entrepreneurs of pornography in the cyber age.* New York: Routledge.

Laumann, E., S. Ellingson, J. Mahay, A. Paik, & Y. Youm (Eds.). (2004). *The sexual organization of the city.* Chicago: University of Chicago Press.

Laumann, E., J. Gagnon, R. Michael, & S. Michaels. (1994). *The social organization of sexuality: Sexual practices in the United States.* Chicago: University of Chicago Press.

Linz, D., & N. Malamuth. (1993). *Pornography.* California: Sage Publications.

Lynxwiler, J., & D. Gay. (2000). Moral boundaries and deviant music: Public attitudes toward heavy metal and rap. *Deviant Behavior 21:* 63–85.

Mahay, J., E. Laumann, & S. Michaels. (2001). Race, gender, and class in sexual scripts." In E. Laumann & S. Michaels (Eds.), *Sex, love, and health in America: Private choices and public policies* (pp. 197–238). Chicago: University of Chicago Press.

Mehta, M. (2001). Pornography in Usenet: A study of 9800 randomly selected images. *Cyberpsychology and Behavior 4:* 695–703.

Mehta, M., & D. Plaza. (1997). Content analysis of pornographic images on the Internet. *The Information Society 13:* 153–161.

Mitchell, K., D. Finkelhor, & J. Wolak. (2003). The exposure of youth to unwanted sexual material on the Internet: A national survey of risk, impact, and prevention. *Youth and Society 34* (3): 330–358.

Norris, P. (2001). *Digital divide: Civic engagement, information poverty, and the Internet worldwide.* New York: Cambridge University Press.

Peek, C., D. Wittred, & D. A. Gay. (1982). "Pornography: Important political symbol or limited political issues?" *Sociological Focus 13:* 41–52.

Potter, G. (1989). The retail pornography industry and the organization of vice. *Deviant Behavior 10:* 233–251.

Rimm, M. (1997). Marketing pornography on the information superhighway: A survey of 917,410 images, descriptions, short stories, and animations downloaded 8.5 million times by consumers in over 2000 cities in forty countries, provinces, and territories. *Georgetown Law Journal 83* (5): 1849–1934.

Sherkat, D., & C. Ellison. (1997). The cognitive structure of moral crusade: Conservative Protestantism and opposition to pornography. *Social Forces 75:* 957–981.

Smith, T. (2003). American sexual behavior: Trends, demographic differences, and risk behavior. (GSS Topical Report number 25). National Opinion Research Center, University of Chicago.

Smith, T. (1990). The sexual revolution? *Public Opinion Quarterly 54:* 415–435.

Stern, S., & A. Handel. (2001). Sexuality and mass media: The historical context of psychology's reaction to sexuality on the Internet. *The Journal of Sex Research 38* (4): 283–291.

Sundholm, M. (1973). The pornographic arcade: Ethnographic notes on moral men in immoral places. *Urban Life 2:* 85–104.

Thomburgh, D., & H. Lin (Eds). (2002). *Youth, pornography, and the Internet.* Washington, D.C., National Academy Press.

Tewksbury, R. (1990). Patrons of porn: Research notes on the clientele of adult bookstores. *Deviant Behavior 11:* 259–271.

Tibbetts, S., & M. Blankenship. (1999). Explaining citizens' attitudes toward pornography: Differential effects of predictors across levels of geographic proximity to outlet sources. *Justice Quarterly 16*: 735–763.

United States Commission on Obscenity and Pornography. (1970). Final Report. Washington, D.C.: U.S. Government Printing Office.

United States Department of Justice. (1986). Attorney General's Commission on Pornography Final Report. Volumes 1 and 2. Washington D.C.: U.S. Government Printing Office.

Waskul, D. 2002. The naked self: Being a body in televideo cybersex. *Symbolic Interaction 25* (2): 188–227.

Weatherford, J. M. (1986). *Porn row.* New York: Arbor House.

Weinberg, M., & C. Williams. (1980). Sexual Embourgeoisment? Social Class and Sexual Activity: 1938–1970. *American Sociological Review 45*: 33–48.

Williams, L. 1989 (1999). *Hard Core: Power, pleasure, and the "frenzy of the visible."* California: University of California Press.

ADULT SOCIAL BONDS AND USE OF INTERNET PORNOGRAPHY

STEVEN STACK   *Wayne State University*
IRA WASSERMAN   *Eastern Michigan University*
ROGER KERN   *Eastern Michigan University*

Pornography has become an enormous commercial success in the last two decades. For example, the number of hard-core video rentals has ballooned from 75 million in 1986 to 665 million in 1996. The United States has become the world's largest producer of hard-core videos with more than 150 titles produced per week. Further revenue is reaped from the sales of sex magazines, Internet porn, phone sex businesses, peep shows, and adult cable programming. In all, the industry grossed eight billion dollars in 1996, more than the entire receipts from all Hollywood's movies put together (Fisher and Barak, 2000; Thio, 2001).

Cyberporn, explicit sexual material available on the Internet, is a relatively new form of pornography. By 1997 there were about 900 pornography sites on the web. Just one year later this had grown to between 20,000–30,000. These websites vary considerably in the number of paid users, from a few hundred to many thousands of people. The sites are nearly as popular as travel and business sites. Cyberporn revenues reached $700 million by the late 1990s (Elmer-DeWitt, 2001; Thio, 2001; Weber, 1997). Observers of cyberporn have speculated that the growth in its popularity is linked to the three "As": accessability, affordability, and anonymity (e.g., Putnam 2000).

Cyberporn has received some scholarly attention in the literature, but most of this coverage has consisted of descriptive treatments of the subject. These analyses do not rigorously test major sociological theoretical perspectives of why some people use cyberporn and others do not.

The present paper makes several contributions to the literature on cyberporn. First, it supplements psychological and descriptive analysis of cyberporn by testing a sociological theoretical framework on the incidence of cyberporn use. In particular, it focuses on an integrated theoretical model that blends together elements from the social control, social learning, and opportunity theories of deviance (Cullen and Agnew, 2003). Second, the present article extends previous work on adult social bonds and deviance (e.g., Benson, 2002; Piqero and Mazzerole, 2000; Sampson and Laub, 1990), to include the neglected ties to religious and political beliefs. Third, the analysis incorporates the neglected knowledge-based dimension of opportunity theory (Kern, 2000). It argues that knowledge of computer techniques relevant to Internet use constitutes an opportunity factor that, in turn, increases the odds of cyberporn use. Fourth, the article also incorporates measures of deviant lifestyles. The use of cyberporn may, for example, reflect a broader engagement in a deviant lifestyle related to sexual freedom. This is the first systematic study to apply these theories to the specific problem of cyberporn.

Previous Literature and Theoretical Framework

Scholarly research on the description and explanation of cyberporn has been dominated by psychologists and clinicians (e.g., Fisher and Barak, 2001; Putnam, 2000; Quayle and Taylor, 2001, 2002; Stein et al., 2001). These have included works in three general categories: proposals to apply psychological antecedents of *pornography* use to the problem of cyberpornography, clinical studies of patients and convicted offenders, and descriptive studies.

Psychological studies of pornography use have *speculated* that factors such as personality disorders (e.g., mood and anxiety disorders and depression), traumas (physical, sexual, family), biological factors (e.g., high testosterone), and substance abuse may be related to cyberporn use (e.g., see reviews in Fisher and Barak, 2001:315–17; Putnam 2000:554). However, these arguments have been based primarily on studies of offline compulsive sexual behavior that includes rape and child molestation. Further, models of offline deviant sexual behavior may not apply to cyberpornography (Fisher and Barak, 2001:315). Psychological researchers have called for theory testing of their suggested models (e.g., Fisher and Barak, 2000; Putnam, 2000), but the one relevant study was unable to find support for most of the hypothesized psychological predictors of cyberporn use among college students (Fisher and Barak, 2001:315).

Clinical work includes case studies of how cyberporn use is related to hypersexual disorders or how continued use is related to deceit (e.g., Quayle and Taylor, 2001; Stein et al., 2001). Given the small, selective samples of the clinical studies, it is difficult to determine to what extent the antecedents of cyberpornography use found would apply to the general population of cyberporn users. Purely descriptive work includes classification schemes of cyberporn images (Mehta, 2001; Rimm, 1995), a content analysis of Internet rape sites (Gossett and Byrne, 2002), and an in-depth study of the motivations for collecting child pornography among 13 convicted offenders (Quayle and Taylor, 2002).

The present study first focuses on social control theory for building its theoretical framework (e.g., Hirschi, 1969; Hirschi and Gottfredson, 2001; Kornhauser, 1978; Sampson and Laub, 1990, 2001). According to control theory, all people are inherently predisposed to deviant behavior. Bonds or stakes in conformity lower the odds of deviance. Deviance threatens loss of such bonds. The bonds that are most salient vary across the life course (Sampson and Laub, 2001). Sampson and Laub (1990) suggest that the more important adult bonds that contribute to the prevention of adult crime and deviant behavior revolve around marriage, work, and ties to the greater community.

Marital Bonds

In particular, marriage per se may not prevent deviance. In extreme cases, for example, a marriage can be so unhappy as to be associated with substance abuse and other social problems such as domestic violence. A meaningful, happy marriage may be a better measure of a marital bond that is most likely to deter deviant behavior among adults (Sampson and Laub, 1990).

Religious Bonds

Among adults, a neglected feature of social control theory is religious ties. A meta-analysis of more than 50 studies on religiosity and deviance determined that there was a highly consistent relationship between the two variables. However, only half a dozen studies are based on adults (Baier and Wright, 2001). Nevertheless, the related literature on attitudes toward pornography often finds a strong link between the strength of religiosity and greater condemnation of pornography (e.g., Hayes, 1995; Sherkat and Ellison, 1997). To the extent that attitudes predict behavior (e.g., Warr and Stafford, 1991), we would predict that condemnation of pornography would make its use less likely. In addition, religious organizations in the United States have often led moral crusades against pornography, and are well known for condemning sexual deviance (e.g., Sherkat and Ellison, 1997). Furthermore, members of organized churches may be under greater surveillance (e.g., by co-religionists), making them less likely to deviate from sexual norms (Tittle and Welch, 1983). Those individuals who attend services more often are most likely to be influenced by religious belief systems and co-religionists.

Some caution should be exercised in interpreting any association between religiosity and deviance in the present study. The effect of religiosity on deviant behavior can be interpreted from an alternative theoretical perspective (e.g., Tittle and Welch, 1983). In addition to acting as an external control to hold back individuals from deviance, religion may function as an internal control. From the standpoint of social learning theory (Akers, 2000), through the process of socialization, persons may learn from religious systems that the use of pornographic sexual materials is inappropriate, and eventually internalize negative definitions of pornography.

Bonds to Conservative Beliefs

A key dimension of the social bond is support for conventional beliefs. Deviance that runs contrary to these beliefs can result in costs to the individual, including guilt and ostracism from the group (Hirschi, 1969). Use of cyberpornography may be constrained by ideological ties to a broader conservative belief system. Political conservatives are more likely than liberals to support traditional behaviors in general (e.g., Peek, Witt, and Gay, 1982). Persons tied to conventional society in terms of their political beliefs may face ostracism and other informal social controls if they are discovered using the Internet for sexual gratification.

Socioeconomic Bonds

Socioeconomic bonds can provide another link to conventional society that may prevent adults from engaging in deviant sexual behavior. Previous research has demonstrated that meaningful work was a key predictor of low adult involvement in a host of deviant behaviors. These behaviors ranged from felony crime to alcohol abuse (Sampson and Laub, 1990). If all else is equal, Internet users (who have higher income, higher educational levels, and more prestigious jobs) might be expected to have lower involvement in cyberpornography. However, given that Internet users are relatively affluent, there may not be enough variation in SES, in this select population, for SES to be related to cyberporn use.

Deviant Sexual Lifestyles

Cyberporn use may be, in part, a derivative of (1) membership in deviant subcultures, including those emphasizing sexual freedom, and (2) a more individual-based sex-drivenness. Deviant subcultures affect individual behavior through shared values, norms, and beliefs (Vold, Bernard, and Snipes, 2002:164-71). A deviant sexual subculture might involve persons engaged in deviant sexual behavior in more general terms. Wysocki's (2001) descriptive work indicates that sex chat rooms attract a high proportion of sexual deviants; in particular, 22 percent of the users reported that they were bisexual and 3 percent reported being transsexuals.

Research on forcible rape has often found that generalized sex-drivenness is a predictor of forcible sex (e.g., Malamuth et al., 1991). In a study of 2,652 men, Malamuth et al. (1991) determined that the number of sex partners (index of sex drive) was the best predictor of rape even after controls were introduced for alternative theories. Sex-drivenness, or hypersexuality, has been hypothesized to be related to the use of cyberporn (e.g., Putnam, 2000:554). The present study cannot resolve the debate over the role of sex-drivenness in sexual deviancy. Nevertheless, it will include indicators of sex drive and deviant sexual behaviors in its model. However, these indicators may be interpreted in other ways besides relying on the concept of biological sex-drivenness. For example, persons with previous exposure to adultery and paid sex may simply have learned a positive attitude toward such behavior, which may contribute to their attraction to cyberpornography. If forms of sexual deviance are related to cyberporn use, the present article cannot determine the exact nature of this association due to data limitations.

It is also possible that involvement in other forms of deviancy and membership in other deviant subcultures may increase the likelihood of cyberporn usage as a pattern of deviance. Various forms of deviance and health risk behaviors are often found to be highly interrelated (Bachman et al., 2002). The general phenomenon of hypersexuality has often been related to substance abuse (Putnam, 2000:554). The present study will incorporate measures of drug use as a possible lifestyle predictor of cyberporn use.

Criminal opportunity theory argues that criminality is most likely to occur at the intersection of three conditions: the presence of a class of motivated offenders, the absence of guardians and other deterrents to crime, and the presence of a suitable target. To date, opportunity theory has been applied mainly to explaining variation in "predatory crime" (e.g., Akers, 2000; Cohen and Felson, 1979; Felson, 1994; Stack, 1982). However, Kern (2000), in a study of motivations of prostitute clients, shows that opportunity can be applied to nonpredatory and/or victimless crimes. It is argued that in place of capable guardians or a lack of suitable victims to block opportunity, a lack of necessary tools, knowledge, and/or expertise can act as similar obstacles to engaging in a chosen criminal or deviant activity.

Internet users vary in the level of their knowledge of computers and software capabilities. To fully utilize cyberporn, for example, it helps if one has the appropriate software and knowledge to download images and video. Hence, persons with greater computer skills and with ownership of the relevant software might be more apt to take advantage of cyberporn opportunities than ones lacking in these resources. Further, the presence of children in the home may reduce opportunities for cyberpornography. Children can act as guardians and report the use of pornography to other adults in the home; children also can reduce opportunities for viewing porn on the family computer by increasing demand for limited Internet time. They may need to use the family's computer for school assignments, computer games, chat rooms, email, and other uses. In particular, the presence of teenage children may represent the greatest threat to discovery and the greatest competing demand for computer time for potential adult cyberporn offenders.

Methods

Data are taken from the General Social Survey for the year 2000 (Davis, 2001). The analysis is restricted to persons who reported having used the Internet and for which complete data were available ($N = 531$). The dependent variable is a dichotomous variable. The respondents were asked if they had visited a sexually explicit website during the last 30 days. Persons who reported that they had are coded as 1, all others are coded 0. Given that the dependent variable is a binary variable, logistic regression techniques are appropriate (Borooah, 2002).

Social Bonds

Religious bonds are measured in terms of three variables. (1) The frequency of church attendance on a seven-point index from never to several times a week or more. The higher the level of attendance the greater the ties to a religious group. (2) Conservative religious orientation is measured by a dichotomous variable, the respondent identifying himself or herself as a fundamentalist (0, 1). (3) The religious dimension of belief is measured as a dichotomous variable, belief in an afterlife (0, 1). Some caution should be exercised in interpreting the results of the present study as it is based on self-report data. Religious persons may be less likely to admit to using cyberporn than their counterparts, unless they have been socialized to value honesty more than their counterparts. However, a meta-analysis of research on religiosity and deviance found that the relationship holds across self-report studies (such as the GSS) and studies based on third-party or official data (Baier and Wright, 2001).

Bonds to a Spouse

Bonds to a spouse refers to the presence of a happy marriage where 1 = respondent reports being very happily married and 0 = all others.

Bonds to Liberal Beliefs

The measure of conservative beliefs is self-reported political liberalism. This is measured on a seven-point index from 1 = very conservative to 7 = very liberal. This variable is predicted to be positively related to cyberporn usage.

Socioeconomic Bonds

Socioeconomic bonds are measured in relation to years of education. Income and occupational status were also used in results not reported here. However, they never emerged as significant predictors of cyberporn use and so were dropped from the analysis. This may be due to a problem of restricted ranges. Given that Internet use requires computer technology, the Internet users are disproportionately from higher socioeconomic groups to begin with. There may not be enough variation in some measures of SES levels to affect deviant behavior.

Opportunity Factors

Opportunity factors are measured in two ways. First, knowledge of computer technology is measured as the sum of four variables: how to download a file from the worldwide web, how to send a file to someone, knowledge of what a virus is, and knowledge of the name of a search engine. Responses were coded as yes/no (0, 1). Scores ranged from zero to four (Davis, 2001:822–23). The alpha reliability coefficient was 0.74, indicating that the measure possesses internal consistency. Second, we measure the presence of a teenage child in the home as a binary variable (0, 1).

Deviant Lifestyles

Three available measures of deviant sexual lifestyles are incorporated into the present analysis. First, lifetime prevalence of ever having strayed (committed adultery) in marriage is coded as a binary variable (0, 1). Second, lifetime prevalence of ever having paid for or been paid for sex (prostitution) is coded as a dichotomous variable (0, 1). Third, the number of sex partners the respondent reported having had in the last five years is a measure of sex-drivenness. A second deviant lifestyle is measured in relation to drug use. Two measures are available in the General Social Survey. These are lifetime prevalence of crack use (0, 1) and lifetime prevalence of intravenous drug use (0, 1).

Demographic Controls

Demographic controls thought to have a bearing on use of cyberporn are taken from the related literature on the correlates of attitudes toward pornography (e.g., Sherkat and Ellison, 1997; Tibbetts and Blankenship, 1999; Wood and Hughes, 1984). Gender is measured as a dichotomous variable where 1 = male. Race is measured as a dichotomous variable where white = 1 and all others = 0. Rural residence is measured as a binary category (0, 1) where 1 = living in open country or in unincorporated and/or incorporated places of less than 2,500 persons. Region of residence is measured as a series of binary variables: Pacific (0, 1), South (0, 1), and the remaining regions serve as the benchmark category.

Analysis

Table 4 presents the results of a logistic multiple regression analysis of the predictors of cyberporn use. Gender (male) is a strong predictor of cyberporn use. From the odds ratio (OR), males are 6.43 times more likely to use cyberporn than females. Three indicators of adult social bonds bore significant relationships to cyberporn use net of controls. A unit change in church attendance was associated with a 26 percent decrease in the odds of cyberporn use

TABLE 4. The Influence of Adult Social Bonds, Opportunity Factors, Deviant Life Styles, and Demographic Controls on Use of Cyberpornography, Logistic Regression Results, Odds Ratios, General Social Survey, 2000 (N = 531 Internet Users)

Independent Variable	Odds Ratio
Gender (M)	6.43*
Adult Social Bonds	
Church attendance	0.74*
Fundamentalist	1.91
Religious belief	1.09
Happy marriage	0.39*
Beliefs: political	1.19*
Education	1.03
Deviant Lifestyles	
Adultery	3.18*
Paid sex	3.70*
Number of sex partners	1.00
Crack use	0.62
IDU drug use	0.85
Opportunity Factors	
Teen children	0.55
Knowledge of PCs	1.12*
Demographic Controls	
White	1.50
Rural	2.49
Pacific region	2.44*
Southern region	1.19
Age	0.96*
Model Fit Indicators	
Model chi-square	140.5*
Nagelkerke R^2	0.40

*Associated logistic regression coefficient significant using Wald chi-square test, $p < 0.05$.

(1.00 – OR 0.74). Further, persons who were reportedly happily married were 61 percent less apt to report cyberporn use. Finally, for the relatively unexplored belief dimension of political liberalism, a one-unit increase in liberalism was associated with a 19 percent increase in the odds of using cyberporn.

Two indicators of deviant lifestyles had significant relationships to cyberporn use. Both indicators of a deviant sexual lifestyle were predictive of cyberporn usage. Persons ever having an extramarital affair were 3.18 times more apt to have used cyberporn than ones who had lacked affairs. Further, those ever having engaged in paid sex were 3.7 times more apt than those who had not to be using cyberporn. Indicators of drug use were, however, unrelated to cyberporn use.

Opportunity theory was supported by the findings on the relationship between knowledge of the Internet and computers. For a one-unit increase in PC knowledge, the odds of cyberporn use rose by 12 percent. Finally, two demographic factors were predictive of cyberporn use net of controls. Persons residing in the Pacific region were 2.44 times more likely than those in other regions to be using cyberporn. Turning to age, for every additional year, the odds of cyberporn use decline by 4 percent.

Three indicators of model fit suggest that the present model represents a strong fit to the data. According to the Nagelkerke R^2 (Borooah, 2002), the model explains 40 percent of the variance in cyberporn use. Further, the model chi-square also indicates a good model fit ($p < 0.000$). Finally, the full model correctly predicted the classification of 87.6 percent the 531 Internet users as either users or nonusers of cyberporn.

In results not reported here, the independent variables from Table 4 were run as predictor variables for predicting several variables with close associations with cyberporn use. The results of the analysis, where church attendance is the dependent variable and the remaining x-variables are the independent variables, determined that controlling for the other variables, the strongest predictor of attendance is being a fundamentalist. Although having no direct effect on cyberporn use, this variable has a powerful indirect effect on cyberporn through promoting church attendance. Other strong predictors of church attendance include education, being happily married, and being politically conservative. The significant predictors of being happily married included political liberalism (negative association), being a parent of teens, being white, and age. Adultery is best predicted by having engaged in paid sex and age. Paid sex is best predicted by gender (male) followed by adultery. Finally, the greater the education level, the greater the knowledge of computer techniques. Although insignificant in Table 4, education has a significant indirect effect on cyberporn use through its association with knowledge of computer techniques.

Discussion

Previous literature on cyberpornography has been dominated by psychological models and descriptive work. Little empirical work has been done on the predictors of cyberpornography use and, in particular, no systematic study has been done on the sociological predictors of cyberporn use. The present study tests a sociological model of cyberpornography use. It finds strong support for the linkages between social control variables and cyberporn use. These direct links include those involving religious, marital, and political bonds. Although religious bonds have been neglected in control theory as it applies to adults, they had a stronger negative influence on cyberporn use than the indicator of marital bonds—being happily married.

The results on religious bonds are consistent with a descriptive study by Wysocki (2001) of a sex chat room on the Internet. Wysocki (2001) briefly mentioned that half the users reported that religion had no influence on their lives and also that half reported no religious affiliation. These figures represent a lower than average level of religiosity (e.g., Davis, 2001). The results of the present study on religious bonds among adults are also consistent with a large body of evidence on the effect of religious bonds on deviance among juveniles (Baier and Wright, 2001; Stack, 1994) and sexual deviance among adults (Stack and Gundlach, 1992).

Past sexual deviant behavior had, however, an even more powerful impact on cyberporn use than religious bonds. In particular, involvement in paid sex was a somewhat more powerful factor in predicting cyberporn use than any significant measure of social bonds. Caution needs to be exercised in interpreting this finding. Due to the lack of relevant data in the GSS, we cannot adequately determine the root cause of this association. One possibility is that cyberporn users may be part of a broader subculture of sexual deviance that legitimizes various forms of deviant sexuality. However, such involvement in a deviant sexual subculture cannot be measured in the data at hand.

There was some support for an opportunity theory of deviance. Persons who reported greater knowledge of Internet-oriented computer techniques were more likely to have used cyberporn. Although having no direct association with cyberporn, being a parent of teenage children influenced cyberporn use through its positive associations with church attendance and marital happiness. Opportunity theory, then, applies to the victimless deviant act of cyberporn use.

Finally, the present study documented a strong relationship between gender and cyberporn. Males were more than six times as likely to use cyberporn than females. Previous work on attitudes toward pornography has shown that men are more approving of pornography than women (e.g., McCabe, 2000:75). To the extent that attitudes are predictive of behavior, a premise central to differential association theory (e.g., Warr and Stafford, 1991), we would expect men to be more involved in the consumption of pornographic materials, including cyberporn. Further, testosterone level is predictive of hypersexual behavior (e.g., Putnam, 2000:554). So from a biological standpoint, to the extent that use of cyberpornography is a sign of hypersexual behavior, we would expect men to be more likely than women to use cyberpornography. Further, to the extent that women are more involved in religion than men, and religion represents a source of sanctions against sexual deviance, we would expect men to be more apt to consume cyberpornography. However, we cannot rigorously test some of these possible interpretations of the gender factor since we do not have data on testosterone level or attitudes toward cyberpornography. Nevertheless, gender continued to influence cyberporn usage even after controls for many covariates of gender. Further work is needed on data sets containing additional theoretically relevant covariates of gender. Such work could determine which covariates account for the strong association between being male and using cyberporn.

The present study is one of a few that try to explain the use of pornography—why some groups may be more apt to use it than others. The results of the present study tend to be consistent with a related theory-testing subfield: the study of factors affecting the formation of *attitudes* toward pornography. These studies generally find that acceptance of pornography is associated with such factors as religious affiliation, self-perceived conservatism, and attitudes toward morality (e.g., Miller, 1994; Sherkat and Ellison, 1997; Tibbetts and Blankenship, 1999; Wood and Hughes, 1984).

The other major theory-testing area in pornography studies concerns the effects of exposure to pornography. This area centers on the question of pornography's effect on sexual violence and sexual aggression. Many studies have reported a positive association between pornography use and sexual violence (Bergen and Bogle, 2000; Boeringer, 1994; Ford and Linney, 1995; Howitt, 1995; Lavoie, Robitaille, and Herbert, 2000; Malamuth and Donnerstein, 1984; Perse, 1994). Future research might explore the effects of exposure to cyberporn on aggressive sexual behavior. The present study could not accomplish this goal, given the limitations of the data in the General Social Surveys.

There has been discussion on the need for more regulation of cyberpornography, especially child pornography, which is a criminal offense (e.g., Durkin, 1997; McCabe, 2000). Children who are sexually molested tend to suffer a variety of negative consequences, including psychological, physical, and social damages. The Internet, which is increasingly the main disseminator of child pornography (Quayle and Taylor, 2002:332), may intensify the incidence of child molestation in two ways. The Internet makes depictions, both pictorial images and films, easily available. Further, the emergence of sexual chat rooms can heighten sexual fantasies and also facilitate actual person-to-person exploitative sexual encounters offline (Durkin, 1997; Quayle and Taylor, 2002). The present study suggests that the strengthening of adult social bonds, especially those to religion and marriage, might reduce the attraction to cyberpornography in general, and, perhaps, child cyberpornography in particular.

References

Akers, Ronald. 2000. *Criminological Theories.* Los Angeles, Cal.: Roxbury.

Bachman, Jerald, Patrick O'Malley, John Schulenberg, Lloyd Johnston, Alison Bryant, and Alicia Merline. 2002. *The Decline of Substance Abuse in Young Adulthood.* London: Lawrence Erlbaum Associates.

Baier, Colin, and Bradley R. E. Wright. 2001. "If You Love Me, Keep My Commandments: A Meta Analysis of the Effect of Religion on Crime." *Journal of Research on Crime and Delinquency* 38:3–21.

Benson, Michael. 2002. *Crime and the Life Course.* Belmont, Cal.: Wadsworth.

Bergen, Raquel, and Katherine Bogle. 2000. "Exploring the Connection Between Pornography and Sexual Violence." *Violence and Victims* 15:227–34.

Boeringer, Scott. 1994. "Pornography & Sexual Aggression." *Deviant Behavior* 15:289–304.

Borooah, Vani. 2002. *Logit and Probit.* Thousand Oaks, Cal.: Sage.

Cohen, Lawrence, and Marcus Felson. 1979. "Social Change and Crime Rate Trends: A Routine Activity Approach." *American Sociological Review* 44:588–608.

Cullen, Francis, and Robert Agnew, eds. 2003. *Criminological Theories.* Los Angeles, Cal.: Roxbury.

Davis, James. 2001. *General Social Surveys, 1972–2000, Cumulative Codebook.* Storrs, Conn.: Roper Center for Public Opinion Research.

Durkin, Keith. 1997. "Misuse of the Internet by Pedophiles." *Federal Probation* 61:14–18.

Elmer-DeWitt, Philip. 2001. "On a Screen Near You: Cyberporn." p. 398 in Nathaniel Terrell and Robert Meier, eds., *Readings in Deviant Behavior.* New York: Harcourt.

Felson, Marcus. 1994. *Crime and Everyday Life.* Thousand Oaks, Cal.: Pine Forge Press.

Fisher, William, and Azy Barak. 2000. "Online Sex Shops: Phenomenological, and Ideological Perspectives on Internet Sexuality." *Cyber Psychology & Behavior* 3:575–89.

————. 2001. "Internet Pornography: A Social Psychological Perspective on Internet Sexuality." *Journal for Sex Research* 38:312–23.

Ford, Michele, and Jean Ann Linney. 1995. "Comparative Analysis of Juvenile Sex Offenders, Violent Nonsexual Offenders, and Status Offenders." *Journal of Interpersonal Violence* 10:56–70.

Gossett, Jennifer, and Sarah Byrne. 2002. "Click Here, a Content Analysis of Internet Rape Sites." *Gender and Society* 16:689–709.

Hayes, Bernadette. 1995. "Religious Identification and Moral Attitudes: The British Case." *British Journal of Sociology* 46:459–74.

Hirschi, Travis. 1969. *Causes of Delinquency.* Berkeley, Cal.: University of California Press.

Hirschi, Travis, and Michael Gottfredson. 2001. "Control Theory and the Life Course Perspective." Pp. 229–41 in Alex Piqero and Paul Mazerolle, eds., *Life Course Criminality: Contemporary and Classic Readings.* Belmont, Cal.: Wadsworth.

Howitt, Dennis. 1995. "Pornography and the Pedophile: Is it Criminogenic?" *British Journal of Psychology* 68:15–27.

Kern, Roger. 2000. *Where's the Action: Criminal Motivations Among Prostitution Clients.* Ann Arbor, Mich.: University Microfilms.

Kornhauser, Ruth. 1978. *Social Sources of Delinquency.* Chicago, Ill.: University of Chicago Press.

Lavoie, Francine, Line Robitaille, and Martiine Hebert. 2000. "Teen Dating Relationships and Aggression." *Violence Against Women* 6:6–36.

McCabe, Kimberly. 2000. "Child Pornography and the Internet." *Social Science Computer Review* 18:73–76.

Malamuth, Neal, and Edward Donnerstein, eds. 1984. *Pornography and Sexual Aggression.* New York: Academic Press.

Malamuth, Neal, Robert Sockloskie, Mary Koss, and J. S. Tanaka. 1991. "Characteristics of Aggressors Against Women: Testing a Model Using a National Sample of College Students." *Journal of Consulting and Clinical Psychology* 59:670–81.

Mehta, Michael D. 2001. "Pornography in Usenet: A Study of 9,800 Randomly Selected Images." *Cyber Psychology & Behavior* 4:695–703.

Miller, Alan. 1994. "Dynamic Indicators of Self-Perceived Conservatism." *Sociological Quarterly* 35:175–82.

Peek, Charles, David Witt, and David Gay. 1982. "Pornography: Important Political Symbol or Limited Political Issue?" *Sociological Focus* 15:41–51.

Perse, Elizabeth M. 1994. "Uses of Erotica and Acceptance of Rape Myths." *Communications Research* 21:488–515.

Putnam, D. E. 2000. "Initiation and Maintenance of Online Sexual Compulsivity. Implications for Assessment and Treatment." *Cyber Psychology and Behavior* 3:553–64.

Quayle, Ethel, and Max Taylor. 2001. "Child Seduction and Self-Representation on the Internet." *Cyber Psychology & Behavior* 4:597–608.

————. 2002. "Child Pornography and the Internet." *Deviant Behavior* 23:331–61.

Rimm, M. 1995. "Marketing Pornography on the Information Superhighway." *Georgetown Law Journal* 83:1849–1934.

Sampson, Robert, and John Laub. 1990. "Crime and Deviance Over the Life Course." *American Sociological Review* 55:609–27.

_____. 2001. "Understanding Variability in Lives Through Time: Contributions of Life Course Criminality." Pp. 242–58 in Alex Piqero and Paul Mazerolle, eds., *Life Course Criminality: Contemporary and Classic Readings*. Belmont, Cal.: Wadsworth.

Sherkat, Darren, and Christopher Ellison. 1997. "The Cognitive Structure of a Moral Crusade: Conservative Protestantism and Opposition to Pornography." *Social Forces* 75:957–82.

Stack, Steven. 1982. "Social Structure and Swedish Crime Rates: A Time Series Analysis, 1950–1979." *Criminology* 20:499–514.

_____. 1994. "The Effect of Geographical Mobility on Premarital Sex." *Journal of Marriage and the Family* 56:204–08.

Stack, Steven, and James Gundlach. 1992. "Divorce and Sex." *Archives of Sexual Behavior* 21:359–67.

Stein, Dan, Donald Black, Nathan Shapira, and Robert Spitzer. 2001. "Hypersexual Disorder and Preoccupation with Internet Pornography." *American Journal of Psychiatry* 158:1590–94.

Thio, Alex. 2001. *Deviant Behavior,* 6th ed. Boston, Mass.: Allyn and Bacon.

Tibbetts, Stephen, and Michael Blankenship. 1999. "Explaining Citizen Attitudes Toward Pornography." *Justice Quarterly* 16:735–63.

Tittle, Charles, and Michael Welch. 1983. "Religiosity and Deviance: Toward a Contingency Theory of Constraining Effects." *Social Forces* 61:653–82.

Vold, George, Thomas Bernard, and Jeffrey Snipes. 2002. *Theoretical Criminology*. New York: Oxford University Press.

Warr, Mark, and Mark Stafford. 1991. "The Influence of Delinquent Peers: What They Say or What They Do?" *Criminology* 29:851–66.

Weber, Thomas. 1997. "The X-Files." *Wall Street Journal* May 20:A1, A8.

Wood, Michael, and Michael Hughes. 1984. "The Moral Basis of Moral Reform: Status Discontent vs. Culture and Socialization as Explanation of Anti-Pornography Social Movement Adherence." *American Sociological Review* 49:86–99.

Wysocki, Diane K. 2001. "Let Your Fingers Do the Talking: Sex on an Adult Chat Line." In Alex Thio and Thomas Calhoun, eds., *Readings in Deviant behavior*. Boston, Mass.: Allyn and Bacon.

Conclusion

These studies illustrate the issue of pornography, that is, the demographics that are most likely to use pornography. Further, these studies indicate that the form of technology is important for the use of pornography. In addition, these studies have identified that better ties to religion and a happy marriage may be insulators from using pornography over the Internet.

Discussion Questions

1. What is Buzzell's definition of pornography?
2. How does Buzzell define technology and how is it similar to the definition of technology used in this book?
3. Why do Stack et al. focus on Internet pornography?
4. Why did Stack et al. focus on social control theory?

4

Identity Theft/Cyberfraud

Cyberfraud includes behaviors that occur with guile and deceit. An example of this behavior is identity theft that may lead to identity fraud. Hoar (2001) argued that identity theft is a criminal activity for the new millennium. Several have defined identity theft by combining it with identity fraud. For instance, one definition of identity theft is "the unlawful use of another's personal identifying information" (Bellah, 2001, p. 222). Others have defined identity theft as "involv[ing] financial or other personal information stolen with intent of establishing another person's identity as the thief's own . . . " (Identity Theft, 2004c). The FTC sees identity theft as "occur[ring] when someone uses your personally identifying information, like your name, social security number, or credit card number without your permission, to commit fraud or other crimes" (www.ftc. gov/bcp/edu/microsities/idtheft/consumers/about-identity-theft.html).

The first paper in this chapter, written by A. J. Elbirt, explores issues surrounding identity theft. Elbirt defines identity theft and provides a list of tactics that may be necessary to reduce instances of identity theft.

The second paper in this chapter, written by Wang, Yuan, and Archer, explores identity theft. Wang et al. provide an overview of the problem of identity theft, followed by a formal definition and a definition of identity thieves. The article includes the views on combating identity theft.

WHO ARE YOU? HOW TO PROTECT
AGAINST IDENTITY THEFT

A. J. ELBIRT   *University of Massachusetts; Center for Network and Information Security*

Identity theft has become one of the most lucrative criminal endeavors, with over half a million cases reported in the United States resulting in annual losses in the billions of dollars. Facilitated by the voluminous information available on the Internet to those who know where to look, the reported incidents of identity theft have grown at an unprecedented rate. Unfortunately, while the victims of identity theft may spend years attempting to clear their credit histories and criminal records, this crime is rarely prosecuted. While numerous laws have been enacted in an attempt by the United States government to address the issue of identity theft, the best protection available to consumers is constant vigilance.

With more than 100 million Americans connected to the Internet [1], information security has become a top priority. Many applications—electronic mail, electronic banking, medical databases, and electronic commerce—require the exchange of private information. As an example, when engaging in electronic commerce, customers provide credit card numbers when purchasing products. Identity theft, the fastest growing type of fraud, affected 500,000 Americans in 2001, resulting in over $2 billion in losses at an average cost of $17,000 per victim of which roughly $1,500 is required just to repair the damage to a victim's credit report. From January through September of 2003, nearly 10 million Americans were identified as victims of identity fraud, resulting in over $5 billion in victim out-of-pocket losses and $48 billion in losses to businesses and financial institutions according to a Federal Trade Commission report [2]–[8], [15], [18], [20]. Through the use of e-mail address hiding, the Internet has enabled identity thieves to flourish, increasing the scale of this type of fraud by a factor of up to 50 when compared to more traditional types of fraud [2], [4], [5], [8], [9]. Moreover, identity fraud is a criminal activity that typically goes un-prosecuted and under-punished. According to a Gartner study, identity thieves have only a 1 in 700 chance of being either exposed or arrested [3].

Identity theft is the assumption of another person's financial identity through the use of the victim's identifying information. This information includes a person's name, address, date of birth, social security number, credit card numbers, and checking account information. With this information, a thief is capable of charging merchandise to the victim's account and changing the billing address for the account so that the unauthorized purchases remain undetected.

Identity theft opens the door to other crimes, such as gaining access to welfare and social security benefits, ordering new checks to a new address, obtaining new credit cards, obtaining the victim's paycheck, taking out loans in the victim's name, and using the victim's name upon arrest [2], [3], [5]–[7], [9], [10], [15], [17]–[20]. The most common forms of identity theft involve credit card usage and social security numbers. According to Garner, 70% of credit card related cases of identity theft involve insiders [3], [6], [8]. Social security numbers also pose a significant problem in that they are overused as customer account numbers and employee numbers, giving a thief a "master key" into an individual's digital identity [2]–[4], [6], [9].

Tactics

Identity thieves are extremely resourceful in their efforts to obtain personal information about their victims. Dumpster diving, i.e., searching someone's garbage, and mail theft are commonly used to obtain credit card numbers and bank account numbers from discarded statements. Preapproved credit card offers are also frequent targets of thieves intent upon establishing a line of credit based on false credentials [2]–[6]. Basic theft of electronic equipment such as laptops and personal digital assistants may yield significant amounts of personal information. Moreover, thieves often pose as legitimate account managers for credit card companies and financial institutions and ask for personal information under the guise of account verification or maintenance [2], [3]. Even worse, an identity thief may legally obtain much of the necessary personal information for perpetrating identity fraud by using public information sources. Examples of these types of sources include online data resellers and information brokers that provide background information on an individual for a small fee [2], [3], [10].

Additional options abound for computer savvy identity thieves. Much like Trojan horse programs and Internet worms, it is possible for an attacker to place a file on a user's computer to track their actions, intercept electronic communications, and snoop through files to gain the desired information. Even more aggressive strategies include [2]:

- Creating fake e-commerce sites with desirable products at cheap prices to lure customers into providing detailed personal information.
- Gaining unauthorized access to online systems and placing programs on servers to allow unauthorized persons to access the system.
- Publicly posting fake product sales information to Usenet forums with links to web pages asking for more detailed personal information.

Laws Designed to Protect Consumers

A number of laws have been enacted in an effort to protect consumer information privacy and deter identity theft. The Health Insurance Portability and Accountability Act (HIPPA) was passed in 1996 and attempted to address the confidentiality of patient information by forbidding the divulgence of individually identifiable health-care information without patient authorization or prior consent. HIPPA covered health-care information obtained both electronically and orally, requiring health-care providers to protect both the confidentiality and integrity of patient information. HIPPA also requires health-care providers to supply patients with a notice of their privacy rights and the privacy practices of the provider. Finally, HIPPA states that health-care providers must safeguard against unauthorized use and disclosure of patient information and these providers must obtain a patient's written authorization in advance if the provider is to use protected health-care information for most purposes not related to treatment or payment. Note that exceptions to this requirement exist for certain public health purposes, law enforcement, and other public purposes [11].

The Identity Theft and Assumption Deterrence Act, passed in 1998, addresses the use of another person's identification information without lawful authority. This law classifies identity theft as a felony violation at the state or local level (whichever is determined to be more appropriate) if the theft results in further activities that violate federal law [6], [10].

The Gramm-Leach-Blily Act of 1999 targets the protection of private consumer information by financial institutions. The law classifies the obtaining of private consumer information via fraudulent means as a federal crime. This law includes fictitious statements made to all employees, officers, or agents of the financial institution or those statements made to customers in an attempt to obtain the desired information. The law also details the obligations that financial institutions have to consumers to guarantee the security and confidentiality of customer records against unauthorized access and use in addition to other likely threats against the nonpublic personal information that these institutions collect from their clients. Moreover, the law specifically enables states to enact and enforce laws that are tougher than the Gramm-Leach-Blily Act [3], [4], [10], [11], [16].

Legislation enacted more recently includes the USA PATRIOT Act of 2001 and the Consumer Privacy Protection Act of 2002. Unlike previously established laws that protect an individual's private information, the USA PATRIOT Act requires financial institutions to maintain records for reporting purposes to aid in identifying money laundering activities as part of the fight against terrorism [11]. In 2002, the Consumer Privacy Protection Act was established to place requirements on data-collection organizations in regards to collection and sale of private information as well as to detail solutions for instances of identity fraud [9].

Two other proposed pieces of U.S. legislation are currently under debate. The Fair and Accurate Credit Transactions Act was proposed in 2003 to enable consumers to obtain one free copy of their credit report each year. This proposed law would also bar merchants from printing all of the numbers of a credit card on receipts in addition to requiring credit card companies to put an automatic fraud alert on all credit files that are considered to be at risk of fraudulent activity [9]. The Social Security Misuse Prevention Act, also proposed in 2003, would require individual consent to allow organizations to sell or display social security numbers on their documentation. This proposed law would also forbid the United States government from displaying an individual's social security number on public records that are either posted to the Internet or distributed to the public via electronic means. Finally, this proposed law would put strict limits upon businesses as to when it would be permissible to require that their customers provide social security numbers [9], [14].

Guarding against Identity Theft

When attempting to minimize the opportunities for identity theft, it is imperative to guard our personal information. This information includes but is not limited to our social security number, maiden name (yours and your mother's), date of birth, past addresses, and driver's license number [2], [4], [6]. To further protect against identity theft, we must remember to be both proactive in our defense efforts and constantly aware of how identity thieves obtain the information they need to be successful. To that end, contact your insurance agent to discuss the purchase of identity theft insurance and be sure to support legislation designed to protect your personal information. In addition, there are a number of measures that any of us can implement to impede the efforts of an identity thief [2]–[4], [6], [8], [9], [12], [13], [18], [19].

Information Confidentiality

Maintaining information confidentiality is the first step in thwarting the efforts of identity thieves. To that end, exercising basic common sense when dealing with sensitive information will serve to mitigate much of the associated risk. Secluding yourself when transmitting vital information via telephone and submitting written requests to organizations that you do business with to not share your personal information with other organizations during unrelated transactions are key steps in minimizing the opportunities for identity theft. Immediately report lost or stolen credit cards, bank cards, and telephone calling cards. Check your creditors' policies for stolen cards and fraudulently accessed accounts to determine your liability. As previously noted, social security numbers are commonly targeted by identity thieves due to their overuse as customer account numbers for organizations such as banks, credit card companies, and hospitals [2]–[4], [6], [9], [18]. As a result, it is critical that you do not carry your social security card in your wallet or purse and that you do not give out your social security number unless it is absolutely necessary and you have initiated the contact with the organization in question. You must also remove your social security number from your driver's license and your checks. Finally, contact any organization that you do business with and ask them to change your identification number to a randomly generated number in place of your social security number.

Information Tracking

Continuous monitoring of high risk targets is the next phase in guarding against identity theft. This includes regular requests for copies of your credit report and constant attention to the billing cycles of your existing credit cards, telephone, cable, Internet, and other bills for unexpected increases in charges. Call the issuer of your credit card if your bill is noticeably late, keep track of what you buy, and check your credit card bill for unusual purchases. Subscribe to your credit bureaus' regular and automatic notification of unusual credit account activity. Check your W-2 tax statements for unexpected extra earnings that would indicate that someone is working under your name. Finally, do not assume that your mail is safe. Safeguard your incoming and outgoing mail by mailing bills and other personal documents at a post office or via a post office box instead of from home. Place change of address cards in an envelope before sending them to the appropriate postmaster.

Information Storage

How and where information is stored significantly impacts the ability of an identity thief to succeed. Store passports, birth certificates, wedding certificates, stocks, social security cards, and savings account books in locked vaults. Keep a written record of the contents of your wallet or purse in a locked vault. Protect personal information stored on your computer with firewalls and passwords. Only use encrypted web sites that have a posted privacy policy. Choose passwords that make sense to you but are not obvious choices for an identity thief to try when attempting to pose as you. Passwords such as birth dates, anniversary dates, names for pets, and maiden names are examples of bad passwords. Finally, be sure to change your passwords often to minimize the damage should one or more become compromised.

Information Disposal

To prevent dumpster diving, shred all personal documents, preapproved credit card solicitations, old bank statements, credit card charge slips, and old credit card statements before putting them in the trash. If possible, use a cross-shredder to further obfuscate the contents of these types of documents. Cancel and cut up unused or expired credit cards, bank cards, and telephone calling cards.

Recovering From Identity Theft

Unfortunately, even the most prepared of us may still become the victim of identity theft. According to most analysts, recovering from identity theft requires an average of almost 200 hours worth of effort expended in contacting creditors, financial institutions, and law enforcement officials. Should you find yourself a victim of identity theft, a number of organizations are available to assist you in your efforts to minimize the impact of the fraudulent act [2], [3], [6], [9], [15], [16], [18], [19]:

- Privacy Rights Clearinghouse, 619-298-3396, http://www.privacyrights. org or http://www.ssa.gov.
- United States Public Interest Research Group, 202-546-9707, http://www. pirg.org.
- National Association of Consumer Advocates, http://www.naca.net/ resource.htm.
- The Education Department, http://www.ed.gov/misused.
- Federal Trade Commission, 877-438-4338 or 877-IDTHEFT, http://www. ftc.gov or http://www.consumer.gov/idtheft.com.
- Federal Bureau of Investigation, http://www.fbi.gov.
- U.S. Postal Inspection Service, http://www.usps.com/postalinspectors.
- U.S. Department of Justice identity theft and fraud information, http:// www.usdoj.gov/criminal/fraud/idtheft.html.
- Identity Theft Prevention and Survival, http://www.identitytheft.org.
- Identity Theft Resource Center, http://www.idtheftcenter.org.
- Internet Fraud Complaint Center, http://ifccfbi.gov.
- Contact the fraud department of your credit card companies to request that fraud alerts be placed on your accounts. The three major credit bureaus are:
  - Experian, 888-397-3742, http://www.experian.com.
  - TransUnion, 800-680-7289 or 800-888-4213, http://www.transunion.com.
  - Equifax, 800-685-1111 or 800-525-6285, http://www.equifax.com.
- Submit a written request to all of the appropriate credit bureaus to have long-term fraud alerts placed on your accounts.

In addition to contacting these organizations, be sure to contact local police, file a report, and obtain an affidavit of fraud and a copy of the police report so that you can give copies of these documents to creditors as proof that you have been a victim of identity theft [2], [3], [9].

Constant Vigilance

The ruthless tactics employed by identity thieves demand our constant vigilance if we are to preserve our credit histories and maintain clean criminal records. While current and pending legislation will continue to assist us in these endeavors, we must also engage in a proactive approach to managing our identities. The recommendations for guarding against identity theft must be integrated into our daily lives to further frustrate the fraudulent efforts of identity thieves. While nothing can guarantee invulnerability to identity theft, savvy consumers can put themselves in the safest possible position to avoid and, if necessary, quickly recover from the damage wrought by this type of fraudulent activity.

References

[1] "The Nielsen NetRatings Reporter." World Wide Web, June 20 1999. http://www.nielsen-netratings.com/weekly.html.

[2] S. E. Arnold, "Internet users at risk: The identity/privacy target zone," *Searcher*, vol. 9, pp. 24–39, Jan. 2001.

[3] L. Bielski, "Identity theft," *ABA Banking J.*, vol. 93, pp. 27–30, Jan. 2001.

[4] J. Bigham Bernstel, "Identity crisis," *Bank Marketing*, vol. 33, pp. 16–20, Jan. 2001.

[5] P. Fichtman, "Preventing credit card fraud and identity theft: A primer for online merchants," *Information Systems Security*, vol. 10, pp. 52–59, Nov.–Dec. 2001.

[6] S. Groves, "Protecting your identity," *Information Management J.*, vol. 36, pp. 27–31, May–June 2002.

[7] O. O'Sullivan, "Who's that knocking on my portal?," *US Banker*, vol. 109, pp. 49–52, Nov. 1999.

[8] I. Schneider, "Intruder alert," *Bank Systems & Technology*, vol. 39, pp. 24–26, 28, 46, July 2002.

[9] D. A. Riordan and M. P. Riordan, "Who has your numbers?" *Strategic Finance*, vol. 84, pp. 22–26, Apr. 2003.

[10] E. H. Freeman, "Pretexting, data mining and personal privacy: The Gramm-Leach-Bliley Act," *Information Systems Security*, vol. 11, pp. 4–8, May–June 2002.

[11] F. Scholl and J. Hollander, "The changing privacy and security landscape," *Business Communications Rev.*, vol. 33, pp. 54–57, May 2003.

[12] R. Stuhlmuller, "User identity: The key to safe authentication," *Communications News*, vol. 37, pp. 32–38, Mar. 2000.

[13] G. V. Hulme, "Slow acceptance for biometrics," *InformationWEEK*, pp. 56–62, Feb. 10, 2003.

[14] *Social Security Number Misuse Prevention Act*, Bill Summary and Status for the 107th Congress, available at http://thomas.loc.gov/cgibin/bdquery/z?d107:SN00848:@@@L&summ2=m&.

[15] J. R. Marbaix, "Lessons in privacy," *U.S. News & World Report*, vol. 137, no. 7, pp. 74–75, Sept. 6, 2004.

[16] "Educating students about identity theft," *Recruitment & Retention in Higher Education*, vol. 18, no. 9, pp. 5–6, Sept. 2004.

[17] D. Graham-Rowe, "Internet fuels boom in ID theft," *New Scientist*, vol. 181, no. 2438, pp. 24, Mar. 13, 2004.

[18] J. Rubenking, S. Carroll, and N. J. Rubenking, "identity theft: What, me worry?" *PC Magazine*, vol. 23, no. 4, pp. 75–77, Mar. 2, 2004.

[19] "Identifying ways to combat identity theft," *Perspective*, vol. 19, no. 2, pp. 1–2, Feb. 2004.

[20] K. Davis and A. Stevenson, "They've Got Your Numbers," *Kiplinger's Personal Finance*, vol. 58, no. 1, pp. 72–76, Jan. 2004.

A CONTEXTUAL FRAMEWORK FOR COMBATING IDENTITY THEFT

WENJIE WANG   *Donghua University*
YUFEI YUAN AND NORM ARCHER   *McMaster University*

Identity theft, in which criminals use someone else's personal identity and other relevant information in unauthorized ways, has become a significant and growing problem in many countries. In the United States, the number of identity theft cases reported to the U.S. Federal Trade Commission (FTC; www.ftc.gov) grew from 161,836 in 2002 to 214,905 in 2003, an annual increase of 33 percent. (www.consumer.gov/sentinel/pubs/Top10Fraud2003.pdf.) Some estimates in 2002 put the number of American identity theft victims at close to 10 million, an 81 percent rise from 2001 and at a cost of nearly US$53 billion. Phonebusters (www.phonebusters.com), a Canadian identity theft-reporting agency, reported that more than 14,599 Canadians became identity theft victims in 2003 (compared with 8,209 in 2002) and at a cost of roughly $21.8 million (compared with $11.8 million in 2002; www.phonebusters.com/english/statistics_E03.html). A major reason for the dramatic rise in identity theft cases is the explosive growth of Internet applications, making identity information more widely used and thus an easy target for criminals. Although identity theft has become one of the top legal concerns of the information age, the more dangerous aspect is how terrorists can use it to breach national security.

Combating identity theft and protecting consumers and society as a whole is of urgent importance to maintain a healthy economy and stable social environment. Toward that end, identity theft has been studied from several different perspectives: Bill McCarty has investigated the motives and tactics of automated identity theft attacks,[1] for example, whereas George Milne and his colleagues have examined online behaviors that could increase or reduce the risk of online identity theft.[2] In the general field of computer security and privacy, technologies such as digital certificate authorization, biometrics authentication,[3] public-key infrastructure (PKI), and digital identity-management systems such as Multiple and Dependable Digital Identity (MDDI)[4] aim to safeguard data, including identity information. The Liberty Alliance (www.projectliberty.org), a consortium representing organizations from around the world, is committed to developing an open standard for federated network identity that supports all current and emerging network devices. However, to the best of our knowledge, there hasn't been a general systematic framework for research on identity theft problems to date.

In this article, we outline our attempt to develop a general framework that shows identity theft in the context of integrated multiparty perspectives. The goal is to combat identity theft more efficiently and effectively.

Identity Theft

Identity theft is a very complex issue. It isn't just technical—it also involves economic, social, and legal issues. Let's take a closer look at the different aspects of identity theft.

Identity Thieves

An identity thief is an individual or organization that tries to steal and use identity illegally for financial fraud or other purposes. An identity thief could be an individual criminal, a terrorist, or a crime ring. Although many people think that identity theft is primarily carried out by faceless strangers, statistics show that the perpetrator is often someone the identity owner knows, such as a relative, family friend, or colleague. Moreover, the thief is frequently somebody who works in an organization of which the victim is a customer. A recent study of more than 1,000 identity theft arrests in the United States revealed that as much as 70 percent of personal data stolen from companies was performed by internal employees (http://msnbc.msn.com/id/5015565). From an outsider's perspective, it's very difficult to deter insider crimes.

Identity thieves typically commit fraud in two steps. The first is to steal an identity or create a fake one. The second is to illegally use a fake identity to gain access to the victim's financial services or to commit crimes.

Stealing

Traditional approaches to stealing identity include "dumpster diving" to retrieve personal data from discarded credit-card or utility bills, stealing personal financial letters from mailboxes, stealing wallets and purses, "shoulder surfing" when individuals input personal identification information, bribing employees to hand over personal customer information, and physically stealing confidential files or computer hard drives in which identity information is stored. Online identity thieves attack databases via *spoofing* (sending a message to a computer from a source that pretends the message is coming from a trusted computer's IP address) or *phishing* (sending an e-mail message to a targeted individual, asking the individual to access a web site that mimics a trusted institution and then divulge private identity information). Identity thieves might also try to break into databases and archives in which identity information is stored.[5] The spoofer could pose as an ISP or even an "identity theft prevention" service provider.

Using a Fake Identity

Identity thieves create fake certificates to misrepresent identity by swapping images on them, altering their validation times or owner names, or, in many cases, creating completely fake ones. Innovations such as low-cost desktop publishing technology and computer-supported devices make it easy for casual counterfeiters to forge fake identity certificates. In fact, a quick search online brings up templates of various documents and other counterfeiting information. Counterfeiters have even been caught issuing forged digital certificates. Naturally, innovations in computer and Internet technology that facilitate identity counterfeiting[6] also make it much more difficult to combat identity theft.

Fraudulent abuse of identity causes financial damage to victims and society in general. Stolen identities can be used to open credit-card accounts, obtain loans or social benefits, open telecommunications or utility accounts, and more. In some cases, abusers even create and use a new fictitious identity to fraudulently gain employment or start a new life, possibly in other countries. Criminals have even committed crimes using stolen or fake identity to evade detection, investigation, and arrest, and, consequently, have ruined many an honest citizen's reputation: in the U.S., innocent identity theft victims have even been jailed for crimes that imposters have committed.[7]

The FTC has reported that the most common identity abuses occur with credit-card, phone, or other utility accounts because of the potential for significant gains to the perpetrators. These three abuses accounted for 54 percent of the total number of victims in 2003 (214,905). In fact, credit-card fraud (at 33 percent of all fraud) was the most common form of reported identity theft, followed by phone or utilities fraud (21 percent), bank fraud (17 percent), and employment fraud (11 percent; www.consumer.gov/sentinel/pubs/Top10Fraud2003.pdf).

Fraudulent abuse of travel documents has begun to receive considerable attention because it can affect national security and social stability. Illegal immigrants or terrorists can use fake passports to enter a country, for example. In North America, social insurance numbers (SINs), social security numbers (SSNs), and drivers' licenses are de facto identifiers, making them the most prized targets for identity thieves.

Understanding and analyzing identity theft is an important and basic step toward combating it. Although identity theft problems can be more clearly understood through improved statistics gathering and analysis, research on preventing, detecting, and prosecuting actual identity theft should be a top agenda item for the future. Toward that end, we present our framework for combating identity theft.

A Contextual Framework for Combating Identity Theft

In this article, we define identity as both the identity certificate and the information that can uniquely identify the owner; as such, they're the main targets of most identity theft.

Our proposed contextual framework for combating identity theft describes the major stakeholders involved. We'll examine each stakeholder in more detail in the next section. Figure 1 shows the stakeholder's roles in the prevention, detection, and legal prosecution of identity theft.

Uses of the Framework

Our framework clearly identifies the major stakeholders and their roles and interactions in the context of combating identity theft. The framework can help multiple parties understand the identity theft problem and develop better identity security solutions. Some potential uses of our framework include:

Understanding. Government, businesses, and individuals will be able to assess identity theft risks and vulnerabilities in current identity management processes.

Additionally, the framework can help solution providers identify the roles of various stakeholders involved in combating identity theft and analyze the relationships and interactions among these stakeholders.

Development. The framework eases the task of identity security solution providers in developing a systematic and effective security strategy and provides application context analysis for developing a multiparty security solution. Additionally, it supports multiparty collaboration in the identity-management process.

Evaluation. Using the framework, identity security solution providers and users can examine the efficiency and effectiveness of various identity theft prevention and detection solutions from multiple perspectives. It can assist in studying how changes in one activity impact other activities and stakeholders, and evaluating the balance between the need for privacy protection by identity owners and the need for combating identity theft by identity issuers and checkers.

Let's look at the framework in more detail.

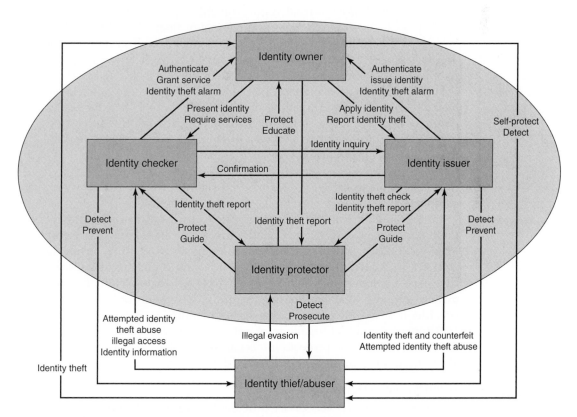

FIGURE 1. The contextual framework for combating identity theft. In the graph, nodes represent the major stakeholders, and arrows indicate their interactions and information flows.

Framework Stakeholders

Four main stakeholders help combat identity theft through a variety of prevention, detection, and legal protection and theft prosecution activities.

Identity owners

An *identity owner* is an individual who is the subject of his or her identity and who has the legal right to own and use it. An identity owner can apply to obtain identity certificates for different purposes related to social activities and financial services throughout the owner's life. This process begins at birth, when a birth certificate is issued as a child's permanent identity. From then on, based on that identifier, an individual can apply for other kinds of identity certificates for the purpose of receiving social welfare, driving a vehicle, traveling abroad, processing financial transactions, and so on.

Because identities belong to identity owners, it's their responsibility to safeguard them. As such, they should be aware of the risk of identity theft and the severe legal and financial damage such theft could cause. In addition, identity owners are responsible for using their identity legally and ethically, and not abusing their rights—such as lending health cards to relatives or acquaintances—which could harm those who issue identity certificates.

Identity Issuers

An *identity issuer* is a trusted government or private institution that issues identity certificates to authorize certain social or financial rights to the identity owner. Such certificates are valid for a person's (or organization's) identification for a specific purpose over a finite time period. They usually consist of six information components: certificate identifier (such as a passport number), certificate receiver (the owner's name), certificate purpose (citizenship), certificate issuer (the government), validation time period, and the issuer's signature or certification. A certificate also contains the information necessary to verify the certificate holder, such as a photograph or fingerprint, and the identity of the certificate authorizer such as a watermark or stamp. A physical token, such as a passport or birth certificate, can represent an identity certificate, or it can take digital form, such as a digital certificate issued by a trusted certificate authorizer (for example, VeriSign on the Internet).

Governments issue identity certificates such as birth certificates, SSNs in the United States or SINs in Canada, drivers' licenses, and passports to eligible individuals. Private institutions issue business identity certificates such as credit cards, debit cards, telephone cards, and digital certificates. An identity issuer's responsibility is to verify the receiver's true identity before issuing a valid certificate that a validating institution can then use to verify this identity. Identity issuers not only issue secure identity certificates but also protect sensitive personal identifiable information held in archives or databases. Issuers must also provide protection mechanisms if identity information is stolen. We'll discuss the protection process in detail later.

Identity Checkers

An *identity checker* is a service provider that verifies identity holders' authenticity and eligibility. Identity checkers must verify that two things are valid: the owner's certificate, and the holder's identity. When authenticating identities, the checker must establish and use strict authentication processes and execution mechanisms. Identity checkers, such as customs officers and traffic police, examine identity certificates and compare them (including photo identity) to other identifying information, such as the physical appearance of identity holders, to verify identity. Credit-card checkers, such as merchants, normally verify credit-card validity through electronic communication with the issuer or the holder's bank. The cardholder's signature, however, usually isn't carefully verified. Such weak verification isn't acceptable in countries such as China, where the identity holder must also provide a personal identification number (PIN). Identity checkers have the responsibility of protecting identity information against incursions and notifying identity owners if such a breach is discovered.

Identity Protectors

An *identity protector* is an individual or organization that works to protect individuals and institutions, including identity owners, issuers, and checkers, from identity theft. Some protectors have legal powers apprehending and punishing criminals. Identity protectors can be government legislators, law enforcement agencies, the legal system, public and private security-service providers, and technical security-solution providers.

Government legislators enact laws to protect victims of identity theft and punish perpetrators. Law enforcement agencies, such as the Royal Canadian Mounted Police (RCMP) and the U.S. Federal Bureau of Investigation (FBI), enforce laws to detect and prosecute violators and give victims legal protection. In the United States, the Identity Theft and Assumption Deterrence Act of 1998 directs the FTC to establish procedures for educating the public, receives complaints, and coordinates enforcement efforts with various investigatory agencies.[7] In support of identity protection, some law enforcement agencies have established identity theft call centers and statistical databases such as the Consumer Sentinel database in the United States (www.consumer.gov/sentinel/) and PhoneBusters in Canada to record and track consumer and business complaints. Such repositories can also be used to build legal cases and detect trends in consumer fraud and identity theft. Credit bureaus such as Experian (www.experian.com), TransUnion (www.transunion.com), and Equifax (www.equifax.com) provide and monitor credit records to prevent and detect identity theft.

Various security technology providers develop technical solutions for the prevention and detection of identity theft. Many active researchers and engineers work in the field of security information technologies. These technologies are essential for building the secure identity management systems that identity issuers, checkers, and owners use.

Combating Identity Theft

To combat identity theft, all stakeholders must interact and collaborate for secure identity management. Because each stakeholders actions impact other stakeholders' effectiveness against identity theft (see Table 1), an integrated view is essential in developing strategies and solutions. Table 1 details the activities of the four main stakeholders in defeating identity theft. These activities are divided into three categories: prevention, detection, and legal protection and prosecution. Obviously, the most effective way to combat identity theft is prevention. However, if identity theft occurs, more damage accumulates if it isn't detected quickly. Moreover, identity theft detection can provide the evidence necessary to punish criminals.

Prevention

Advanced technologies and education can help prevent identity theft. Let's look at the various measures more closely.

Education and guidance. Educating the public is an effective way to prevent identity exposure and subsequent theft. The more aware people are of possible threats and severe damage from identity theft, the more motivated

TABLE 1. Stakeholders' Activities to Combat Identity Theft.

Identity Theft	Identity Protector	Identity Issuer	Identity Checker	Identity Owner
Identity stealing or counterfeiting	Educate or guide identity issuer and identity checker to educate identity owner to self-protect identity certificates and information. Develop prevention or detection technologies. Prevent sensitive information exposure (such as social security numbers) in public reports. Develop anti-counterfeiting techniques.	Prevent identity information exposure by using biometric verification. Protect identity information in databases. Prevent internal theft through screening and management mechanisms. Educate identity owners to prevent identity theft. Apply anti-counterfeiting techniques in identity certificate production. Apply advanced technology (smart card) to produce physical tokens.	Use security measures to prevent online identity theft. Use security technologies to protect identity information database. Apply screening and management mechanisms to prevent internal theft. Educate identity owners.	Become aware of severe damage possible from identity theft. Take effective measures to self-protect identity certificates and other personal information.
Identity abuse	Enact laws relevant to identity theft. Gather identity abuse evidence. Find and prosecute criminals. Develop identity abuse prevention and detection technologies.	Tighten identity application requirements. Apply effective authentication (such as biometrics). Monitor abnormal transaction patterns. Notify affected identity owners of breaches in databases.	Restrictive authentication execution. Notify affected identity owners of breaches in databases.	Regularly check personal and financial information.

they'll be to take measures to prevent it. Identity protectors play a major role in public education, as do identity issuers and checkers who focus on customer education under protectors' guidance. In North America, for example, governments broadcast television programs that warn of potential damage from identity theft, and some companies have put identity theft alerts in their advertising materials or directly on their web sites.

The public should also know which measures they should take to protect identity and other relevant information. For example, government education materials and programs, such as an Ontario, Canada, government pamphlet on identity theft prevention (www.cbs.gov.on.ca) and an Australian Government National Crime Prevention Program (www.ema.gov.au/), provide simple tips for preventing identity theft, such as guarding against exposure when entering information into public online terminals, not giving out personal information to strangers over the phone or by e-mail, and using a separate bank account with a low credit limit for online transactions. Immediately informing police, credit bureaus, and financial institutions of such occurrences is important to minimize loss. In particular, financial institutions can mitigate the risk by canceling existing credit cards, accounts, passwords, and PINs when identity theft is detected or reported.

Prevention Technologies. Identity theft prevention technologies such as biometrics and smart cards are continually evolving. Some of them even endow identity certificates with secure features that are hard to counterfeit or abuse. Database security technologies can also prevent identity information theft, and PKI technologies can protect digital certificates and identity information in online transactions. These technologies can be applied separately or jointly within identity protection activities. Biometrics information, for instance, can be collected at an identity check point, encrypted, and then transmitted through PKI to make comparisons at the identity issuer's centralized database for authentication checks.

Biometrics can reduce identity theft by identifying the owner through unique human characteristics such as fingerprints, voiceprints, or retinal eye scans. An advantage of biometric authentication is that it requires the person being identified to be physically present at the point of identification. This makes it difficult, if not impossible, to impersonate the identity owner. Moreover, authentication based on biometric techniques eliminates the need to remember a password, PIN, or carry a token, thus reducing identity information exposure. Many governments and other institutions around the world have begun to use biometrics to prevent identity theft. The United States, for example, now requires the inclusion of biometric identifiers such as digital photos and electronic fingerprints in U.S. visas (www.epic.org/privacy/us-visit/). The Canadian government is debating the use of a biometric national identity card for Canadian citizens, as landed immigrants are already required to carry a biometric Maple Leaf Card. (www.mapleleafweb.com/features/privacy/id_cards/cards.html). However, biometric solutions also have their drawbacks. Biometric profiles can't easily be changed if illegal access is gained, whereas if a password or PIN is lost, it's possible to get a new one.

Digital certificates, often called online passports, work with PKI to prevent online identity theft. PKI integrates digital certificates, public-key cryptography, and trusted online certificate authorities (CA) into a total network security architecture, which can create a secure online transaction environment for digital certificate owners. Two well-known federated identity management (FIM) solutions, Liberty Alliance (www.projectliberty.org) and Microsoft Passport (www.passport.com), are an attempt to develop an open, interoperable standard for digital identity management and to manage web-based identification and authentication.

Smart cards, which embed integrated circuits (ICs) that contain microprocessors and enhanced memory to store information and processing capacity, are normally used in conjunction with other technologies to prevent identity theft. Smart cards can store biometric information to deliver secure and accurate identity verification; they can also store and program private keys and digital certificates with the help of PIN encryption to secure online transactions. Moreover, they're much more difficult to counterfeit than ordinary magnetic strip cards.[8]

Advanced anticounterfeiting techniques—watermarks, chemical voids, optically variable ink, holograms, embossed characters and numbers, tamper-evident signature panels, and magnetic stripes with improved card validation technologies—bestow identity certificates with features that are hard to counterfeit or alter. Canadian passports (www.ppt.gc.ca/passports/book_e.asp), for example, have five anticounterfeiting features, including digital photos, holograms, optically variable inks, ghost photos, and digitally printed information.

The development of advanced technology creates new and secure features to prevent identity theft. However, criminals can also exploit technological advances to steal identities and commit fraud. The result is a never-ending race between industry, in developing new security features, and criminals, in their attempts to compromise technology and commit fraud. As long as the cost for committing any kind of fraud is significantly lower than the gains, the race will continue.

Prevention Mechanisms. Identity issuers and checkers can adopt simple, inexpensive, and yet effective mechanisms for preventing identity theft. Internal theft is a major threat to an organization's identity information, but internal screening and managerial mechanisms can minimize this. The Industrial and Commercial Bank of China's home page (www.icbc.com.cn), for example, clearly states that the bank will never request account numbers and passwords from customers by e-mail, letter, or telephone, except when customers log in to the bank's official site. To prevent sensitive identity information exposure, credit bureaus and banks have stopped printing SINs and other identifying numbers on hard copy reports mailed to customers. Moreover, to effectively prevent identity abuse, the Canadian government has tightened its requirements for obtaining passports and SINs.

Identity Theft Detection

Identity theft often isn't detected until long after the subsequent damage has occurred. The FTC reports that the average time between an identity theft event and the date of discovery is 12 months (www.consumer.gov/sentinel/

pubs/Top10Fraud2003.pdf.) Early detection of identity theft will clearly reduce potential loss, as well as provide better evidence that's essential for prosecuting criminals.

Restrictive authentication is the best way to detect identity abuse. Identity issuers and checkers can more effectively detect potential theft when executing well-designed authentication processes aided by advanced technologies. It's much easier to detect an imposter if his or her fingerprint (captured on the checker's site) doesn't match the encrypted fingerprint stored in the issuer's online database. Identity and user authentication technologies[9] continue to evolve to combat the increasing sophistication of identity thieves. Some department stores capture customer signatures for credit-card payment authentication with an automated signature check. This process can also detect stolen credit cards.

All of the stakeholders need to take effective measures to detect identity theft as early as possible. Security expert Bruce Schneier pointed out that we should be moving our identity authentication efforts toward detecting fraudulent transactions (www.schneier.com/crypto-gram-0504.html). According to FTC statistics, credit-card fraud accounts for the greatest proportion of identity theft, as we have mentioned before, and has attracted much attention in identity theft prevention. Using data mining and other automatic monitoring technologies, banks can monitor account activity continuously with a view to identifying abnormal transactional patterns that suggest fraud. If they detect such patterns, they simply contact cardholders immediately to confirm transactions or identify potential fraud. Identity owners can also detect theft quickly by regularly checking their personal and financial information through online banking services rather than waiting for their monthly paper statements. Recently, banks in China have provided a mobile banking service that immediately sends a short confirmation message to the customer's cell phone when a credit-card payment is authorized. This significantly increases credit-card holders' awareness of transactions (english.cmbchina.com/corporate+business/firmbank/Functions.htm). However, identity thieves have managed to defeat this move by sending massive numbers of false transaction alarm messages to people, purportedly in the name of identity theft protection, in order to steal credit-card holders' money. This has become a widespread form of identity theft crime in China (www.fcc.com.cn/2005/11-10/142218.html).

Legal Protection and Prosecution

If identity theft does occur, victims must rely on protectors, issuers, and checkers to stop or recover their losses and apprehend and prosecute criminals. Certain laws[10] have been enacted specifically to help in such situations. The U.S. Identity Theft and Assumption Deterrence Act of 1998 ensures that private consumers who were targets of identity theft are viewed as victims in federal criminal cases, forcing courts to consider damage to these consumers by including them in restitution orders. The act also calls for stiffer penalties for perpetrators and implements procedures for investigation and enforcement.[7] In January 2001, the Canadian Personal Information Protection and Electronic Documents Act (PIPEDA) passed; it requires that organizations protect personal information against loss or theft as well as unauthorized access, disclosure, copying, use, or modification. It also mandates that the level of security surrounding the data should be appropriate to the information's sensitivity. People with access to the information must also sign confidentiality agreements.

To prosecute identity thieves, law enforcement agencies must be able to gather evidence of their criminal activities. Identity thieves can be detected and their criminal activities captured by monitoring measures when they use fake identities to obtain a certain right or financial benefit. Cameras already monitor ATM users, but criminal evidence is difficult to gather in certain situations, such as data fraudulently copied from a database.

Future Research

Within the framework described in Table 1, we've thus far described an overall view of combating identity theft. This lets governments and businesses design proper management strategies and technical security solutions to efficiently combat identity theft. However, problems revealed in the discussion of the framework (see Table 2) must be addressed by further research. In the following section, we propose some potential research directions.

Risk Management

Identity theft is a risk that businesses must manage. Unfortunately, most organizations don't know how or, if they do, they typically don't put enough effort into it. Although our framework can help clarify the issues in identity theft, organizations must build an action plan to combat it on more general principles. Risk management is one such concept that would be very useful in establishing proper security policies and solutions.

TABLE 2. Current Problems in Combating Identity Theft.

Major Activities	Problems
Prevention	Lack of systematic identity theft prevention action plans and prevention policies.
	No effective mechanism to manage, control, and protect sensitive identity information, such as fingerprints.
	Lack of evaluation for technical solutions, such as biometrics, smart cards, and experiences in implementation.
	Limited education programs and public media usage and weak impact of existing education programs on public and society.
	Many countries pay little attention to identify theft problems.
Detection	No comprehensive restrictive authentication process or other effective methods for detecting identity theft occurrences.
	Careless checking by front-line employees and lack of administrative mechanism to regulate checking execution of front-line employees.
	Poor criminal evidence tracking techniques and methods.
Protection and prosecution	Existing identify theft laws don't cover many aspects of identify protection, such as limiting excessive information requirements in order to protect privacy.
	Low level of resources invested in time-wasting identity theft crime investigation and prosecution.
	Poor cooperation between law enforcement agencies among jurisdictions (national or international).

Risk management is the systematic application of management policies, processes, procedures, and technologies to the tasks of identifying, analyzing, assessing, treating, and monitoring risk.[11] Its objective is to protect assets from all external and internal threats so that the losses resulting from the realization of such threats are minimized.

Risk is determined by three primary factors: assets, threats, and vulnerabilities. *Assets* represent anything of value, such as identity that is worth securing, so it can be relied on to access valuable services and privileges. *Threats* are any eventualities that represent a danger to an asset, such as internal theft or Internet hacking. *Vulnerabilities* are weaknesses existing in the identity safeguard system, such as the exposure of identity information during an authentication process. After identifying a risk, a risk management professional assesses the risk by identifying and evaluating assets, threats, and vulnerabilities. Then, he or she develops a risk management solution on the basis of information derived from the assessment process. The security solution providers select countermeasures to protect assets from possible threats depending on the likelihood of each threat and develop relevant security policies to reduce potential threats and vulnerabilities, thereby successfully reducing the overall risk of identity theft. Moreover, business managers can separate acceptable and unacceptable risk events, and thus rationally invest resources in the prevention of unacceptable and high-probability risk events that can affect the business. Low probability and low-impact risk events might receive a low priority or be ignored entirely.

It's important for identity security managers to study how to apply risk management in the context of combating identity theft, considering such aspects as identity theft risk assessment and security policy development and implementation. Specifically, we need to answer the following questions: How do we measure and assess the three primary risk factors in the context of identity theft? How should organizations establish a practical and rational solution for combating identity theft based on the risk management concept? What kinds of countermeasures and security policies will reduce vulnerability in identity management systems? How should these countermeasures and security polices be evaluated and selected?

Countermeasure Costs and Benefits

It's imperative for identity security managers to analyze costs and benefits of all identity theft countermeasures in order to achieve an effective level of security management. In most Western countries, for example, signatures authorize a credit-card payment, but they're almost never verified. However, in China, PINs are required in the credit-card authentication process. Customers must enter their PINs via a handheld device when making a purchase. In North America, PINs are also used in debit-card transaction authorizations. The PIN countermeasure still must be evaluated in terms of its cost and effectiveness in enhancing credit-card security management—such data would help determine if this measure should be adopted in the North American credit-card system. The cost and benefit analysis of some new technologies, such as biometric and smart-card technology, can also push forward their applications. Such financial analysis appears to be relatively rare for identity theft countermeasures, and more research is needed. The U.S. government, for example, invested US$380 million in fiscal year 2003 and more than US $330 million in fiscal year 2004 in its new biometric U.S. Visitor and Immigrant Status Indicator Technology (US-VISIT) program (www.epic.org/privacy/us-visit/). These data show the program's direct cost, but what are its indirect costs? How effective is this fingerprint-checking system? What is the effectiveness and cost of adding the owner's photo to a credit card or using a PIN or password in the credit-card system? What types of data should be collected and how?

Multiparty Coordination

The success in combating identity theft relies on joint efforts and coordination among all stakeholders in every relevant activity. In the process for issuing U.S. biometric visas, for instance, the applicant's fingerprints are electronically compared with fingerprint records in criminal databases. Coordination between the visa issuer (consular posts abroad) and protectors (such as the U.S. Department of Homeland Security or the FBI) effectively blocks terrorists or other criminals via this comparison process.

Such coordination activities should be considered in combating future identity theft. International cooperation, for example, is required in combating identity theft across the border. If U.S. biometric visa or passport abusers haven't committed a crime in the United States, their criminal records could be in the archives or databases of their home countries. An effective biometric terrorist defense system requires a worldwide network that supports online identity matching; otherwise, the effectiveness of such a biometric system could be undermined.

Privacy Protection Issues

Authentication requires collecting valid identity information. However, excessive and inappropriate collection without the owner's consent could result in privacy violations and damage to customer trust, effectively driving customers away from the business.[12] In addition, new technology for authenticating identity might bring privacy problems that will impact consumer acceptance. Potential abuses of biometric information, such as tracking individuals and their transactions without their consent, are of concern due to possible individual privacy violations,[3] such as in the new U.S. visa and passport application program. Privacy protection must be balanced against the collection of identity information for authenticating and preventing nonpermitted, illegal, or unethical use of private information.

Combating identity theft is a very complex task. It requires collaboration from all involved stakeholders, through efforts in education, technology development, security management, and law enforcement. No single silver bullet can solve the problem. As our framework demonstrates, dependencies among the stakeholders prevent any single stakeholder from making major reductions in identify theft without the collaboration of the others. The framework does not provide any specific solutions but rather helps us to organize our thinking and our efforts. Research on identity theft is urgently needed if the rise in identity theft incidence is to be stopped, and we believe that our framework will help further that effort.

Acknowledgments

A grant from the China Scholarship Council, Canada's Social Sciences and Humanities Research Council, and the Natural Sciences Research Council of Canada supported this research. The authors are grateful for the valuable comments and suggestions from the editor and five anonymous reviewers who made significant contributions to the improvement of the article.

References

1. B. McCarty, "Automated Identity Theft," *IEEE Security & Privacy*, vol. 1, no. 5, 2003, pp. 89–92.
2. G. R. Milne, A. J. Rohm, and S. Bahl, "Consumers' Protection of Online Privacy and Identity," *J. Consumer Affairs*, vol. 38, no. 2, 2004, pp. 217–232.
3. S. Prabhakar, S. Pankanti, and A. K. Jain, "Biometric Recognition: Security and Privacy Concerns," *IEEE Security & Privacy*, vol. 1, no. 2, 2003, pp. 33–42.
4. E. Damiani, S. De Capitani di Vimercati, and P. Samarati, "Managing Multiple and Dependable Identities," *IEEE Internet Computing*, vol. 7, no. 6, 2003, pp. 29–37.
5. B. Schneier, "Risks of Third-Party Data," *Comm. ACM*, vol. 48, no. 5, 2005, p. 136.
6. F. W. Abagnale, *The Art of the Steal—How to Protect Yourself and Your Business from Fraud, America's #1 Crime*, Broadway Books, 2001, p. 63.
7. K. M. Saunders and B. Zucker, "Counteracting Identity Fraud in the Information Age: The Identity Theft and Assumption Deterrence Act," *Int'l Review of Law Computers & Technology*, vol. 13, no. 2, 1999, pp. 183–192.
8. W. Kou, S. Poon, and E. M. Knorr, "Smart Card and Application," *Payment Technologies for E-Commerce*, Weidong Kou, ed., Springer, 2003, p. 95.
9. L. O'Gorman, "Comparing Passwords, Tokens and Biometrics for User Authentication," *Proc. IEEE*, vol. 91, no. 12, 2003, IEEE Press, pp. 2021–2040.
10. R. Lepofsky, "Preventing Identity Theft," *Risk Management*, vol. 51, no. 10, 2004, pp. 34–40.
11. A. R. Bowden, M. R. Lane, and J. H. Martin, *Triple Bottom Line Risk Management: Enhancing Profit, Environmental Performance, and Community Benefits*, John Wiley & Sons, 2001, p. 15.
12. M. Head and Y. Yuan, "Privacy Protection in Electronic Commerce—A Theoretical Framework," *Human System Management*, vol. 20, no. 2, 2001, pp. 149–160.

Conclusion

Identity theft is an important behavior that takes place on the Internet. The papers in this chapter focus on the tactics that are necessary to help protect individuals from identity theft. These tactics are easy and simple to perform, but people often do not think about them until after their identity is taken.

Discussion Questions

1. How is identity theft defined?
2. How is an identity thief defined?
3. Summarize and discuss some of the tactics that are used to avoid being a victim of identity theft.

5

Intellectual Property Theft

Intellectual property is the result of any creative or innovative endeavor from a human and the expression of this endeavor (Stim, 2000; Piquero, 2005). Intellectual property is deeply embedded in copyright statutes. These statutes span from state to state and country to country. Legal statutes may call the unauthorized use of intellectual property a criminal activity—specifically, this is intellectual property theft. The two articles in this section introduce intellectual property theft, provide rationales for its causes and preventions, and show how criminological theories may relate to a specialized form of intellectual property theft.

The first paper in this chapter, written by Nicole Leeper Piquero, defines intellectual property crime (theft). Then the paper shifts into the nature and extent of the behavior. This is followed by an explication of the causes of intellectual property theft. Piquero provides specific explanations of the theoretical rationales for intellectual property theft, then offers innovative prevention strategies.

The second paper in this chapter, written by George E. Higgins, Brian D. Fell, and Abby L. Wilson, defines a specific form of intellectual property theft—digital piracy. They present the legal rationale and statutes that make digital piracy illegal. Higgins et al. provide a rationale as to why criminological theory is relevant to understanding digital piracy and illustrate a rationale for why two popular criminological theories are important in understanding this behavior. Higgins et al. empirically examine their views using data from university students that show how self-control theory and social learning theory come together to understand digital piracy.

CAUSES AND PREVENTION OF INTELLECTUAL PROPERTY CRIME

NICOLE LEEPER PIQUERO

Introduction

Intellectual property refers to any product that results from the creativity and innovation of the human mind and the original expression of those ideas

(Stim, 2000; Ronkainen and Guerrero-Cusumano, 2001; Luckenbill and Miller, 1998). In other words, intellectual property covers just about every possible idea or invention from the arts and literary fields (i.e., books, photographs, recordings, choreography, etc.) to science and technology. Intellectual property right laws in the United States grant the exclusive ownership and rights to use, produce, and distribute creative work to the creator or author.

According to the World Intellectual Property Organization (WIPO), "intellectual creation is one of the basic prerequisites of all social, economic, and cultural development" (WIPO, 2001: 41). Therefore, the absence of laws and regulations governing the rights of individuals to freely create and develop innovations may stymie technology, cultural, and intellectual advancements. So why is the protection of intellectual property so important? Does it matter if the production of ideas and innovations slows to a snail's pace or stops all together? Intellectual property is believed to form the backbone of economic activity and give a competitive advantage in the world marketplace particularly to industrialized nations (Ronkainen and Guerrero-Cusumano, 2001: 59). In the United States, copyright industries rather consistently account for approximately 5% of the country's Gross Domestic Product (GDP). In order to protect economic interest and promote innovation and advancement, it is important to protect intellectual property from piracy and theft.

However, some in the legal arena disagree and argue that the obsessive American concern with protecting intellectual property is counterproductive and oppressive in various ways (see Lessig, 2001). Additionally, other legal scholars have addressed many important matters of relevance designed to produce a more complete understanding of intellectual property rights and violations such as the intersection of freedom of speech and intellectual property rights (Yen, 2003; Volokh, 2003), the challenge to preserve works that are created in a digital format while not violating the exclusive rights of the copyright owner (Gasaway, 2003), the role of applying criminal laws to copyrighted material and how the imposition of these laws can stifle creativity and reduce innovation (Moohr, 2003), the creation of the "copyleft"—an anti-law movement that emphasizes the free availability of art (Dusollier, 2003), as well as the implication of intellectual property issues in an international context (Endeshaw, 2002; Patry, 2003; Story, 2003). Although these efforts have certainly provided important evidentiary background regarding the legal issues associated with intellectual property rights, they have offered little help in understanding the social science assessment of the causes and prevention efforts of intellectual property violations.

There are generally four recognized types or categories of intellectual property: copyright, patents, trademarks, and trade secrets. Copyrights deal largely with forms of creativity concerning mass communications such as novels, music, song lyrics, motion pictures, plays, computer programs, and choreography to list a few examples (WIPO, 2001: 40). Patents are used to protect new inventions so that they cannot be exploited or used without the authorization of the patent owner (WIPO, 2001: 17). Trademarks are designed to individualize goods and services (referred to as service marks) in order for consumers to distinguish the source (Poltorak and Lerner, 2002). A trademark can be a symbol, a word, a design, a logo, a slogan, or any combination thereof that distinguishes one brand from another. Trade Secrets refer to business information that is kept in confidence such as formulas, patterns, devices, strategies, techniques that are used to obtain and advantage over competitors (Stim, 2000).

Violations of intellectual property rights have long been an issue receiving at least some attention but the level of attention has been ratcheted up considerably in recent years. Of course, the real challenge is to understand why "copying" as a form of theft—a view widely held by copyright holders—is not more widely shared by members of the public. Through a series of high profile lawsuits (*RIAA v. John Does*; *A and M Records v. Napster*, *RIAA v. Napster*; *Metallica v. Napster*) the music and motion picture industries have recently raised the general awareness of copyright violations. The copying of computer software, movies, video games, and music deny publishers and authors' economic returns on their property, and with the adaptations constantly being made to the definition of "property" this really amounts to nothing more than theft (Carruthers and Ariovich, 2004). Unfortunately, despite the increased attention, very little is actually known about the extent of the problem; the costs associated with the misuse and theft of intellectual property; the causes of intellectual property theft; the policy responses to intellectual property violations; and the effectiveness of existing responses. The current research attempts to fill this void by providing a review of the current state of research regarding these issues, as well as outlining an agenda for future research.

Nature and Extent of Intellectual Property Theft

Though the rights of intellectual property are related to and oftentimes suggested to be similar to the ownership of other forms of physical property (e.g., tangible property), there are several unique features of intellectual property that separate it from tangible property (Seale et al., 1998). First, there is a nonexclusive dimension of intellectual property. Unlike tangible goods, intellectual property is not consumed by its use. In other words, intellectual property can be used in many places at once. Computer software provides a perfect illustration of intangible property that does not need to be removed from the owner's possession in order to be useful to another (Thong and Yap, 1998). With the theft of tangible property the owner is deprived of the use of his or her property but this is not the case with the theft of intellectual property. Hence, the nonexclusive nature of intellectual property makes it harder to maintain exclusive use over intellectual property than it is to control tangible property (Seale et al., 1998: 29). Second, retail costs rarely reflect production costs (Seale et al., 1998). Since perceptions of price and value matter to consumers (Zeithaml, 1988), a sense of unfairness may surface when faced with a discrepancy between manufacturing costs and purchase price (Seale et al., 1998). This sense of unfairness matters to the point that consumers believe they are getting their money's worth. When consumers believe that they are paying more than what is deserved for a desired good (or service), the perceived unfair price may become the needed motivation to find cheaper ways to obtain the product, including piracy. Finally, many forms of intellectual property theft require skills and expertise as well as opportunity to offend

(Seale et al., 1998). Unlike tangible property, the theft of many (but not all) forms of intellectual property requires a certain level of skill and know-how, such as how to use a computer or how to navigate the Internet, as well as exposure to equipment (i.e., computer) to aid in the theft. While it is assumed that opportunities for street crimes (e.g., theft of tangible property) are generally available to everyone (Gottfredson and Hirschi, 1990; Cohen and Felson, 1979), the same is not true with regard to intellectual property theft—not everyone possesses the skills nor has the opportunity readily available to engage in intellectual property theft. This last feature is important in that it limits who is capable of engaging in intellectual property theft.

Similarities are drawn between tangible property and intellectual property theft in order to explain the behavior in familiar terms. In some instances the law is able to change and adapt in order to incorporate new forms of intangible property under its purview. For example, property now includes intangibles such as bonds, shares, trademarks, and patents (Carruthers and Ariovich, 2004). However, the relevance of the unique features of intellectual property cannot be overlooked. They matter to the point that it is hard for the public to not only comprehend that a theft has occurred—after all no tangible product has been taken; but, also to the point that the public becomes outraged at such behavior. Once the public becomes outraged, it becomes a social problem that needs to be addressed and corrective actions can be put into place to prohibit the behavior. Up until now, those most likely to abhor the behavior are those who would benefit from its protection. Business groups and trade associations such as the Business Software Alliance (BSA), the Recording Industry Association of America (RIAA), and the Motion Picture Association of America (MPAA) are lobbying the government to become more involved in protecting intellectual property rights domestically and abroad (Carruthers and Ariovich, 2004).

Because the breadth of intellectual property is so wide, it is difficult to obtain precise measurements as to how much theft is actually occurring. Luckenbill and Miller (1998) suggest that the quantity of intellectual property at least in the United States has considerably increased over the past century. By examining the number of pieces of intellectual property (i.e., copyrights, patents, and trademarks) registered annually with the U.S. federal government, they concluded that the increase over the past century has been roughly on the order of four to five times more pieces of intellectual property (Luckenbill and Miller, 1998: 94). This growth in volume, they suggest, has allowed intellectual property to become more vulnerable to misuse. The latest developments in technology allow for easy duplication with minimal flaws (Christensen and Eining, 1991). Therefore, copyrighted materials have been the easiest targets.

Estimating the costs of intellectual property theft also is not an easy task. Each industry calculates its own losses, but one thing is certain: across all industry estimates, the losses incurred are significant. In 1997, the U.S. theft of intellectual property rights were estimated to cost $300 billion with high technology corporations the most frequently targeted (Maher and Thompson, 2002). The music industry places the value of the sales of pirated recordings at $4.6 billion for 2002, an increase of seven percent from the proceeding year (IFPI, 2003). The motion picture industry estimates that $1.25 billion were lost between 1998 and 2002 due to audiovisual piracy (not including the impact on Internet piracy nor losses stemming from signal theft) in the United States alone (MPA, 2003). Meanwhile, worldwide estimates on the annual dollar amount of software pirated range anywhere from $7.5 to $17 billion (Ronkainen and Guerrero-Cusumano, 2001; Christensen and Eining, 1991: 68). Regardless, one overall conclusion, made recently by the Office of the U.S. Trade Representative 2004 Annual "Special 301" report, is that the lack of intellectual property rights protection and enforcement continues to be a global problem.

Since industrialized nations are believed to most benefit from intellectual property rights protection, it should come as no surprise that the U.S. government has been particularly instrumental in pushing for international protections for intellectual property rights (USTR, 2004). The U.S. government works closely with the World Trade Organization (WTO), an international organizational designed to deal with the rules of trade between nations, in order to ensure that WTO members adhere and uphold the rules established by the Trade-Related Aspects of Intellectual Property Rights (TRIPS) by providing extensive technical assistance and training on implementing the TRIPS agreement. This agreement established in 1994 set forth rules to govern the rights of intellectual property as part of worldwide trade negotiations such as requiring a minimum standard of protection for many forms of intellectual property (i.e., patents, copyrights, trademarks, trade secrets, geographical indicators), providing effective enforcement of these rights, and allowing disputes to be settled through the WTO's dispute settlement mechanism (Carruthers and Ariovich, 2004; USTR, 2004).

The Office of the U.S. Trade Representative (USTR) annually reports on the adequacy and effectiveness of intellectual property rights protection with the countries that serve as trading partners to the United States. They monitor and categorize countries that are not complying with the TRIPS regulations. This year, 52 countries have been designated as either Priority Foreign Countries, Priority Watch List, Watch List, or those that fall under Section 306 monitoring. Priority Foreign Countries are those that have the most onerous and egregious policies that have the greatest adverse impact on relevant U.S. products and who are not involved in good faith negotiations to make significant progress in addressing these problems (USTR, 2004). These countries are subject to intense investigation and possible sanctions. This year, only the Ukraine made the Priority Foreign Countries list. Countries are placed on the Priority Watch List when they do not provide an adequate level of intellectual property rights protection and enforcement or market access for persons relying in intellectual property protection. Fifteen countries were placed on the Priority Watch List (Argentina, Bahamas, Brazil, Egypt, European Union, India, Indonesia, Korea, Kuwait, Lebanon, Pakistan, Phillippines, Russia, Taiwan, and Turkey). Thirty-four countries made the Watch List indicating that they merit bilateral attention to address the underlying intellectual property right problems they face. These countries include Azerbaijan, Belarus, Belize, Bolivia, Canada, Chile, Colombia, Costa Rica, Croatia, Dominican Republic, Ecuador, Guatemala, Hungary, Israel, Italy, Jamaica, Kazakhstan, Latvia, Lithuania, Malaysia, Mexico, Peru, Poland, Romania, Saudi Arabia, Slovak Republic, Tajikistan, Thailand, Turkmenistan, Uruguay, Uzbekistan,

Venezuela, and Vietnam. Finally, two countries, China and Paraguay, fall under the category of Section 306 monitoring because of serious intellectual property problems and previous bilateral agreements reached with the United States to address specific problems. From this report one thing is clear: the U.S. government is keeping a close eye on the steps and efforts taken by foreign countries in order to help protect the intellectual property rights of U.S. products.

With this background in hand, the next section outlines a series of different theoretical explanations that have been put forth to account for intellectual property violations.

Causes of Intellectual Property Theft

In order to understand and combat the theft of intellectual property, it is important to examine the underlying motivations and justifications of such behavior. Most research seeking to understand the causes of the behavior is limited to the violation of copyright realm of intellectual property theft with an even more specific focus on software piracy. Despite the narrow definition of intellectual property, much insight can be gained by understanding the motivation and reasoning behind this specific form of intellectual property theft. The opportunities to offend are first discussed followed by different theoretical models that have been used to explain the theft of intellectual property.

Opportunity to Offend

Advances in information technology have not only provided worldwide access to creative works for the consuming public but have also posed a serious threat to authors of copyrighted material (Luckenbill and Miller, 1998). With each passing decade, new technological advances created challenges for the protection of intellectual property (Luckenbill and Miller, 1998). The proliferation of photocopying machines throughout the 1960s raised copyright concerns for the literary field with regards to published materials such as journal articles and novels. The 1970s ushered in the era of the personal computer and home video (e.g., VCR) posing serious threats to the software and the motion picture industry. Digital audiotape recorders threatened the music industry throughout the 1980s while the 1990s have brought about the development of portable mediums with large data storage capacity as well as advancing the network infrastructures to allow for greater speed in data transmission (i.e., cable modems and digital subscriber lines) (Luckenbill and Miller, 1998; Hinduja, 2001). All of these technological advances have not only made the accessing of information easier but have also made it easier to copy and distribute copyrighted materials such as computer software, motion pictures, and music.

Piracy is the unauthorized copying of copyright material for commercial purposes and the unauthorized commercial dealing in copied materials (WIPO, 2001: 51). The advancements made in technology have made piracy not only much easier to accomplish, but also provide the tools at little or minimal costs and almost no risk. As the price of personal computers drop, so too do the costs associated with piracy since most of the equipment needed to engage in piracy (e.g., CD recording devices or "burners") is readily available with most personal computers. Since most households contain personal computers and dedicated Internet connections, the ease of copying and distributing pirated materials can he accomplished in the ease of one's own home with little risk of detection (Hinduja, 2001). Due to the simplicity and inexpensive nature of copying materials, some have argued that piracy (particularly software piracy) is extremely widespread (Christensen and Eining, 1991).

Certain environments such as universities, governmental agencies, and businesses are conducive or supportive of piracy (primarily software piracy). In fact, the levels of piracy have become so widespread in these environments that some have argued that the behavior has become socially acceptable (Christensen and Eining, 1991). Environments, such as university settings, are actually considered to be breeding grounds for certain types of piracy (primarily software piracy) because of the heavy reliance upon computers in the environment (Sims et al. 1996; Hinduja, 2001) and the ready and sometimes required access and use of computers to perform functions (for administrators, faculty, staff, and students alike).

Demographic or Personal Attribute Factors

Early research on the causes of intellectual property violations focused on identifying demographic and personal attribute correlates of pirating behavior in order to develop or establish a profile of those who pirate copyrighted material. The belief was that once a profile was developed it might be possible to gain insights into those who are most likely to engage in pirating behavior. Once the pirates are identified, measures and actions can then be taken to address and stop the problem of piracy. The vast majority of this research relied on student samples (both undergraduate and graduate) and inquired about computer crimes and software piracy. Student populations, it is argued, are appropriate for study for several reasons. First, software piracy is more prevalent in academia than in business and the university setting is believed to be a breeding ground for such behavior because of the large role that computers play in the daily lives of students (Sims et al., 1996; Hinduja, 2001). Second, today's students are tomorrow's managers and the behaviors that they learn in school are likely to be carried over into the workplace (Sims et al., 1996). Similarly, parental socialization (particularly in terms of parental control) can also influence youths' risk-taking attitudes and freedom to deviate from social norms (Hagan and Kay, 1990). As such these values and lessons learned early in life are likely to remain a part of the individual's repertoire. Finally, students provide a captive audience that allows researchers to inquire about causes and correlates of behavior including criminal behaviors such as software piracy.

Gender, age, level of schooling, levels of computer usage, and personal attributes are among the most commonly examined correlates. The evidence is mixed regarding the effects of gender. Some studies suggest that gender is a significant predictor of (primarily software) pirating with males more likely to engage in piracy than females (Solomon and O'Brien, 1990; Hagan and Kay, 1990; Hollinger, 1993; Simpson et al., 1994; Sims et al., 1996; Seale et al., 1998). Other studies, however, find no significant differences across gender in the willingness to engage in the behavior (Sacco and Zureik, 1990; Tsalikis and

Ortiz-Buonafina, 1990; Davis and Welton, 1991). The effects of age indicate that younger individuals are more likely to engage in pirating behavior than older individuals though this finding is somewhat tempered by level of schooling. Research suggests that age has an indirect effect on piracy (Solomon and O'Brien, 1990; Seale et al., 1998) indicating that younger individuals are more likely to self-report engaging in the behavior. Other studies indicate that the more years of schooling, the more likely one is to pirate software. It appears that that older (college) students are more likely to pirate than younger ones (Hollinger, 1993; Sims et al., 1996). Graduate students were found to be more likely to pirate than undergraduate students (Sims et al., 1996) though several studies were unable to find significant differences between upper division undergraduates (e.g., juniors and seniors) and graduate students (Davis and Welton, 1991; Hollinger, 1993). Not surprisingly, a positive relationship has been found between levels of computer usage and piracy with those who use computers more frequently more likely to engage in software piracy (Eining and Christensen, 1991; Sims et al., 1996). In addition, various other personal attributes of self-reported pirates have been examined. These traits include intelligence, eagerness, aggressiveness, motivation, courageousness, adventuresome, and being qualified (see Seale et al., 1998 for review). It is interesting to note that this last set of characteristics are the exact same set of traits valued by society and are sought after in a good employee (Seale et al., 1998). In this way, it seems as though software piracy can be related to more general forms of white-collar crime in that the same traits that make individuals "criminal" are the same traits that make them good at their jobs. In sum, the evidence is clearly mixed regarding the relationship between demographic and personal attributes and piracy.

Deterrence

Modern deterrence theory is indebted to the Classical School of Criminology (Beccaria, 1963; Bentham, 1967) and assumes that humans are guided by reason, have free will, and are responsible for their own actions. Deterrence theory, therefore, assumes that individuals are deterred or dissuaded from criminal activities if they perceive legal sanctions to be certain, swift, and severe. The certainty of punishment refers to the probability of apprehension and being sanctioned; the swiftness of punishment refers to how quickly sanctions are imposed after the commission of the act; and severity refers to the notion that the punishment should be severe enough to outweigh the benefits gained by the commission of the crime. Hence, the deterrence approach presumes a causal effect of sanctions or the threat of imposing such sanctions (Reiss, 1984). Such a presumption assumes that the power of sanctioning violators will prohibit future violations. This presumed deterrent effect is hypothesized to operate in two ways: specific and general deterrence. The deterrence doctrine assumes that offenders who have been apprehended and punished will cease offending provided that their punishments are perceived to be severe enough (e.g., specific deterrence) and/or that those severely punished will serve as an example for the general public to instill enough fear of punishment that they will not engage in criminal behavior (e.g., general deterrence).

As originally formulated, deterrence dealt strictly with the fear of the law and legal sanctions, a notion which is commonly referred to as "mere deterrence" (Gibbs, 1975). Researchers expanded the concept of deterrence beyond the strict legal concept of formal sanctions to include "informal deterrence" or the actual or anticipated social sanctions and other consequences of crime that prevent their occurrence or reoccurrence (Akers, 2000: 22). Informal sanctions may include external factors such as the perception of family members, friends, and business associates who may disapprove of the act, and internal factors such as one's own conscience and moral beliefs. Informal sanctions operate in the same manner as formal sanctions in that individuals will not engage in the prospective act for fear of the informal punishment that would ensue.

Therefore, in order for formal deterrence to work there must first be a law prohibiting the behavior. In terms of intellectual property rights, there are both criminal and civil statutes designed to prevent the theft of intellectual property (see Maher and Thompson, 2002 for an overview). Deterrence assumes that people are not only aware of the laws that prohibit the behavior but are also fearful of the sanctions (both formal and informal) that may ensue. Christensen and Eining (1991) and Reid, Thompson, and Logsdon (1992) examined the impact of student knowledge of copyright laws and found that students tend to be relatively uninformed about the laws pertaining to software copyrights. Other research suggests that even when individuals are aware of the copyright laws that knowledge does little to deter the behavior. Swinyard, Rinne, and Keng (1990) found that some individuals were more influenced by the benefits of their actions than with the legal costs of their actions. Maher and Thomson (2002) report that civil sanctions are also insufficient at deterring the theft of intellectual property rights. The lack of deterrence in this case is not because the individuals do not know the law exists but precisely the opposite: the punitive damages that result from the illegal act are simply viewed as a "cost of doing business" (Maher and Thomson, 2002: 765).

The effects of informal sanctions do not fare much better in explaining theft of intellectual property rights. Seale and his colleagues (1998) found no relationship between university software policies and the reported piracy practices of university employees. Taylor and Shim (1993) also found no effect. Harrington (1989) found that situational factors such as a low likelihood of being caught and punished, behavior referent to others, and a perceived lack of clear standards of conduct were better predictors of software copying among a sample of students than were individual factors (e.g., age, socioeconomic status, and level of education). In sum, the extant research on the deterrent effects of intellectual property theft seem to show little effect. Hollinger and Lanza-Kaduce (1988) suggest that computer laws seem to serve more as a symbolic function rather than as a deterrent. The same general conclusion could be made for all of intellectual property laws.

Equity Theory

Closely related to the deterrence perspective, is the notion of equity theory (Adams, 1963: 436). Equity theory, like deterrence, is a perceptual theory that assumes individuals are rational beings and calculate the costs and benefits of an act before choosing a course of action. The underlying impetus for equity theory is that individuals search for fairness or equity in social exchanges with the desire to maximize one's own personal outcomes. Social exchanges can include goods and services as well as conditions that affect an individual's well-being such as psychological and emotional aspects (Glass and Wood, 1996). Individuals are assumed to engage in acts as long as they perceive an equitable relationship: "An equitable relationship exists when the individual perceives that the participants in the exchange are receiving equal relative outcomes from the relationship" (Glass and Wood, 1996: 1191).

Reciprocation is one major class of social exchange that exists when there is a direct exchange between two parties (Eckhoff, 1974; Glass and Wood, 1996). The pirating of copyrighted goods falls within this category. For example, two friends, Heather and Jennifer, each want the most recent CD from their two favorite artists, No Doubt's *The Singles 1992–2003* and Train's *My Private Nation*, but neither girl has enough money to buy more than one CD. So, the girls decide that Heather will buy the No Doubt CD while Jennifer will buy the Train CD and then will exchange the CDs in order for each to make a copy of the other. In this instance, from the perspective of each girl, an equitable exchange has occurred. Each individual will allow the other to illegally copy the CD she purchased because they each anticipate the outcomes will outweigh or be equal to the inputs they bring to the exchange (Glass and Wood, 1996). In other words, each girl feels as though the exchange is fair and equitable and she is getting out of the exchange what she put into it, a copy of a latest CD.

While equity theory offers little explanation in terms of why one begins offending in the first place, it does offer an explanation as to why the illegal behavior continues and why it ceases. Piracy and illegal swapping of copyrighted materials are likely to continue as long as the situation and exchange is perceived by all parties to be fair and equitable. As long as the exchange is viewed by all parties to be fair and equitable, meaning that each side of the exchange feels like they are maximizing their own benefits, the more likely the motivation will remain to continue the behavior. On the other hand, as soon as one party feels that there is inequity in the exchange the behavior is likely to cease. Inequity in the exchange causes individuals to become distressed, and in order to end the distress the individual is motivated to reduce the inequity of the situation (Glass and Wood, 1996).

There are two possible avenues to restore the equity in the relationship. The first enables the cessation of the criminal activity all together while the second calls for adjustment to the perceived value of the goods to be exchanged. One way to acquire equity is to restore "actual equity" by altering inputs or outcomes of the exchange (Glass and Wood, 1996). In other words, the individual can altogether remove himself from the exchange or he can alter how much he puts into the exchange. The second way is by restoring psychological equity in which the individual changes his perceptions of the value of his inputs or outcomes (Glass and Wood, 1996). In this second situation, the actual good or product being exchanged does not get altered but instead the perceived value of the object is changed.

Research has examined equity theory by focusing on the cost of the product to be copied. Parker (1976) and Harrington (1989) both find that the higher the costs of the software, the more likely it is to be copied. In terms of equity theory, individuals were more likely to engage in the behavior when they believed the results would come out in their favor. In other words, the high price of the desired outcome (i.e., the copied product) maximized their outcomes. Glass and Wood (1996) examined equity theory from a slightly different angle. They used a sample of undergraduate business students to examine how much an individual is willing to put into the exchange. By using a scenario design, Glass and Wood (1996) asked respondents how likely it would be that they would allow a fellow classmate to copy software that they had purchased for a class at varying dollar amounts ($10, $75, and $100). Consistent with equity theory, they found that the higher the cost of the software, the lower the subject's intention to allow another to copy it. Glass and Wood (1996) also included other positive and negative situational factors into the questionnaire and found that in the instances of the positive situational factors (i.e., positive social outcome or fulfilling debt requirement), the subjects were inclined to allow the software to be copied whereas with the negative situational variable (i.e., being caught in the act), the subjects were not likely to permit the copying of the software.

Ethical Decision-Making Process

The premise behind the ethical decision-making process is that ethics or morals influence the decision an individual will ultimately make. Those individuals who have and adhere to a high moral standard are believed to be less likely to engage in unethical behavior while those with low morals are believed to be more likely to engage in unethical behaviors. Ethical behavior refers to actions that would be both legal and morally acceptable to the larger community (Glass and Wood, 1996). Engaging in any type of criminal activity including piracy could be considered an unethical decision. This decision making model is predicated on the assumption that a person can recognize and distinguish unethical behavior. If a person is unable or unwilling to recognize the moral issue at hand, he/she will fail to use his/her morals or ethics in the decision-making process (Jones, 1991).

A substantial amount of evidence indicates that individuals do not perceive piracy to be an ethical problem. Among a sample of college students, Cohen and Cornwell (1989) found that software piracy was viewed as both acceptable and normal. Solomon and O'Brien (1990) indicate that most of their sample of college students had pirated or allowed a friend to pirate software. These same students indicated that they viewed the pirating behavior to be socially and ethically acceptable. Shim and Taylor (1989) report that in a sample of faculty members most believe that their colleagues were engaging in software piracy but did not support the pirating of software for teaching purposes.

Some research has suggested that the relationship between gender and willingness to engage in unethical behavior, such as piracy, is not well understood (Gilligan, 1982; Oz, 1990). Gilligan (1982: 19), for example, argues that the developmental processes of men and women differ such that female moral development focuses on the understanding of responsibility and relationships whereas male moral development centers around fairness and the under-standing of rights and rules. These differences lead to distinctive ways of interpreting experiences and choices that ultimately lead to different paths for resolution. For example, males may view actors in a dilemma as opponents, whereas females will view those same actors as members of a social network upon which they all depend (Gilligan, 1982: 30). Therefore, males will tend to rely on logic and rules to dictate the path to resolution while females tend to rely on communication and care for resolution. The evidence to date is mixed regarding the differences between men and women on unethical behavior in general and pirating behavior in particular (Sims et al., 1996).

Cultural differences may also influence the ethical decision-making process in that ethics and morality judgments may differ by culture or national origins. Swinyard and colleagues (1990) conducted a cross-cultural study between Singapore and the United States in order to examine differences in morality and software piracy. Using student samples in both countries, they found that Singaporean subjects were more familiar with copyright laws but were less supportive of the laws and more likely to engage in software piracy than the American subjects. In order to explain this difference, the authors provide an explanation that focuses on cultural differences in moral decision making. They suggest that Americans tend to be rule-oriented when it comes to making decisions while Asians lean more toward being circumstance-oriented. It appears as though Americans tend to have fundamental values of right and wrong and apply those standards to all situations. Asians, on the other hand, tend to focus more on the totality of the circumstances when making decisions.

Theory of Reasoned Action

The central feature of the theory of reasoned action is that an individual's intention to perform a given behavior is a function of the sum of their motivational influences (Ajzen and Fishbein, 1980). The main premise, then, is that a person's intention to engage in some action is the main predictor and influencer of attitude. To the extent that a person intends to do something, they will more than likely do it. But if they do not intend to do something, then they will more than likely not do it. Two main determinants of an individual's behavior under this theory are (1) personal, or attitudinal factors, defined as the favorable (or unfavorable) evaluation of behavior, as a function of an individual's salient beliefs (i.e., suggesting that people think about their decisions and possible outcomes before making their decision), and (2) social or normative factors which includes a person's perception of what important referent groups think s/he should do (i.e., asking others their opinion before engaging in the act). At the point of decision or when confronted with a moral situation in which a choice is to be made, the theory of reasoned action argues that individuals will decide on the basis of their attitudes toward the behavior and their perceptions of what others think is appropriate.

Recently, Ajzen (1991) extended his formation of the theory of reasoned action because this earlier theory was limited in dealing with behaviors over which people had incomplete volitional control. Termed a theory of planned behavior, Ajzen argues that intentions to perform behaviors of different kinds can be predicted with high accuracy from attitudes toward the behavior, subjective norms, and perceived behavioral control. Common to both models, however, is the key assumption that "intentions are assumed to capture the motivational factors that influence a behavior; they are indications of how hard people are willing to try, of how much of an effort they are planning to exert, in order to perform the behavior" (Ajzen, 1991: 181).

Much research examining the theory of reasoned action has relied on scenario or vignette research designs in which the respondent is presented with a scenario, or hypothetical story in which a character portrayed in the story engages in a particular act, and asked if they would respond as the actor in the scenario did. This method has been used to examine a variety of criminal behaviors including tax evasion (Nagin and Klepper, 1989), drunk driving, and shoplifting (Nagin and Paternoster, 1993; Piquero and Tibbetts, 1996) as well as corporate offending decisions (Simpson and Piquero, 2002). Research has recently applied the theory to account for software piracy, though instead of examining intentions to offend they rely on self-reported measures of piracy. Seale and his colleagues (1998) surveyed employees at a large southwestern university in order to determine if two separate factors, attitudinal and normative, existed. They were unable to identify the two separate factors as predicted by the theory. However, they did find several factors that affected an individual's social or normative beliefs. Specifically, they found that perceived behavioral control as measured by expertise required had a direct effect on self-reported piracy. Christensen and Eining (1991) used a sample of business students in order to examine the influence of subjective or social norms (e.g., influence of organization including schools and companies and influence of friends) on self-reported piracy behavior and found a significant and positive relationship. This suggests that when an individual believes that friends and social organizations (i.e., school and place of employment) favorably view software piracy, they are more likely to report engaging in the behavior.

Learning Theory

At its core, Sutherland's (1947) theory of differential association argues that criminal behavior is learned much like noncriminal behavior is learned, through interaction with other persons in a process of communication. According to differential association, a person becomes delinquent because of an excess of definitions favorable to violation of law over definitions unfavorable to law violation. These definitions have been the source of much debate in criminology but generally involve both attitudes and behaviors. When attitudes and behaviors are more prone to crime than noncrime, the chances of criminal activity increase.

Building off the pioneering work of Sutherland regarding his differential association theory, Burgess and Akers (1966) and later Akers (1985), specified a social learning theory of criminal activity that makes use of the central concepts and principles of behaviorism. Like differential association, social learning theory maintains that criminal behavior is learned, but the way its learned is through direct operant conditioning and imitation or modeling of others.

According to Akers, behavior is learned or conditioned as a result of the effects (outcomes, consequences) it has on an individual (i.e., instrumental conditioning). There are two major processes involved in instrumental conditioning, reinforcement and punishment, and each of these may take two forms, negative and positive. Reinforcement causes a behavior to increase in frequency. This can occur through positive reinforcement (rewarding of behavior) or negative reinforcement (if engaging in a behavior allows a person to prevent an unpleasant stimulus). Punishment can be positive (e.g., when an unpleasant response follows a behavior) or negative (e.g., if a reward is removed in response to a behavior). According to Akers, Krohn, Lanza-Kaduce, and Radosevich (1979: 638), "whether deviant or conforming behavior is acquired and persists depends on past and present rewards or punishments for the behavior and the rewards and punishments attached to alternative behavior." Recently, Akers (1998) further extended his individual social learning theory to include the influence of the social structure (SSSL). The basic assumption behind SSSL is that social learning is the primary process linking social structure to individual behavior. The main proposition of SSSL is that variations in the social structure, culture, and locations of individuals and groups in the social system explain variation in crime rates, principally through their information on differences among individuals on the key social learning theory variables (Akers, 1998: 322). In sum, social learning theories of criminality contend that individuals learn to engage in crime primarily through their associations with others and in particular through the constellation of rewards and punishments.

More often than not the primary variable that is used in testing social learning theory is the behavior of peer groups. Several studies of software piracy also rely on this variable to examine the influence of peers on an individual's self-reported pirating behavior. For example, using a sample of college students, Hollinger (1993) examined two types of computer crime, giving or receiving pirated computer software and accessing another's computer account or files without the owner's knowledge or permission. He found that friends' involvement in piracy was strongly correlated with self-reported computer crime. More specifically, only 2% of the sample was likely to engage in computer crime when they reported that their best friends were not likely to engage in computer crime. However, almost 40% of the sample admitted to engaging in computer crime when they reported that more than half of their best friends engage in the same behavior.

Skinner and Fream (1997) conducted a direct test of social learning theory using a sample of undergraduate students who reported their involvement in five types of computer crime: software piracy, guessing a password to gain unauthorized access, gaining unauthorized access for the purpose of browsing, gaining unauthorized access for the purpose of changing information, and wrote or used a program that would destroy someone's computerized data (i.e., creating a computer virus). They found that associating with peers who participate in computer crime was the strongest predictor of their computer crime index (which was created by summing the frequency measure that asked students how often in the past year they committed each of the five computer crimes). In addition, they found that the source of imitation is learned not only from peer groups, but from a variety of sources including parents, siblings, teachers, and virtual peer groups or computer bulletin boards where interaction occurs electronically.

Prevention of Intellectual Property Theft

One of the primary reasons we attempt to understand the causes and correlates of criminal behavior is so that we are able to develop intervention and prevention efforts designed to control the behavior. Strategies to control behavior can be regarded as either primarily focusing on preventive behaviors (front-end strategies) or as deterrents (backdoor strategies), and even further some strategies do not simply attempt to make the offense "harder" or less rewarding, but to reduce or eliminate opportunity. Preventive controls are designed to make criminal activities harder or less rewarding for perpetrators by increasing the costs of engaging in the criminal act (Gopal and Sanders, 1997). Deterrent controls, on the other hand, intend to avoid criminal activities altogether by dissuading the users from even considering engaging in the act (Gopal and Sanders, 1997). A variety of different prevention techniques have been employed in order to prevent the theft of intellectual property rights but these efforts have primarily been designed on an ad hoc basis.

One of the most common prevention strategies employed is to use technological advances to increase the costs of engaging in piracy. These antipiracy technologies include strategies such as using encryption technology to make it harder for pirates to intercept the information while it is being transmitted, the use of special codes that would only allow access to the authorized owner, offering customer support to only the legal owner, and using hardware locks. Each technological advancement is designed to try and stay one step ahead of the pirates in order to dissuade them from engaging in piracy. The problem with this type of strategy is that some may find the challenge of breaking the new protective barrier as a rewarding experience rather than a hindrance to pirating (Sims et al., 1996). Another approach that also utilizes technological advancements is to use the technology to give the public what it wants. In other words, rather than trying to fight the use of new advances in technology some companies are finding ways to use the technology in their favor. For example, the prolific Internet source, Napster, drew much attention for the illegal downloading and sharing of copyrighted music. Napster provided a peer-to-peer file sharing service that allowed individuals to post and download music through the transmission of MP3 music files without legally purchasing the songs. Record companies along with artists fought hard and won the battle to shut down the illegal Napster service but recognized the potential of peer-to-peer file sharing services (*AandM et al., v. Napster*; *Metallica v. Napster*). New legal music services are now available that allow individuals to download their favorite music for either a one-time download fee (e.g., iTunes) or as a monthly service (e.g., Napster).

Since many students reported not knowing intellectual property laws (see Christensen and Eining, 1991), roughly 50 percent had indicated they had read the licensing agreement that appears on most copyrighted software programs, another deterrent strategy, educating the public, may be warranted.

(Note: Still, it remains unknown if 100 percent read these agreements—i.e., were knowledgeable about the legal rights of copyright holders—patterns of behavior would change.) One such method that is being used is a public educational campaign. The MPAA continues to engage in this effort in order to teach the public that movie piracy is illegal, to explain how it impacts the economy and impacts the jobs of many people who work in the motion picture industry. The current phase of the educational program is designed to target daily newspapers, consumer magazines, college newspapers, as well as anti-piracy messages appearing in local theaters to help inform the public about the negative consequences of pirating behavior. Other industries, such as the software industry, maintain anti-piracy speaker bureaus and distribute informational videos to their consumers how their goods should and should not be used (Luckenbill and Miller, 1998). Finally, educators are also advocating for the inclusion of ethical components into courses in order to educate students about the proper uses of intellectual property (Simpson et al., 1994).

Industries have also created or hired units, such as trade associations, to look after and protect their property. For example, the MPAA has its own security office to aid in the fight against film piracy (Luckenbill and Miller, 1998). The duties of the MPAA security office include setting up hotlines that allow them to receive tips or reports of pirating behavior, tracking the process of cases as they move through our legal system, and keeping records (Luckenbill and Miller, 1998). In addition to these private policing responsibilities, trade associations also allow the industry to have a collective voice and more resources to help mobilize legal resources against the pirating behavior. Trade associations can lobby for the interest of the industry as a whole and in some instances have proven to be quite successful. For example, the U.S. Senate Bill 893 (effective October 28, 1992) was created as a response to the pressure of the software industry and increased the penalties for copyright infringement (Cheng et al., 1997: 50).

The last strategy used to try and control the theft of intellectual property is by means of lawsuits (both civil and criminal) and legal statutes in order to deter pirating behavior. Enlisting the help of the government by means of legislative action is an avenue that is being aggressively pursued. Many trade associations have not only fought to get laws passed that prohibit the theft of intellectual property rights but have also filed their own lawsuits against individuals. Many criminal statutes against theft of intellectual property are currently on the books with many of the laws specific to certain forms of intellectual property. For example, the Economic Espionage Act of 1996 makes the theft of trade secrets a federal crime while the Trademark Counterfeiting Act of 1984 criminalizes the trafficking of counterfeit goods and services (Maher and Thompson, 2002).

Unfortunately, while each of these strategies in isolation has been well documented and implemented in a number of arenas, there have been no outcome evaluation efforts that have examined the effectiveness of each of the interventions. In addition, we know almost nothing about the changes in intellectual property violations (both by amount and type) that have occurred in response to these prevention and intervention efforts. This is unfortunate since many of these efforts are costly in terms of both time and financial resources that are needed for proper implementation. A clear understanding of the impact of these efforts on intellectual property violations is imperative to help guide public policies designed to combat piracy and protect the rights of intellectual property owners.

Agenda for Future Research

As has been made clear, the current state of knowledge regarding the nature and prevalence of intellectual property theft is scant. A three-pronged research effort is suggested that may be ambitious—but always relevant in helping to begin to fill some of the gaps that remain in the knowledge base regarding the theft of intellectual property rights. These three priorities surround data collection efforts, theoretical tests, and cataloging and evaluating the knowledge base regarding the effects of policy efforts.

First, just as the U.S. Bureau of Census together with the Bureau of Justice Statistics conducts a nationwide survey of crime victims, efforts must be developed to initiate a nationwide data collection effort that targets information regarding the prevalence of intellectual property theft with special attention made to include all varieties of intellectual property violations (i.e., copyright, patents, trademarks, and trade secrets). This data collection effort need not be separate from those that are currently conducted but new questions will obviously need to be added. This nationwide data collection would also benefit from asking respondents about their knowledge of laws pertaining to and regarding intellectual property rights (e.g., copyright laws). It would be useful to understand whether persons are knowledgeable about such laws in an effort to aid public policy responses for intervention and prevention efforts. Although there are industry specific measures available on trends regarding violations of intellectual property rights (e.g., copyright violations including music piracy), this data has been gathered by those agencies and organizations that have a vested interest in the outcome (e.g., RIAA) so an independent source of information would help to aid in the understanding of the nature and prevalence of this kind of theft here in the United States. Ideally, international victimization data would also be collected as well in order to understand the global impact of these types of offenses.

Second, currently there is very little information known about the causes and correlates of intellectual property theft and what little information is known seems to raise more questions than it answers. For example, do the theoretical explanations offered earlier predict all types of intellectual property theft equally well or does theft of intellectual property fall better under the purview of one theory (i.e., social learning) than another (i.e., ethics)? Or is an integration of various frameworks best suited for the understanding of this type of behavior? Some of the theories already outlined seek to explain the onset of this kind of behavior while others focus on explaining persistence and desistence of intellectual property right violations. Ideally we would want to understand why individuals start offending, what causes them to continue, and why they stop. In addition, very little is known about the differences at the individual (i.e., micro) and group (i.e., macro) level. Are some theories better equipped to understand intellectual property violations at the micro-level while others better inform us of offending at the macro-level? While some research has suggested that piracy is more prevalent among younger individuals (i.e., college students) we know nothing regarding this type of crime over an individual's life course (though Oz (1990) suggests that the offending behavior is established long before the individual enters the workforce). Therefore, are some theories more relevant to an earlier phase as opposed to later part of an individual's life-course? Other issues regarding the opportunity to offend also arise. Do the correlates of intellectual property violations (as well as the various types) differ across samples (i.e., general population, business executives and managers, high school students, college students) both domestically and abroad? Similarly, how are the opportunities to offend distributed across different populations? Some evidence seems to suggest that those who use the computer more often are more likely to report engaging in software piracy (Eining and Christensen, 1991; Sims et al., 1996) but as of yet no study has directly examined the influence of exposure time and access to the computer or access to Internet services on pirating behavior. In short, a series of small-scale well-designed surveys could provide important baseline information regarding the causes of intellectual property theft.

Third, policy options, responses, intervention, and prevention efforts aimed at curtailing intellectual property violations seem to be changing almost daily. It would be useful for researchers to catalog these efforts and explain their changing manifestations over time. For example, many of the prevention efforts that have been put into place are industry specific. The efforts put into place that surround music piracy, such as only allowing a song to be copied a certain number of times, may and often times do differ from the efforts aimed at deterring individuals from copying the latest movies. Many of these efforts have considered and implemented technological advancements that make it more difficult to copy products. In that regard, it would be interesting to understand individual's responses to these efforts and if they have become deterred or more determined to engage (or continue) the behavior.

Copyright laws and enforcement of their violations have been ill studied in the social sciences. While legal studies have kept track of and documented the ever-changing laws and legal statutes regarding the theft of intellectual property rights (see Maher and Thomson, 2002 for review), very little is known on how these laws impact the public at large and more specifically the effects the laws have on the offending behavior. For example, record shows that were prevalent during the 1980s where it was common to buy bootlegged records and concerts have pretty much ceased to exist. It is unclear if these outlets were shut down due to the changes in laws protecting copyrighted works, such as the bootlegged music being sold, or if the sales of such illegal goods simply was displaced to other venues (many are found on eBay). Recent news reports have indicated that local area flea markets have become targeted locations cracking down on the illegal sales of copyrighted CDs and DVDs. Such interventions require the cooperation of local and federal law enforcement as well as the cooperation of the recording and/or the motion picture associations. Understanding not only the costs and consequences of such actions but the larger impact on society is only one piece to the overall puzzle regarding the full range of available responses to the theft of intellectual property rights.

In short, although the legal arena has been witness to much research on the theft of intellectual property rights, the same cannot be said from the social scientific community generally, and the criminological community in particular. This is a bit surprising since criminology contains the theories and requisite methodological tools needed to effectively understand and document the problem of intellectual property theft. The Department of Justice and its research arm, the National Institute of Justice, stands in a good position to begin local and nationwide efforts together in an effort to document the nature and prevalence of intellectual property rights violations as well as cataloging and evaluating policy efforts already put into place. It is important that such research-based efforts are stepped up and executed quickly so that the needed data can be collected and used to help inform the public policy issues, discussions, and decisions that surround the theft of intellectual property rights. Nowhere and at no time has this been as important of an issue as it is in today's digital age. If America wants to continue to be a world leader in the production of intellectual property, a more complete understanding of the prevalence and causes of the problem are needed as well as avenues which can help prevent the theft from occurring.

References

Adams, J. S. (1963). "Toward an Understanding of Inequity," *Journal of Abnormal and Social Psychology, 67*, 422–436.

Ajzen, I. (1991). "The Theory of Behavior," *Organizational Behavior and Human Decision Processes, 50*, 179–211.

Ajzen, I., and Fishbein, M. (1980). *Understanding Attitudes and Predicting Social Behaviour*. Englewood Cliffs, NJ: Prentice Hall.

Akers, R. L. (1985). *Deviant Behavior: A Social Learning Approach* (3rd ed.). Belmont, CA: Wadsworth.

Akers, R. L. (1998). *Social Learning and Social Structure: A General Theory of Crime and Deviance*. Boston, MA: Northeastern University Press.

Akers, R. L. (2000). *Criminological Theories: Introduction, Evaluation, and Application* (3rd ed.). Los Angeles, CA: Roxbury Publishing Company.

Akers, R. L., Krohn, M. D., Lanza-Kaduce, L., and Radosevich, M. (1979). "Social Learning and Deviant Behavior: A Specific Test of a General Theory," *American Sociological Review, 44*, 635–655.

Beccaria, C. (1963). *On Crimes and Punishment*. New York: MacMillan Publishing.

Bentham, J. (1967). *A Fragment on Government and an Introduction to the Principal of Morals and Legislation*. Oxford: Basil Blackwell.

Burgess, R. L., and Akers, R. L. (1966). "A Different Association-Reinforcement Theory of Criminal Behaviors." *Social Problems, 14*, 128–147.

Carruthers, B. G., and Ariovich, L. (2004). "The Sociology of Property Sights. *Annual Review of Sociology, 30*, 23–46.

Cheng, H. K., Sims, R. R., and Teegen, H. (1997). "To Purchase or to Pirate Software: An Empirical Study," *Journal of Management Information Systems, 13*, 49–60.

Christensen, A. L., and Eining, M. M. (1991). "Factors Influencing Software Piracy: Implication for Accountants." *Journal of Information Systems, Spring*, 67–80.

Cohen, L. E., and Felson, M. (1979). "Social Change and Crime Rate Trends: A Routine Activities Approach." *American Sociological Review, 44*, 588–608.

Cohen, E., and Cornwell, L. (1989). "A Question of Ethics: Developing Information Systems Ethics. *Journal of Business Ethics, 8,* 431–437.

Davis, J. R., and Welton, R. E. (1991). "Professional Ethics: Business Students Perceptions." *Journal of Business Ethics, 10,* 451–463.

Dusollier, S. (2003). "Open Source and Copyleft: Authorship Reconsidered?" *Columbia Journal of Law and the Arts, 26,* 281–296.

Eckhoff, T. (1974). *Justice: Its Determinants in Social Interaction.* Rotterdam, Netherlands: Rotterdam University Press.

Eining, M. M, and Christensen, A. L. (1991). "A Psycho-Social Model of Software Piracy: The Development and Test of a Model," In R. M. Dejoie, G. C. Fowler, and D. B. Paradice (Eds.), *Ethical Issues in Information Systems* (pp. 182–188). Boston, MA: Boyd and Fraser.

Endeshaw, A. (2002). "The Paradox of Intellectual Property Lawmaking in the New Millennium: Universal Templates as Terms of Surrender for the Non-Industrial Nations; Piracy as an Offshoot," *Cardozo Journal of International and Comparative Law, 10,* 41–77.

Gasaway, L. N. (2003). "America's Cultural Record: A Thing of the Past?" *Houston Law Review, 40,* 643–671.

Gibbs, J. N. (1975). *Crime, Punishment, and Deterrence.* New York: Elsevier.

Gilligan, C. (1982). *In a Different Voice: Psychological Theory and Women's Development.* Cambridge, MA: Harvard University Press.

Glass, R. S., and Wood, W. A. (1996). "Situational Determinants of Software Piracy: An Equity Theory Perspective," *Journal of Business Ethics, 15,* 1189–1198.

Gopal, R. D., and Sanders, G. L. (1997). "Preventive and Deterrent Controls for Software Piracy," *Journal of Management Information Systems. 13,* 29–47.

Gottfredson, M., and Hirschi, T. (1990). *A General Theory of Crime.* Palo Alto, CA: Stanford University Press.

Hagan, J., and Kay, F. (1990). "Gender and Delinquency in White-Collar Families: A Power-Control Perspective," *Crime and Delinquency, 36,* 391–407.

Harrington, S. (1989). "Why People Copy Software and Create Computer Viruses: Individual Characteristics or Situational Factors," *Information Resource Management Journal,* 28–37.

Hinduja, S. (2001). "Correlates of Internet Software Piracy," *Journal of Contemporary Criminal Justice, 17,* 369–382.

Hollinger, R. C. (1993). "Crime by Computer: Correlates of Software Piracy and Unauthorized Account Access," *Security Journal, 2,* 2–12.

Hollinger, R. C., and Lanza-Kaduce, L. (1988). "The Process of Criminalization: The Case of Computer Crime Laws," *Criminology, 26,* 101–126.

IFPI. (2003). *The Record Industry Commercial Piracy Report, 2003.* London: IFPI.

Jones, T. M. (1991). "Ethical Decision Making by Individuals in Organizations: An Issue-Contingent Model," *Academy of Management Review, 16,* 366–395.

Lessig, L. (2001). *The Future of Ideas: The Fate of the Commons in a Connected World.* New York: Random House.

Luckenbill, D. F., and Miller, S. L. (1998). "Defending Intellectual Property: State Efforts to Protect Creative Works," *Justice Quarterly, 15,* 93–120.

Maher, M. K., and Thomson, J. M. (2002). "Intellectual Property Crimes," *American Criminal Law Review, 39,* 763–816.

Moohr, G. S. (2003). The Crime of Copyright Infringement: An Inquiry Based on Morality, Harm, and Criminal Theory," *Boston University Law Review, 83,* 731–783.

MPA. (2003). *2003 Piracy Fact Sheets: US Overview.* MPA Worldwide Market Research.

Nagin, D., and Klepper, S. (1989). "Tax Compliance and Perceptions of the Risks of Detection and Criminal Prosecution, " *Law and Society Review, 23,* 209–240.

Nagin, D., and Paternoster, R. (1993). "Enduring Individual Differences and Rational Choice Theories of Crime," *Law and Society Review 27,* 461–496.

Oz, E. (1990). "The Attitude of Managers-To-Be toward Software Piracy," *OR/MS Today,* August, 24–26.

Parker, D. B. (1976). *Crime by Computer.* New York: Charles Scribner and Sons.

Patry, W. (2003). The United States and International Copyright Law: From Berne to Eldred. *Houston Law Review, 40,* 749–762.

Piquero, A., and Tibbetts, S. (1996). "Specifying the Direct and Indirect Effects of Low Self-Control and Situational Factors in Offenders' Decision Making: Toward a More Complete Model of Rational Offending," *Justice Quarterly, 13,* 481–510.

Poltorak, A. I., and Lerner, P. J. (2002). *Essentials of Intellectual Property.* New York: John Wiley and Sons, Inc.

Reid, R. A., Thompson, J. K., and Logsdon, J. M. (1992), "Knowledge and Attitudes of Management Students toward Software Piracy," *Journal of Computer Information Systems, 33,* 46–51.

Reiss, Jr., A. J. (1984). "Selecting Strategies of Social Control over Organizational Life," In K. Hawkins and J. M. Thomas (Eds.), *Enforcing Regulation* (pp. 23–35). Boston, MA: Kluwer-Nijoff Publishing.

Ronkainen, L. A., and Guerrero-Cusumano, J. (2001). "Correlates of Intellectual Property Violations," *Multinational Business Review, 9,* 59–65.

Sacco, V. F., and Zureik, E. (1990). "Correlates of Computer Misuse: Data from a Self-Reporting Sample," *Behaviour and Information Technology, 9,* 353–369.

Seale, D. A., Polakowski, M., and Schneider, S. (1998). "It's Not Really Theft!: Personal and Workplace Ethics That Enable Software Piracy," *Behaviour and Information Technology, 17,* 27–40.

Shim, J. P., and Taylor, G. S. (1989). "Practicing Manager's Perception/Attitude toward Illegal Software Copying," *OR/MS Today, 16,* 30–33.

Simpson, S. S., and Piquero, N. L. (2002). "Low Self-Control, Organizational Offending, and Corporate Crime," *Law and Society Review, 36,* 509–547.

Simpson, P. M., Banerjee, D., and Simpson, Jr., C. L. (1994). "Softlifting: A Model of Motivating Factors," *Journal of Business Ethics, 13,* 431–438.

Sims, R. R., Cheng, H. K., and Teegen, H. (1996). "Toward a Profile of Student Software Pirates," *Journal of Business Ethics, 15,* 839–849.

Skinner, W., and Fream, A. M. (1997). "A Social Learning Analysis of Computer Crime among College Students," *Journal of Research in Crime and Delinquency, 34,* 495–522.

Solomon, S. L., and O'Brien, J. A. (1990). "The Effect of Demographic Factors on Attitudes toward Software Piracy," *Journal of Information Systems, 30,* 40–46.

Stim, R. (2000). *Intellectual Property: Patents, Trademarks, and Copyrights* (2nd ed.), Albany, NY: West Thomas Learning.

Story, A. (2003). "Burn Berne: Why the Leading International Copyright Convention Must Be Repealed," *Houston Law Review, 40,* 763–801.

Sutherland, E. (1947). *Principles of Criminology.* Philadelphia, PA: Lippincott.

Swinyard, W. R., Rinne, H., and Keng Kau, A. (1990). "The Morality of Software Piracy: A Cross-Cultural Analysis," *Journal of Business Ethics, 9,* 655–664.

Taylor, G. S., and Shim, J. P. (1993). "A Comparative Examination of Attitudes toward Software Piracy among Business Professors and Executives," *Human Relations, 46,* 419–433.

Thong, J. Y. L., and Yap, C. (1998). "Testing an Ethical Decision-Making Theory: The Case of Softlifting, " *Journal of Management Information Systems, 15,* 213–237.

Tsalikis, J., and Ortiz-Buonafina, M. (1990). "Ethical Beliefs' Differences of Males and Females," *Journal of Business Ethics, 9,* 509–517.

109

Digital Piracy:
Assessing the
Contributions of
an Integrated
Self-Control Theory
and Social Learning
Theory Using
Structural Equation
Modeling

USTR. (2004). *2003 Special 301 Report.* Washington, D.C.: Office of the U.S. Trade Representative.

Volokh, E. (2003). "Freedom of Speech and Intellectual Property: Some Thoughts after Eldred, 44 Liquormart, and Bartnicki," *Houston Law Review, 40,* 697–748.

WIPO. (2001). *WIPO Intellectual Property Handbook: Policy, Law, and Use.* Geneva, Switzerland. WIPO Publication. No. 489(E).

Yen, A. C. (2003). "Eldred, the First Amendment, and Aggressive Copyright Claims," *Houston Law Review, 40,* 673–695.

Zeithaml, V. (1988). "Consumer Perceptions of Price, Quality, and Value: A Means-End Model and Synthesis of Evidence." *Journal of Marketing, 52,* 2–22.

DIGITAL PIRACY: ASSESSING THE CONTRIBUTIONS OF AN INTEGRATED SELF-CONTROL THEORY AND SOCIAL LEARNING THEORY USING STRUCTURAL EQUATION MODELING

GEORGE E. HIGGINS   *University of Louisville*
BRIAN D. FELL   *University of Louisville*
ABBY L. WILSON   *University of Louisville*

Computer crime is on the rise and is a substantial social problem, and one of the most common forms of computer crime is software piracy (Britz, 2004). Software piracy is often referred to as the illegal copying of commercially available software so that the individual may avoid fees, or the making of unauthorized copies of an organization's internally developed software for an individual's personal use (Straub & Collins, 1990). This definition can be extended to include digital piracy—the illegal act of copying digital goods, software, digital documents, digital audio (including music and voice), and digital video for any reason other than to backup without explicit permission from and compensation to the copyright holder (Gopal, Sanders, Bhattacharjee, Agrawal, & Wagner, 2004).

The Internet has provided a haven for pirates. According to Wall (2005), the Internet provides a challenge for law enforcement because it provides individuals with four different avenues for criminal activity. First, the Internet allows criminals to maintain their criminal behavior through semi-anonymous communications. Second, the Internet has created an environment that is anonymous and transnational that can be used for criminal activity. Third, the Internet has created a shift in thinking from the ownership of physical property to the ownership of ideas (i.e., the shift to intellectual property) stifling creativity and advancements. Fourth, digital piracy is relatively easy to perform and takes place away from the copyright holder, so the impression is given to the pirate that the behavior is victimless. The ownership of ideas includes film, music, and software that can be pirated without the copyright owner's knowledge creating subforms of digital piracy.

Subforms of digital piracy (i.e., audio arid video piracy—the illegal act of uploading or downloading digital sound or video without explicit permission from and compensation to the copyright holder) have recently been on the rise (Gopal et al., 2004; Hinduja, 2003). These forms of digital piracy are influenced by the growth of the Internet and economic incentives to perform these acts. The speed and accessibility of the Internet coupled with the writable CD and compression technologies make digital piracy accessible and easy. According to the International Federation of Phonographic Industries (2004), a watchdog group for the music industry, audio piracy via the Internet has grown by 25 times in the past three years. That translates into 3 million downloads of music a day, which is an estimated loss of 4.1 billion dollars and the motion picture industry loses 3 billion dollars annually (Motion Picture Association of America, 2004).

Digital media falls under the context of intellectual property, which has protections under U.S. copyright laws (see Luckenbill & Miller, 1998). The Copyright Act of 1976 provided the basic framework for the current copyright laws (Im & Koen, 1990). This piece of legislation made copyright violations a federal misdemeanor offense with stiff penalties for repeat offenders. In 1982, The Piracy and Counterfeiting Amendments Act made mass Copyright violations of movies and music a felony. The Copyright Felony Act of 1992 made the reproduction of software and copyright violations involving 10 or more copies a felony (Koen & Im, 1997). The No Electronic Theft (NET) Act made distributing copyrighted materials over the Internet a felony offense (Koen & Im, 1997). Therefore, digital piracy is a form of white-collar crime (see Motivans, 2004, for reviews of these laws). These factors point to digital piracy as a white-collar crime that is a substantial problem needing examination so that it may be reduced.

To date, a few studies have examined this form of white-collar crime. Specifically, Hinduja (2001) used a sample of college students to show that Internet software piracy (a semantic for digital piracy) takes place most often among college students and is much greater for those with a high-speed Internet connection. Hinduja (2003) used a sample of college students to show that Internet software piracy took place most among males who were younger (17–20 years old) who were majoring in the liberal arts and who used their computers. Overall, the Hinduja (2001, 2003) studies suggest that college students are likely to perform digital piracy because of the lax enforcement of computer rules and laws by university officials and because they have a high level of curiosity that does not seem to occur among those with lower levels of education or those in the "working world." This presents a substantial problem for college and university administrators who may be held responsible through fines and negative publicity for their students' intentional or unintentional digital piracy (Koen & Im, 1997). Further, Hinduja (2003) argued that digital piracy may indicate the beginning of a serious crime trajectory.

Bhattacharjee, Gopal, and Sanders (2003) used a sample of college students to show that individuals with low incomes are more likely to pirate a new song than purchase it. Gopal et al. (2004) used a sample of undergraduates ($n = 133$) and structural equation modeling to show that ethical predispositions indirectly affect digital piracy through ethical intentions. From these studies, it is evident that the literature is quite sparse concerning digital piracy. A gap exists in the literature concerning an understanding of why individuals commit digital piracy using criminological theory.

Theories of criminal behavior allow criminologists to organize their empirical data in a rational way. The application of criminological theory to digital piracy will provide assistance in the search for a new empirical understanding. Without the application of these theories, criminologists may be left with fragmented correlates of why individuals perform digital piracy. Two leading criminological theories are attractive in the explanation of digital piracy—Gottfredson and Hirschi's self-control theory and Akers's social learning theory. These two theories claim to account for all forms of crime and deviance, including white-collar crime. Therefore, the present study seeks to understand the individual links that low self-control and social learning theory have with digital piracy. In addition, the present study attempts to integrate these two theories to provide a richer understanding of digital piracy. Some argue that understanding crimes on the Internet with conventional crime theories is a fruitless endeavor because crimes on the Internet maintain different qualities than street crime (Wall, 2003, 2004, 2005).

111

Digital Piracy: Assessing the Contributions of an Integrated Self-Control Theory and Social Learning Theory Using Structural Equation Modeling

The present study offers an understanding of digital piracy using criminological theory that is not present in the current literature. First, the study examines how low self-control and social learning theory can assist in understanding digital piracy. Second, the study attempts to integrate self-control theory and social learning theory to provide a deeper understanding of digital piracy. Third, the present study uses structural equation modeling for analysis. With these three advances, the present study provides information that may lead to policy development for reducing the instances of digital piracy.

Self-Control Theory

Gottfredson and Hirschi's (1990) self-control theory suggests that low self-control is a relatively time-stable individual difference that is developed in early childhood. Low self-control is the result of poor or ineffective parenting practices (i.e., ineffective emotional bonding, monitoring, recognition of deviant behavior, and discipline). Individuals with low self-control are characterized as impulsive, insensitive, physical (instead of mental), risk-taking, short-sighted, and nonverbal. These individuals may be attracted to criminal acts, which are short-lived, immediately gratifying, easy, simple, and exciting. The attraction to criminal acts is shaped by low self-control because

> . . . the dimensions of self-control are, in our view, factors affecting the calculation of the consequences of one's acts. The impulsive or shortsighted person fails to consider the negative or painful consequences of his acts; the insensitive person has fewer negative consequences to consider; the less intelligent person also has fewer consequences to consider (has less to lose). (Gottfredson & Hirschi, 1990, p. 95)

Crime, then, is attractive because it provides immediate benefits for the individual with low self-control without considering the long-term impact of the act for themselves and for others.

While under scrutiny from several researchers, the theory has some empirical support (Pratt & Cullen, 2000). In particular, the research has shown that low self-control remains relatively stable throughout life (Arneklev,

Cochran, & Gainey, 1998; Turner & Piquero, 2002). Some research has supported the link between parenting practices and low self-control (Gibbs, Giever, & Martin, 1998; Hay, 2003; Higgins, 2002, 2004), but the majority of the research has focused on the link between low self-control and street crime (Arneklev, Grasmick, Tittle, & Bursik, 1993; Avakame, 1998; Bichler-Robertson, Potchak, & Tibbetts, 2003; Evans, Cullen, Burton, Dunaway, & Benson, 1997; Forde & Kennedy, 1997; Gibbs & Giever, 1995; Grasmick, Tittle, Bursik, & Arneklev, 1993; Higgins & Makin, 2004a; Keane, Maxim, & Teevan, 1993; Li, 2004; Piquero, Gibson, & Tibbetts, 2002; Piquero & Tibbetts, 1996; Pratt & Cullen, 2000; Tibbetts, 1997; Tibbetts & Herz, 1996; Tibbetts & Myers, 1999; Unnever & Cornell, 2003; Winfree & Bernat, 1998).

Gottfredson and Hirschi (1990) make it clear that their theory can account for white-collar crime. They specifically stated:

> There is no reason to think that the offenders committing these crimes are causally distinct from other offenders. The assumption that white-collar criminals differ from other criminals is simply the assumption, in another guise, that offenders specialized in their particular crimes, an assumption for which there is no good evidence. The central elements of our theory of criminality are easily identifiable among white collar criminals. (Gottfredson & Hirschi, 1990, pp. 190–191)

The research to date does not necessarily support the direct link between low self-control and general forms of white-collar crime (Benson & Moore, 1992; Simpson & Piquero, 2002). However, some research has shown that low self-control has a link with physical media software piracy (Higgins & Makin, 2004a, 2004b). On the other hand, some have suggested that physical media and digital piracy are substantially different behaviors (see Gopal et al., 2004; Hinduja, 2001, 2003; Wall, 2005), making it unclear whether low self-control has a link with digital piracy.

It is expected that low self-control will have a link with digital piracy. This expectation is derived from the following analysis of the characteristics of low self-control in the context of digital piracy. That is, individuals with low self-control may impulsively pirate digital media because they cannot wait to purchase their own copy. Individuals with low self-control may not care about the trust in the licensing agreement between the digital media's creator and its owner. Although digital piracy is not a physical act, it may provide the individual with low self-control a sense of thrill, excitement, or even risk. Digital piracy may be attractive to those with low self-control because it is relatively simple and easy to perform. Finally, individuals with low self-control may perform digital piracy because they believe that no one is being harmed or may not even care if anyone is harmed by their behavior.

Social Learning Theory

Social learning theory has been presented by several theorists in different disciplines (Bandura, 1986; Skinner, 1953). In criminology, the theory most often given this label is Akers's (1985, 1998) version of social learning. Akers's version of social learning theory is a continuous effort to refine and expand the statements made by Sutherland (1949). Thus far, Akers's efforts have involved refining key concepts such as differential association and definitions, while adding the concepts of imitation and reinforcement and the language of behavioralists.

113

*Digital Piracy:
Assessing the
Contributions of
an Integrated
Self-Control Theory
and Social Learning
Theory Using
Structural Equation
Modeling*

For Akers's (1985, 1998) social learning theory, differential association refers to an individual's primary interaction with others in a group. Definitions refer to an individual's attitudes toward a specific behavior including techniques, rationalizations, motivations, and drives. Imitation refers to an individual's emulation of behavior after witnessing another individual's performance of the behavior and the consequences that follow their performance. Differential reinforcement refers to the anticipated and actual rewards and punishments that may promote the initiation and continuation of a behavior.[1]

The process of social learning theory is complex, containing direct, indirect, and reciprocal effects. That is, social learning theory suggests that individuals differentially associate with peers who are deviant or who demonstrate a tolerance for deviance. The individual then learns deviant definitions. Next, the individual is exposed to deviant models that reinforce deviance, the individual initiates or increases his or her involvement in crime, which has implications for further associations and attitudes. To date, the research literature has supported this process (Akers, 1998; Akers, Krohn, Lanza-Kaduce, & Radosevich, 1979; Akers & Lee, 1996; Esbensen & Deschenes, 1998; Esbensen & Huizinga, 1993; Krohn, Skinner, Massey, & Akers, 1985). Sellers, Pratt, Winfree, and Cullen (2000) have supported social learning theory through a meta-analysis of more than 100 studies. Although the research has supported the process of social learning theory, a complete test of this theory would require measuring the concepts with a specific causal structure. This is beyond the scope of the present study, but social learning theory does provide a foundation for developing specific hypotheses among select concepts that may be important to digital piracy. According to Akers (1998), positive findings from these hypotheses can be treated as support for social learning theory.

Therefore, the present study expects social learning theory to have a link with digital piracy based on the following application: digital piracy may be expected to the extent that the individual has differentially associated with family or peers who have performed digital piracy; that the individual has been exposed to digital pirating models; that the individual has been (or anticipates to be) differentially reinforced for digital piracy; and that the individual does not define digital piracy as being morally or situationally wrong and thinks that under select circumstances digital piracy is justified, appropriate, or proper behavior.

To date, the literature shows that social learning theory has a link with physical media software piracy. Skinner and Fream (1997) showed that differential association and definitions had direct links to software piracy, but imitation and differential reinforcement do not have direct links with software piracy. Higgins and Makin (2004a) used a sample of university students to show that differential association and definitions had a link with physical media software piracy when the piracy was for sharing software with a friend. Higgins and Makin (2004b) used a sample of university students to show that only differential association had a link with software piracy when the piracy was for their own interests. Overall, these studies suggest that differential association and definitions are most important for software piracy. Unfortunately, no study in criminology has linked these social learning theory measures to digital piracy leaving a gap in our understanding.

Integrating Self-Control Theory and Social Learning Theory

Social learning theory has important implications for self-control theory in two ways. First, because low self-control remains relatively stable, the dynamic measures of social learning theory may be suitable for policy development (see Arneklev, Grasmick, & Bursik, 1999; Turner & Piquero, 2002, for support of the relative stability hypothesis). Second, some research recognizes that self-control theory and social learning theory may overlap and be connected in complicated ways (Agnew, 1995; Evans et al., 1997). For instance, Gottfredson and Hirschi (1987, 1990) anticipated that the effect of self-control depends to a large extent on various forms of opportunity and other constraints (e.g., deviant peer association). At its core then, self-control theory is inclusive and sensitive to the implications of measures of deviant peer association. Gottfredson and Hirschi (1987) recognized substantial support for the link between deviant peer association and crime and by stating, "that people acquire the propensity to delinquency, find delinquent friends, and then commit delinquent acts, including serious criminal acts" (p. 597). This view suggests a process of acquiring a self-control level followed by delinquent friendships and delinquency. Gottfredson and Hirschi (1990) argued:

> . . . adventuresome and reckless children who have difficulty making and keeping friends tend to end up in the company of one another, creating groups made up of individuals who tend to lack self-control. The individuals in such groups will therefore tend to be delinquent, as will the group itself, (p. 158)

This view implies that groups themselves may facilitate or reduce the difficulty for crime to occur. This view has been supported in the empirical literature (Gibson & Wright, 2001; Higgins & Makin, 2004a, 2004b; Longshore, Chang, Hsieh, & Messina, 2004; Wright, Moffitt, & Caspi, 1998).

In addition to deviant peer association, the empirical literature has shown that low self-control has helped shape an individual's definitions of crime (i.e., attitudes for crime). The shaping of an individual's attitudes toward crime occurs through a subtle peer influence process where peers reinforce definitions toward behavior.[2] Two studies (Bolin, 2004; Longshore et al., 2004) empirically supported this view. Gottfredson and Hirschi (1987, 1990) and Hirschi and Gottfredson (1993, 1994) are clear that low self-control is the most important measure in the theory, the effect of low self-control on crime may not be independent of other influences, for example, differential association (i.e., deviant peer association) and definitions (i.e., attitudes).

While social learning theory and self-control theory differ about the use of deviant peer associations and the development of definitions, Gottfredson and Hirschi (1987, 1990) and Bolin (2004) suggest a process for deviant peer association and attitudes in self-control theory. Higgins and Makin (2004) found that definitions and differential association moderated the link between low self-control and physical media piracy (i.e., software piracy). However, no study, to our knowledge, has examined the mediating qualities of social learning theory for the link that low self-control has with digital piracy. Therefore, to fill this gap in our knowledge of digital piracy, the present study expects that low self-control will have a link with digital piracy through social learning theory and that it will remove the direct link between low self-control and digital piracy.

115

Digital Piracy: Assessing the Contributions of an Integrated Self-Control Theory and Social Learning Theory Using Structural Equation Modeling

Present Study

Research suggests that digital piracy is an emerging white-collar crime that is a substantial social problem (Gopal et al., 2004; Hinduja, 2001, 2003). Recognizing that no criminological theory research has been used to explain digital piracy, we examine the mediating links that self-control and social learning theory have with each other to provide an explanation for digital piracy.

The present study presents the first systematic investigation of this issue using self-control theory and can be seen as contributing to the literature on Gottfredson and Hirschi's theory. Regarding the study of social learning theory, this is the first systematic investigation to our knowledge that examines the link between the theory and digital piracy. In addition, the present study goes beyond previous research (Bolin, 2004; Gibson & Wright, 2001; Longshore et al., 2004; Wright et al., 1998) by also examining the roles of both differential association and definitions as measures of social learning theory that mediate the effect that low self-control has on digital piracy.

Method

This section presents the sample, procedures, and measures that were used in this study.

Sample and Procedures

After obtaining Institutional Review Board and Human Subject Protection Review approval, the researchers gave a self-report questionnaire to college students at an eastern university in the USA, in the fall 2004 semester. The students for this study came from four classes that were open to all majors and three classes that were open only to Justice Administration majors. All of the classes were housed in the College of Arts and Sciences (i.e., Liberal Arts). The researchers asked the students that were present the day of questionnaire administration to take part in the study. The researchers told the students of the voluntary nature of the study, and that all responses were anonymous and confidential. This set of procedures produced 392 completed questionnaires.

The sample was on average 21.37 years old (±2.27). The sample was 61% females and 39% males. The average major for the sample was business administration. Finally, the average class rank for the sample was sophomore.

The nature of the sample may be questioned based on population and cross-sectional design. The nature of digital piracy dictates that a university sample—like the one used in the present study—is warranted. That is, Hinduja (2001, 2003) has identified that the individuals most likely to perform digital piracy from the Internet are in college as opposed to those not in college or those in the working world. Further, the cross-sectional nature of the data may be problematic for some because the present study expects a specific causal logic. Two points speak to this concern. First, Gottfredson and Hirschi (1987, 1990) argued that cross-sectional data were most appropriate to examine their theory. Second, the present study will examine alternative models. With these arguments in mind, the cross-sectional sample of university students is suitable for the present study.

Measures

The measures for this study included low self-control, differential association, definitions, and intentions to commit digital piracy.

Intentions for Digital Piracy

The dependent measure for the present study is an individual's intention to perform digital movie piracy that is derived from three scenarios that were modified from Shore et al. (2001) (see Appendix A for the scenarios). Each scenario was followed by a question that asked the students the likelihood that they would engage in the behavior in the scenario. The students marked the likelihood that they would engage in the behavior in the scenario on a five-point Likert-type scale anchored by "not very likely" and "very likely." Higher scores on the scale represented stronger intentions to perform digital movie piracy.

Low Self-Control

The low self-control measure for this study was the popular 24-item Grasmick et al. (1993) scale. The scale is a second-order factor. That is, the 24 items of the scale coalesce into six subscales (i.e., impulsivity, simple tasks, risk-taking, physical, self-centered, and temper) and then form self-control (Tittle, Ward, & Grasmick, 2003). The students marked their responses to the items using a four-point Likert-type scale. The answer choices ranged from 1 (strongly disagree) to 4 (strongly agree). We then used each subcomponent of the scale as an indicator of low self-control in the structural equation modeling analysis, similar to Longshore et al. (2004). Therefore, the psychometric properties of the subscales of the scale become important. The impulsivity scale had an acceptable internal consistency of 0.73 and a mean of 7.91 and standard deviation of 2.08. The simple tasks scale had an acceptable internal consistency of 0.74 and mean of 8.01 and standard deviation of 1.90. The risk-taking scale had an acceptable internal consistency of 0.77 with a mean of 9.51 and standard deviation of 2.15. The physical scale had an acceptable internal consistency of 0.78 with a mean of 10.58 and a standard deviation of 2.39. The self-centered scale had acceptable internal consistency

117

*Digital Piracy:
Assessing the
Contributions of
an Integrated
Self-Control Theory
and Social Learning
Theory Using
Structural Equation
Modeling*

(0.78) with a mean of 7.46 and a standard deviation of 2.11. The anger scale had acceptable internal consistency (0.80) with a mean of 8.44 and a standard deviation of 2.45.

Differential Association

The association with digital pirating peers (i.e., differential association) measure was a composite of six items from Krohn et al. (1985). The items asked students the following: how many of their best (male/female) friends performed digital piracy from the Internet, how many of the friends (male/female) that they have known the longest have performed digital piracy from the Internet, and how many of the friends (male/female) whom they are around the most pirated digital media from the Internet. The students provided this information using five answer choices (1 = none, 2 = just a few, 3 = about half, 4 = more than half, and 5 = all or almost all). Higher scores on the scale indicated more differential association. Each male or female model had acceptable internal consistency (males = 0.97 and females = 0.98) and the mean of the male scale was 8.29 with a standard deviation of 3.92. The female scale had a mean of 6.39 and a standard deviation of 3.60.

Definitions

The measure of definitions was the students' attitudes toward software piracy in general from Rahim, Seyal, and Rahman (2001). This scale captured definitions using 11 items. This measure was relevant because Rahim et al. (2001) hypothesized that the scale is a general measure of attitudes toward piracy that would account for all forms of this behavior. Further, the scale is designed to capture the beliefs that are favorable or unfavorable to software piracy, which is consistent with social learning theory. The students marked their responses using a four-point Likert-type scale using "strongly disagree" and "strongly agree" as anchors. Higher scores on the scale indicated stronger or more favorable attitudes toward software piracy. The scale had acceptable internal consistency (0.85) and a scree test showed that the scale was unidimensional. The scale had a mean of 28.71 and a standard deviation of 5.77.

Results

The analysis for this study is structural equation modeling (SEM) via Mplus (3.11). SEM is a process that allows for the testing of theories that are hypothesized a priori to explain the observed correlations (i.e., variances and covariances) among measures (Kline, 2005). This process tests these theoretical pathways simultaneously. Using maximum likelihood estimation, that is robust when the data depart from normality, SEM is able to use psychometric information to provide estimates that are polluted with measurement error. SEM takes place in a three-step process. First, a measurement model produces confirmatory factor analysis to assess the construct validity of the items by determining how well the model fits the data and to examine the psychometric qualities of the estimates (i.e., the size of the factor loadings) (Model One). Second, the main structural model is examined to find out if the link between low self-control and digital piracy is mediated by social learning theory (Model Two).

Third, alternative models are examined to determine if the main structural model is the soundest model in these data (Models Three through Four). That is, low self-control and social learning theory have independent direct links with digital piracy (Model Three). Further, low self-control has an indirect effect on digital piracy, but low self-control maintains a direct effect on digital piracy (Model Four).

However, before the SEM analysis, the correlations and covariance were generated.[3] The correlations among the indicators ranged from −0.04 to 0.60. Overall, the correlations demonstrate enough shared variance to suggest proceeding to the SEM analysis.

Model One

To develop the measurement model, we used the subscales of the Grasmick et al. (1993) scale to form the low self-control measure. This method reflects our understanding that the Grasmick et al. scale forms a second-order low self-control measure (see Arneklev et al., 1999; Delisi, Hochstetler, & Murphy, 2003; Flora, Finkel, & Foshee, 2003). In addition, we used the composite measures of differential association (i.e., male and female differential association) and definitions to indicate social learning theory. Finally, we used the three individual indicators of the scenarios to represent digital media piracy.

The measurement model for this study demonstrated a good fit of the data (see Appendix B). Specifically, the chi-square estimate was statistically significant suggesting a misfit of the model to the data. However, Schumacker and Lomax (1996) have argued that chi-square is sensitive to sample size and may provide misleading results. Therefore, additional fit statistics were consulted (comparative fit index [CFI] = 0.95, standardized root mean square residual [SRMR] = 0.06, and the root mean square error of approximation [RMSEA] = 0.05) that show that the model does have a good fit of the data suggesting that the measurement model has found proper construct validity for the measures used in this study (see Gibbs, Giever, & Higgins, 2003; Hu & Bentler, 1999, for a description of the fit statistics along with their standards).[4]

The measurement model shows that the factor loadings for the observed indicators are all above Kline's (1998) standard of 0.50 for a large factor loading, with the exception of two indicators, and all of the factor loadings are statistically significant. The physical measure of low self-control does not provide a large factor loading (0.34). This measure is retained because it is theoretically relevant (Gottfredson & Hirschi, 1990; Grasmick et al., 1993). Further, the attitude measure does not provide a strong factor loading as an indicator of social learning theory (0.32). This measure was retained because of theoretical (Akers, 1998; Sutherland, 1949) and empirical relevance to the present study and past research (Higgins & Makin, 2004; Skinner & Fream, 1997). The size and significance of the factor loadings suggest that the measures are suitable indicators of their hypothesized latent measures.

Model Two

To examine whether the link between low self-control and digital piracy is mediated by social learning theory, it is necessary to examine the structural model. The fit of the structural model is comparable to the fit of the measurement

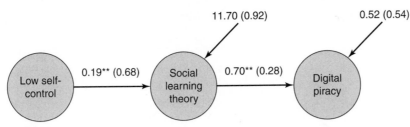

119

*Digital Piracy:
Assessing the
Contributions of
an Integrated
Self-Control Theory
and Social Learning
Theory Using
Structural Equation
Modeling*

FIGURE 1. Structural Model—Indirect Effect of Low Self-Control Effects on Digital Piracy through Social Learning Theory

model (chi-square = 123.78, p = 0.00; CFI = 0.94; RMSEA = 0.04; SRMR = 0.06). Figure 1 shows that low self-control has a positive link with social learning theory (0.68*) and social learning theory has a positive link with digital piracy (0.28**). The link between low self-control and social learning theory suggests that those with low self-control are likely to learn how to digitally pirate. Further, those that have learned how to digitally pirate are likely to pirate software. The results show an indirect effect of low self-control on digital piracy that is positive (0.19**). This result suggests that social learning theory does mediate the link between low self-control and digital piracy. Overall, this model supports the expectation of the present study that the effect of low self-control on digital piracy is mediated by social learning theory.[5]

Model Three

The third model examines the first alternative model—that low self-control and social learning theory have independent direct effects. The fit of this model is similar to the other models (chi-square = 118.64, p = 0.00; CFI = 0.95; SRMR = 0.06), with the exception of the RMSEA (0.06) that suggests the model does not fit as well as the previous models. Figure 2 shows that low self-control

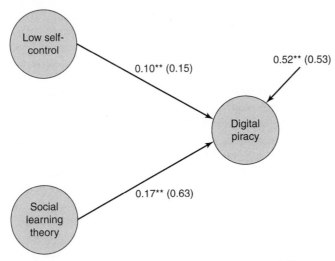

FIGURE 2. Structural Model—Direct Effect of Low Self-Control and Social Learning Theory on Digital Piracy

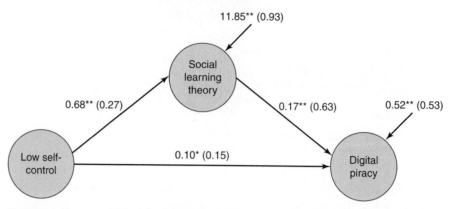

FIGURE 3. Structural Model—Direct and Indirect Effects of Low Self-Control and Social Learning Theory on Digital Piracy

(0.15[*]) and social learning theory (0.63[**]) have independent significant links with digital piracy. The findings from this model support the expectations of both theories.

Model Four

The fourth model tests whether low self-control has an indirect effect on digital piracy, but maintains a direct effect on digital piracy. The fit of this model is better than any of the other models (chi-square = 118.64, p = 0.00; CFI = 0.95; SRMR = 0.05; RMSEA = 0.05), with the fit indices suggesting proper fit. Figure 3 shows that low self-control has a direct effect on social learning theory (0.27[*]) and that social learning theory has a direct effect on digital piracy (0.63[**]). The direct effect of low self-control on digital piracy is 0.15[*]. Further, the indirect effect of low self-control on digital piracy through social learning theory is 0.17[**]. Overall, this model suggests that social learning theory is not capable of removing the effects of low self-control on digital piracy. However, the indirect effect is larger than the direct effect, suggesting that including social learning theory in the model is important.[6]

Discussion

The purpose of the present study was to shed light on an emerging form of white-collar crime—digital piracy—by applying crime theories. The study examined the links between self-control theory and social learning theory and digital piracy. The current literature acknowledges that low self-control remains relatively stable (Turner & Piquero, 2002) and suggests that self-control theory and social learning theory may be linked theoretically (Akers, 1985, 1991, 1998; Evans et al., 1997; Gottfredson & Hirschi, 1987, 1990) and empirically (Gibson & Wright, 2001; Higgins & Makin, 2004; Longshore et al., 2004; Wright et al., 1998). The results from the present study show support for both self-control theory and social learning theory adding to the growing body of research using both theories (Pratt & Cullen, 2000; Sellers et al., 2000).

121

*Digital Piracy:
Assessing the
Contributions of
an Integrated
Self-Control Theory
and Social Learning
Theory Using
Structural Equation
Modeling*

Specifically, the present study develops a three-factor model (low self-control → social learning theory → digital piracy) that was compared to two theoretically derived alternative models. The three-factor model is superior to the four-factor model because all of the standardized effects were larger in the three-factor model, especially for the direct effect of social learning theory. In addition, the three-factor model is more parsimonious. This supports Hirschi and Gottfredson's (1993) contention that self-control is sensitive to constraints. The data suggest that one of the constraints is that individuals need to learn the behavior they intend to perform. In addition, this study supports previous research (Higgins & Makin, 2004) that has found support for the connection between differential association and definitions with low self-control but goes beyond previous research in this area (Gibson & Wright, 2001; Longshore et al., 2004; Wright et al., 1998). Therefore, digital piracy is attractive to those individuals that have low self-control and have socially learned digital piracy. The results also add to the substantial body of research on social learning theory that suggests that criminal behavior is learned (Akers, 1998; Sellers et al., 2000). This result is not possible without including social learning theory measures in the three-factor model. Thus, from these data, the three-factor model that includes low self-control, social learning theory, and digital piracy is important for understanding this behavior.

Given the support for the three-factor model, university administrators may be interested in developing policy that may aid in the reduction of digital piracy. The focus of these programs should come from social learning theory. These policies should emphasize developing proper friendships with non-digital pirating peers. Further, the programs may emphasize definitions that are favorable to not performing digital piracy. Large-scale implementation of these policies may need to be controlled until these policies are evaluated for effectiveness.

Although the results of this study support the three-factor model, this study has limits that future researchers should consider. Future research should collect data from several universities instead of only one. Further, future research should consider using different measures of digital piracy to broaden our understanding of the behavior. Future research should consider the theoretical links that low self-control has with additional theories, which may have substantial implications for understanding digital piracy. Although against the wishes of Gottfredson and Hirschi (1990), future researchers may consider using a longitudinal design.

Despite these limits, the present study provides evidence that low self-control, social learning theory, and digital piracy have a link. Specifically, the results suggest that the link between low self-control and digital piracy is partially mediated by social learning theory. Future studies that collect longitudinal data from students from more than one university and that use different measures of digital piracy will be particularly useful in our understanding. For now, the present study supports the proposition that social learning theory mediates the link between low self-control and digital piracy.

Acknowledgement

A previous draft of this paper was presented at the Annual Meeting of the Academy of Criminal Justice Sciences in March 2005 in Chicago, IL.

Notes

[1] It is important to note that Akers's (1998) version of the theory also includes the development and use of social structure in the theory. That is, Akers proposed that individuals are sensitive to the social structure (i.e., environment) and that this shapes an individual's penchant for crime. However, the effects of social structure on an individual's crime are mediated by the social learning concepts.

[2] This view reduces the emphasis on the overt and challenging qualities of peer pressure.

[3] The correlations and covariance are available from the first author upon request.

[4] The original measurement model does not fit the data as well as the final model presented here. The original measurement was modified by allowing the covariances of impulsivity and simple tasks to freely covary with anger. Our view is that these subscales are designed to be indicators of low self-control. Therefore, allowing these subscales to covary does not take away from their development or indication of low self-control. Further, the digital piracy indicators were allowed to freely covary. This modification was performed because the observed indicators of digital piracy use the same statement "stems" (see Kline, 2005, for a complete explanation of this process). Further, the differential association measures were allowed to freely covary because their items utilize the same stem as well—similar to the digital piracy items.

[5] To determine the validity of the first model, we developed a simulation study to examine parameter and standard error bias and statistical power. To develop this study, we used the parameters from our results of the first model as the population parameters for the simulation study. In developing the simulation study, we followed Muthen and Muthen's recommendation of 500 repetitions, with the estimates and the same sample size as in the original study. In the simulation study, we discovered that the parameters and their standard errors had a little bias, but these biases were within acceptable ranges (see Muthen & Muthen, 2002, for standards). In addition, the simulation study demonstrated that enough statistical power was available in the present study for estimation of all parameters (the lowest amount of power = 1.00) (see Cohen, 1988, for standards for statistical power). The complete findings of this analysis are available upon request from the first author.

[6] In addition to these models, we examined interaction effects. We performed these interactions in two ways. First, we split the sample at its median using an aggregate measure of social learning theory. In this measure of social learning theory, all of the measures were added together. We then made multiple group comparisons where the two samples were empirically compared after simultaneously running the variables together (see Kline, 1998, for details about multiple group models in SEM). We did not find an interaction between the two theories with this technique. Second, we examined the interaction using the random slopes technique from Muthen and Muthen (1998–2004). This technique comprises of interacting the slopes from the latent variables (i.e., low self-control and social learning theory) to form the interaction. This analysis did not reveal an interaction between these measures. Therefore, we concluded that, in these data, low self-control and social learning theory do not interact to performing digital piracy. The results of these analyses are available from the first author on request.

References

*Digital Piracy:
Assessing the
Contributions of
an Integrated
Self-Control Theory
and Social Learning
Theory Using
Structural Equation
Modeling*

Agnew, R. (1995). Testing the leading crime theories: An alternative strategy focusing on motivational process. *Journal of Research in Crime & Delinquency, 32*, 363.

Akers, R. (1985). *Deviant behavior: A social learning approach.* Belmont, CA: Wadsworth.

Akers, R. (1991). Self-control as a general theory of crime. *Journal of Quantitative Criminology, 7*, 201–211.

Akers, R. (1998). *Social learning and social structure: A general theory of crime and deviance.* Boston, MA: Northeastern University Press.

Akers, R. L., Krohn, M. D., Lanza-Kaduce, L., & Radosevich, M. (1979). Social learning and deviant behavior: A specific test of a general theory. *American Sociological Review, 44*, 636–655.

Akers, R. L., & Lee, G. (1996). A longitudinal test of social learning theory: Adolescent smoking. *Journal of Drug Issues, 26*, 317.

Arneklev, B. J., Cochran, J. K., & Gainey, R. R. (1998). Testing Gottfredson and Hirschi's "low self-control" stability hypothesis: An exploratory study. *American Journal of Criminal Justice, 23*, 107–127.

Arneklev, B. J., Grasmick, H. G., & Bursik, R. J., Jr. (1999). Evaluating the dimensionality and invariance of "low self-control." *Journal of Quantitative Criminology, 15*, 307–331.

Arneklev, B. J., Grasmick, H. G., Tittle, C. R., & Bursik, R. J., Jr. (1993). Low self-control and imprudent behavior. *Journal of Quantitative Criminology, 9*, 225–247.

Avakame, E. F. (1998). Intergenerational transmission of violence, self-control, and conjugal violence: A comparative analysis of physical violence and psychological aggression. *Violence and Victims, 13*, 301–316.

Bandura, A. (1986). *Social foundations of thought and action: A social cognitive theory.* Englewood Cliffs, NJ: Prentice Hall.

Benson, M. L., & Moore, E. (1992). Are white-collar and common offenders the same? An empirical and theoretical critique of a recently proposed general theory of crime. *Journal of Research in Crime & Delinquency, 29*, 251–272.

Bhattacharjee, S., Gopal, R. D., & Sanders, G. L. (2003). Digital music and online sharing: Software piracy 2.0? *Communications of the ACM, 46*, 47–76.

Bichler-Robertson, G., Potchak, M. C., & Tibbetts, S. (2003). Low self-control, opportunity, and strain in students' reported cheating behavior. *Journal of Crime and Justice, 26*, 23–53.

Bolin, A. U. (2004). Self-control, perceived opportunity, and attitudes as predictors of academic dishonesty. *Journal of Psychology: Interdisciplinary & Applied, 138*, 101–114.

Britz, M. T. (2004). *Computer forensics and cyber crime: An introduction.* Upper Saddle River, NJ: Prentice Hall.

Cohen, J. (1988). *Statistical power analysis for the behavioral sciences.* Hillsdale, NJ: Lawrence Erlbaum Associates.

Delisi, M., Hochstetler, A., & Murphy, D. S. (2003). Self-control behind bars: A validation study of the Grasmick et al. scale. *Justice Quarterly, 20*, 241–263.

Esbensen, F.-A., & Deschenes, E. P. (1998). A multisite examination of youth gang membership: Does gender matter? *Criminology, 36*, 799–827.

Esbensen, F. A., & Huizinga, D. (1993). Gangs, drugs, and delinquency in a survey of urban youth. *Criminology, 31*, 565–589.

Evans, D. T., Cullen, F. T., Burton, V. S., Dunaway, R. G., & Benson, M. L. (1997). The social consequences of self-control: Testing the general theory of crime. *Criminology, 35*, 475–501.

Flora, D. B., Finkel, E. J., & Foshee, V. A. (2003). Higher order factor structure of a self-control test: Evidence from confirmatory factor analysis with polychoric correlations. *Educational & Psychological Measurement, 63*, 112–127.

Forde, D., & Kennedy, L. W. (1997). Risky lifestyles, routine activities, and the general theory of crime. *Justice Quarterly, 14,* 265–294.

Gibbs, J. J., & Giever, D. M. (1995). Self-control and its manifestations among university students: An empirical test of Gottfredson and Hirschi's general theory. *Justice Quarterly, 12,* 231–255.

Gibbs, J. J., Giever, D. M., & Higgins, G. E. (2003). A test of Gottfredson and Hirschi's general theory using structural equation modeling. *Criminal Justice and Behavior, 30,* 441–458.

Gibbs, J. J., Giever, D., & Martin, J. S. (1998). Parental management and self-control: An empirical test of Gottfredson and Hirschi's general theory. *Journal of Research in Crime & Delinquency, 35,* 40–70.

Gibson, C., & Wright, J. (2001). Low self-control and coworker delinquency. A research note. *Journal of Criminal Justice, 29,* 483–192.

Gopal, R., Sanders, G. L., Bhattacharjee, S., Agrawal, M., & Wagner, S. (2004). A behavioral model of digital music piracy. *Journal of Organizational Computing and Electronic Commerce, 14,* 89–105.

Gottfredson, M. R., & Hirschi, T. (1987). The methodological adequacy of longitudinal research on crime. *Criminology, 25,* 581–614.

Gottfredson, M. R., & Hirschi, T. (1990). *A general theory of crime.* Stanford, CA: Stanford University Press.

Grasmick, H. G., Tittle, C. R., Bursik, R. J., & Arneklev, B. J. (1993). Testing the core empirical implications of Gottfredson and Hirschi's general theory. *Journal of Research in Crime and Delinquency, 35,* 42–72.

Hay, C. (2003). Family strain, gender, and delinquency. *Sociological Perspectives, 46,* 107–135.

Higgins, G. E. (2002). General theory of crime and deviance: A structural equation modeling approach. *Journal of Crime and Justice, 25,* 71–95.

Higgins, G. E. (2004). Gender and self-control theory: Are there differences in the measures and the causal model? *Criminal Justice Studies, 17,* 33–55.

Higgins, G. E., & Makin, D. A. (2004a). Does social learning theory condition the effects of low self-control on college students' software piracy? *Journal of Economic Crime Management, 2,* 1–22.

Higgins, G. E., & Makin, D. A. (2004b). Self-control, deviant peers, and software piracy. *Psychological Reports, 95,* 921–931.

Hinduja, S. (2001). Correlates of Internet software piracy. *Journal of Contemporary Criminal Justice, 17,* 369–382.

Hinduja, S. (2003). Trends and patterns among online software pirates. *Ethics and Information Technology, 5,* 49–61.

Hirschi, T., & Gottfredson, M. R. (1993). Commentary: Testing the general theory of crime. *Journal of Research in Crime & Delinquency, 30,* 47–54.

Hirschi, T., & Gottfredson, M. R. (1994). The generality of deviance. In T. Hirschi & M. R. Gottfredson (Eds.), *Generality of deviance* (pp. 1–22). New Brunswick, NJ: Transaction.

Hu, L. T., & Bentler, P. M. (1999). Cutoff criteria for fit indexes in covariance structure analysis: Conventional criteria versus new alternatives. *Structural Equation Modeling, 6,* 1–55.

Im, J. H., & Koen, C. (1990). Software piracy and responsibilities of educational institutions. *Information & Management, 18,* 189–194.

International Federation of Phonographic Industries (2004). *One in three music discs is illegal but fight back starts to show results.* Retrieved from http://www.ifpi.org.

Keane, C., Maxim, P. S., & Teevan, J. J. (1993). Drinking and driving, self-control, and gender: Testing a general theory of crime. *Journal of Research in Crime & Delinquency, 30,* 30–46.

125

Digital Piracy: Assessing the Contributions of an Integrated Self-Control Theory and Social Learning Theory Using Structural Equation Modeling

Kline, R. B. (1998). *Principles and practice of structural equation modeling.* New York: The Guildford Press.

Kline, R. B. (2005) *Principles and practice of structural equation modeling* (2nd ed.). New York: The Guildford Press.

Koen, C. M., & Im, J. H. (1997). Software piracy and its legal implications. *Security Journal, 31,* 265–272.

Krohn, M. D., Skinner, W. F., Massey, J. L., & Akers, R. L. (1985). Social learning theory and adolescent cigarette smoking: A longitudinal study. *Social Problems, 32,* 455–473.

De Li, S. (2004). The impacts of self-control and social bonds on juvenile delinquency in a national sample of midadolescents. *Deviant Behavior, 25,* 351–373.

Longshore, D., Chang, E., Hsieh, S.-C., & Messina, N. (2004). Self-control and social bonds: A combined control perspective on deviance. *Crime & Delinquency, 50,* 542–564.

Luckenbill, D. F., & Miller, S. L. (1998). Defending intellectual property: State efforts to protect creative works. *Justice Quarterly, 15,* 93–120.

Motion Picture Association of America. (2004). *Worldwide Internet piracy study.* Retrieved November 12, 2004, from http://www.mpaa.org/anti-piracy/content.htm

Motivans, M. (2004). *Intellectual property theft, 2002.* United States Department of Justice, Bureau of Justice Statistics.

Muthen, L. K., & Muthen, B. O. (1998–2004). *Mplus users' guide* (3rd ed.). Los Angeles, CA: Muthen and Muthen.

Muthen, L. K., & Muthen, B. O. (2002). How to use a Monte Carlo study to decide on sample size and determine power. *Structural Equation Modeling 9,* 599–620.

Piquero, A. R., Gibson, C. L., & Tibbetts, S. G. (2002). Does self-control account for the relationship between binge drinking and alcohol-related behaviours? *Criminal Behaviour & Mental Health, 12,* 135.

Piquero, A. R., & Tibbetts, S. (1996). Specifying the direct and indirect effects of low self-control and situational factors in offenders' decision making: Toward a more complete model of rational offending. *Justice Quarterly, 13,* 481–510.

Pratt, T. C., & Cullen, F. T. (2000). The empirical status of Gottfredson and Hirschi's general theory of crime: A meta-analysis. *Criminology, 38,* 931–964.

Rahim, M. M., Seyal, A. H., & Rahman, M. N. A. (2001). Factors affecting softlifting intention of computing students: An empirical study. *Journal of Educational Computing Research, 24,* 385–405.

Schumacker, R. E., & Lomax, R. G. (1996). *A beginner's guide to structural equation modeling.* Mahwah, NJ: Lawrence Erlbaum Associates.

Sellers, C., Pratt, T., Winfree, L. T., & Cullen, F. T. (2000). *The empirical status of social learning theory: A meta-analysis.* Paper presented at the annual meeting of the American Society of Criminology.

Shore, B., Venkatachalam, A. R., Solorzano, E., Butn, J. M., Hassan, S. Z., & Janczewski, L. J. (2001). Softlifting and piracy: Behavior across cultures. *Technology in Society, 23,* 563–581.

Simpson, S. S., & Piquero, N. L. (2002). Low self-control, organizational theory, and corporate crime. *Law & Society Review, 36,* 509–548.

Skinner, B. F. (1953). *Science and human behavior.* New York: Macmillan.

Skinner, W. F., & Fream, A. M. (1997). A social learning theory analysis of computer crime among college students. *Journal of Research in Crime & Delinquency, 34,* 495–518.

Straub, D. W., & Collins, R. W. (1990). Key information liability issues facing managers: Software piracy, proprietary databases, and individual rights to privacy. *MIS Quarterly, 14,* 143–156.

Sutherland, E. H. (1949). *White-collar crime.* New York: Holt, Rinehart, & Winston.

Tibbetts, S. G. (1997). Shame and rational choice in offending decisions. *Criminal Justice & Behavior, 24,* 234–255.

Tibbetts, S. G., & Herz, D. C. (1996). Gender differences in factors of social control and rational choice. *Deviant Behavior, 17,* 183–208.

Tibbetts, S. G., & Myers, D. L. (1999). Low self-control, rational choice, and student test cheating. *American Journal of Criminal Justice, 23,* 179–200.

Tittle, C. R., Ward, D., & Grasmick, H. (2003). Self-control and crime/deviance: Cognitive vs. behavioral measures. *Journal of Quantitative Criminology, 19,* 333–365.

Turner, M. G., & Piquero, A. R. (2002). The stability of self-control. *Journal of Criminal Justice, 30,* 457.

Unnever, J. D., & Cornell, D. G. (2003). Bullying, self-control, and ADHD. *Journal of Interpersonal Violence, 18,* 129.

Wall, D. S. (2003). Mapping out cybercrimes in a cyberspatial surveillant assemblage. In F. Webster & K. Ball (Eds.), *The intensification of surveillance: Crime, terrorism, and warfare in the information age* (pp. 112–136). London: Pluto.

Wall, D. S. (2004). Surveillant Internet technologies and the growth in information capitalism: Spams and public trust in the information society. In R. Ericson & K. Haggerty (Eds.), *The new politics of surveillance and visibility.* Toronto: University of Toronto Press.

Wall, D. S. (2005). The Internet as a conduit for criminal activity. In A. Pattavina (Ed.), *Information technology and the criminal justice system* (pp. 78–94). Thousand Oaks, CA: Sage.

Winfree, L. T., & Bernat, F. P. (1998). Social learning, self-control and substance abuse by eighth grade students: A tale of two cities. *Journal of Drug Issues, 28,* 539–558.

Wright, B. R., Moffitt, T., & Caspi, A. (1998). *Predispositions, social environments, and crime: A model of varying effects.* Paper presented at the annual American Society of Criminology, Washington, DC.

Appendix A. Scenarios

Scenario 1

A popular movie has just been released in theaters nationwide. All of your friends have seen the movie and told you that it is great and that you have to see it! Unfortunately, every time that you try to go see the movie, you cannot because the tickets are always sold out. However, a friend tells you about an online website that has posted an underground copy of the entire movie. The site will only allow visitors to download the movie before it can be viewed. You really want to see the movie.

Scenario 2

A popular CD has just been released to music stores nationwide. All of your friends have heard the CD and told you that it is great and that you have to get it! Unfortunately, every time that you try to go to get the CD, you cannot because it is always sold out. However, a friend tells you about an online website that has posted an underground copy of the entire CD. The site will only allow visitors to download the CD before visitors can listen to it. You really want the CD.

Scenario 3

You own a popular CD that has just been released to music stores nationwide. You have listened to the CD and told your friends that it is great and that they have to get it! Unfortunately, every time that they try to go to get the CD, they cannot because it is always sold out. Your friends really want the CD.

127

Digital Piracy: Assessing the Contributions of an Integrated Self-Control Theory and Social Learning Theory Using Structural Equation Modeling

Appendix B. Measurement Model

Measure	Unstandardized Estimate	Standardized Estimate	Residual Variance (standardized residual variance)
SC1 Impulsive	1.00	0.70	2.39 (0.52)
SC2 Simple tasks	0.75**	0.53	2.92 (0.72)
SC3 Risk-taking	0.91**	0.59	3.33 (0.66)
SC4 Physical	0.61**	0.34	6.00 (0.88)
SC5 Self-centered	0.91**	0.58	3.37 (0.66)
SC6 Anger/temper	1.24**	0.69	3.45 (0.52)
SLT1 Female peers	1.00	0.88	3.56 (0.22)
SLT2 Male peers	0.86**	0.84	3.85 (0.29)
SLT3 Definitions	0.80**	0.33	69.46 (0.89)
DP1 Scenario 1	1.00	0.69	1.06 (0.53)
DP2 Scenario 2	0.99**	0.65	1.28 (0.58)
DP3 Scenario 3	0.86**	0.60	1.27 (0.64)

Conclusion

Intellectual property theft is a pervasive behavior. The behavior may seem minor, but much has yet to be learned about it. Piquero shows that a number of theoretical and demographic perspectives may be used to understand intellectual property theft. The preventative measures to reduce the instances of this behavior, from her perspective, seem logical and grounded in theory.

In the short term, Higgins et al. illustrate that digital piracy is an important social problem. Their study illustrates that an individual's level of self-control has implications for his or her learning to digitally pirate. The digital piracy is influenced by both self-control theory and social learning theory. In the long run, Higgins et al. show that some of the implications from Piquero are relevant and that others need to continue to provide better understandings and consequences of this behavior.

Discussion Questions

1. What is the formal definition of intellectual property? How does this definition pertain to theft?
2. Define and describe the different theoretical perspectives that Piquero uses as possible causes of intellectual property theft.
3. Summarize the different preventative strategies from Piquero's study. What theoretical perspectives do these preventative strategies come from?
4. What rationale did Higgins et al. use to link criminological theory to digital piracy?
5. How does digital piracy fit into the larger realm of intellectual property theft?
6. Summarize Higgins et al.'s substantive results.

6

Hackers

The Internet provides a place for cybercriminal communities to exist and flourish. The communities may be seen as subcultures. Subcultures are cohesive cultural systems that vary in form and substance from the dominant culture. To be clear, a subculture maintains its own values, beliefs, and traditions that differ from the dominant culture. Thus, the individual performs behaviors that are consistent with those of his or her subculture, but that differ from the dominant culture. Some subcultures may be based on ethnic groups, delinquent gangs, and religious sects. Others may take place through the Internet or the cyber-environment. For instance, subcultures harbor some of these individuals that seek to understand computer operating systems (i.e., hackers).

The paper in this chapter, written by McKenzie Wark, defines and describes hacking. Wark discusses the issues surrounding the hacking community and subculture. He describes the unwritten rules of hacking.

HACKERS

McKENZIE WARK   *Eugene Lang College; The New School for Social Research*

The figure of the "hacker" is a new and distinctive one in the social history of the late 20th century. The hacker probably first emerged out of the electrical engineering labs at the Massachusetts Institute for Technology (MIT). As on many campuses, MIT students had a tradition of creating attention-seeking pranks—which at MIT were called "hacks." The term *hack* migrated from this general student inventiveness to a more specific sense of creative invention with given materials in the context of electrical engineering, out of which computing as a distinct discipline was to grow.

Not all computing at MIT or elsewhere qualified as "hacking." It had distinct qualities. "To qualify as a hack, the feat must be imbued with innovation, style and technical virtuosity" (Levy, 1994: 23). Hacking was at once an aesthetic and an ethic, in which cooperation among hackers was achieved through their mutual desire for recognition, achieved via improvements or modifications to each other's programming code. As Richard Stallman, a legendary figure in hacker culture, says: "It was a bit like the garden of Eden. It hadn't occurred to us not to cooperate" (Williams, 1992: 76).

The academic environment in which hacking first emerged contributed greatly to the ethic of collaboration on shared goals via competition for recognition. What was distinctive was the extension of recognizably academic social processes into this new technical area. Hackers were, at the same time, largely indifferent to formal recognition within the academy or industry. The recognition of one's peers was what mattered.

Early development of computing at MIT, Stanford, and elsewhere was heavily dependent on funding provided by the Pentagon, which offered very broad support for basic computing research in the 1950s and 1960s. This certainly contributed to the rather special culture of hacking. As the Pentagon narrowed its research interests, and commercial computing industries grew, hacker culture came under pressure from administrative and commercial imperatives. It survived, for a time, due to the high demand for scarce computing skills.

Hacking persists as something of a governing ideal in programming. A "hacker ethic," with roots in early computing research experience, exists as something like a craft sense of what programming as a kind of labor ought to be. Hackers, who "want to realize their passions," present "a general social challenge," but the realization of the value of this challenge "will take time, like all great cultural changes" (Himanen, 2001: 7, 18, 13).

As computing became a pervasive force with the rise of the Internet, "hacking" developed a second meaning—it named the process of exploring computer networks. In many cases this was benign. The Internet was a new and not well-understood phenomenon, and hackers in this sense were explorers of this new terrain. However, once computer networks were conceived as a new form of "property," transgressions of these putative property boundaries were quickly criminalized (Sterling, 1993). A "moral panic" ensued, in which the hacker appeared as a new kind of folk devil, recklessly invading networks, interrupting essential services, stealing state secrets or credit card numbers. In order to preserve the original meaning of the term hacker, those who exploit weaknesses in computer networks for criminal reasons are sometimes referred to as "crackers."

Nevertheless, even the most benign, creative, ethical and aesthetic version of the idea of the "hacker" presents something of a challenge to the social order, for the hacker is a figure that speaks to the ideal of a kind of labor that finds its own time, that sets its own goals, and that works on common property for the good of all. As Michael Hardt and Antonio Negri argue, many of the new kinds of labor processes that emerged in the late 20th century have a distinctively cooperative element. "The central forms of productive cooperation are no longer created by the capitalist as part of the project to organize labor but rather emerge from the productive energies of labor itself" (Hardt and Negri, 2004: 113). The hacker is the embodiment of this self-organized labor.

The rise of the hacker meets an antithetical development in the rise of strict and extensive intellectual property law. At MIT, hackers worked freely on each other's code, gave code to others and did not secure their files—to do so would only invite others to circumvent the security. This model of free, self-organized labor took place under very special conditions—in research labs with large amounts of Pentagon funding. Yet it provided an ethic of working with information that spread far beyond this academic setting. The sharing of information became a hallmark of early Internet culture. This was perceived to be an obstacle to its development as a commodity by the new forms of business that wanted to invest in it.

The crackdown on hacker culture in its more transgressive sense, and the containment of the hacker ethic in its more benign sense, are two parts of the process of the commodification of computing networks in the interests of restricting the free movement of information and the expansion of the concept of information as private property. If an early slogan of hacker culture has it that "information wants to be free," it finds itself, to borrow from Rousseau, "everywhere in chains" (Wark, 2004: 126).

With the rise of corporations based on computing as labor and information as property, hacker culture responded with new legal models within which hacker culture might survive. These would include the Free Software Movement, and its more corporate offshoot, the Open Source Movement (Moody, 2001). The Creative Commons Movement seeks a broader platform for collaborative labor with information (Lessig, 2004). Where corporations dependent on information generally seek policy solutions that turn copyrights and patents into absolute private property rights, the Creative Commons Movement extends the hacker ethic to all information, seeking forms of legal protection for collaborative labor.

More broadly still, the hacker may be the symptom of a broader class struggle over information, which pits those who produce it—hackers in the very broadest sense—against those who own the means of realizing its value—the corporations whose value is increasingly defined not by tangible assets, but by portfolios of patents, copyrights and brands. Thus, the hacker may turn out to be a very important social category for understanding labor, the commodity and private property in the information age.

References

Hardt, M. and A. Negri. (2004). *Multitude.* New York: Penguin Books.

Himanen, P. (2001). *The Hacker Ethic and the Spirit of the Information Age.* New York: Random House.

Lessig, L. (2004). *Free Culture.* New York: Penguin.

Levy, S. (1994). *Hackers: Heroes of the Computer Revolution.* New York: Penguin.

Moody, G. (2001). *Rebel Code.* Cambridge, MA: Perseus Publishing.

Sterling, B. (1993). *The Hacker Crackdown.* New York: Bantam.

Wark, M. (2004). *A Hacker Manifesto.* Cambridge, MA: Harvard University Press.

Williams, S. (1992). *Free as in Freedom: Richard Stallman's Crusade for Free Software.* Sebastapol, CA: O'Reilly.

Conclusion

Internet crimes are often part of larger communities. These communities are often seen as subcultures. The subcultures come with their own set of unwritten rules. Wark masterfully defines and describes this subculture. He goes on to provide a clear and concise depiction of the rules that surround the hacking subculture.

Discussion Questions

1. What is a hacker?
2. What are the key components of the hacking subculture?
3. According to Wark, what is the evolution of hacking?

7

Criminal Justice and Cyberspace

Thus far, the issues pertaining to the Internet indicate that criminal activity takes place in this environment. In fact, a large portion of the papers in this text have indicated that these activities not only take place, but they are also rising. The criminal justice community may have specific needs to help control and combat criminal activity on the Internet.

The first paper in this chapter, written by Sameer Hinduja, examines the requirements of law enforcement in dealing with cybercrime. Hinduja's paper is a needs analysis of the technology and training that are necessary to be able to properly control and combat cybercrime. Using data from one state, Hinduja shows that the largest need in law enforcement is training, followed by personnel and equipment.

The second paper in this chapter, written by Pollitt, provides an overview of the different models that are generally used in digital forensics. Pollitt reviews different function points for data collection, storage, and admissibility. The paper does not provide an exhaustive list, but it does offer a cogent introduction to different views of digital forensics.

PERCEPTIONS OF LOCAL AND STATE LAW ENFORCEMENT CONCERNING THE ROLE OF COMPUTER CRIME INVESTIGATIVE TEAMS

SAMEER HINDUJA *Michigan State University*

Introduction

For two decades, information technology (IT) has progressed exponentially, and most Americans have seen computers become a vital part of their daily lives. The growth in this area, while introducing unparalleled advances in productivity, commerce, communication, entertainment, and the dissemination of information, has precipitated new forms of antisocial, unethical, and illegal behavior. Moreover, as more and more users have become familiar with computing, the scope and prevalence of the problem have grown. Computer fraud, child pornography, hacking, and software piracy have all achieved notoriety and prominence due to technological developments. These categories fall under the broader heading of a deviance currently receiving deeper examination and unprecedented focus and interest from state, national, and international entities, as well as the general public. This phenomenon is "computer crime," defined as "any illegal act fostered or facilitated by a computer, whether the computer is an object of a crime, an instrument used to commit a crime, or a repository of evidence related to a crime" (Royal Canadian Mounted Police, 2000).

Computer- and Internet-related crimes pose a significant threat to the well-being of individuals and businesses, and none are immune from the repercussions that can result. Our nation's functionality and security are dependent on the persistent and punctual flow of information and services, and this need is met by the computer and network infrastructure in place. As such, the task of preservation assigned in part to local, state, and national law enforcement is of critical value. The general consensus among computer security specialists, however, is that no more than 10% of computer crimes are reported to authorities (Kabay, 2000); in this author's opinion, even this statistic seems generous. The "dark figure" (of at least 90% unreported) stems from at least two factors. First, high-tech criminality is extremely hard to detect, due in part to the power of computers to process and disseminate electronic information rapidly, and the fact that many people have access to the Internet at universities, businesses, libraries, and homes (United Nations, 1994). One of the Internet's most appealing qualities is the ease with which huge volumes of information can be moved from one source to thousands of destinations, virtually instantly and at no cost (Wittes, 1994). While the prevalence of high-speed dedicated connections among the general population is increasing, one need only to have a dial-up connection to the Internet through a telephone line to delve into the cyber-underworld of electronic deviance. Second, computer crime is technologically advanced and cannot be tackled through tactics learned at the local police academy (Leibowitz, 1999).

Waging war against the miscreants who perpetrate these computer- and Internet-related offenses appears to warrant the undivided attention of a team solely dedicated to eradicate or at least curb their vast number. Just as law enforcement agencies have developed specialized criminal investigative units and prevention programs for crimes of violence and drug abuse, a similar program has seemed requisite for computer crime (Carter and Katz, 1996). For example, the Federal Bureau of Investigation, the U.S. Secret Service, the U.S. Customs Service, and a number of companies in the computer and communication industries maintain squads of investigators to ferret out wrongdoing (Wise, 1997).

Only recently have state and local police departments pioneered task forces consisting of personnel, prosecutors, and computer technicians. One of the primary aims of these entities is to follow up on tips given to them by the public and to discover forms of computer wrongdoing (such as the transmission of digital images of children engaged in sexual activities, the posting of fraudulent advertisements online, or file archives consisting of pirated software). A second is to find out what Internet service provider hosts the offending web pages or provides online access to the perpetrator. A third and fourth objective is to determine who exactly is uploading or downloading the illegal data, and then either sternly warn, or take legal action against, the offender (Appelman, 1996; Jefferson, 1997; Wittes, 1994).

Still other agencies have networking specialists employed specifically to deal with security breaches of business and governmental agencies stemming from hacking, the introduction of Trojan horses (backdoors allowing future access into the system), or virii (malicious program code that attaches itself to legitimate or illegitimate files introduced into the system and destroys or corrupts data) (Denning, 1996). Departments with sufficient resources are also training individuals to competently analyze the contents of computer hard drives and to lawfully discover, preserve, and utilize such evidence in the construction of a legal case. Such practices and skills are increasingly essential in order to properly police the cyber-frontier, and to preclude the victimization of innocent societal members. The Michigan State Police (MSP) is one such agency that has fully realized the gravity of the situation, and has collaborated with other influential public sector entities in the state of Michigan to address computer- and Internet-related criminality.

National Assessment of State and Local Law Enforcement Needs

The National Institute of Justice (NIJ) funded a study in 1998 to assess specific needs that law enforcement departments on the state and local level had in terms of capably responding to electronic crime. Individuals from 114 agencies participated in the inventory, and a great deal of salient information was obtained through literature reviews, interviews, discussion groups, and workshops that sought to identify current capabilities, strengths, and weaknesses. In accordance with intuition, the research found that police around the nation require more resources and assistance to succeed in their endeavor. Ten specific needs were characterized as top priorities (Borrowman et al., 2001):

1. *Public awareness.* Individuals in corporate, governmental, public service, and society in general must be advised and educated about computer crimes, their significance and impact, the need for competent response, and practical suggestions which can preempt victimization.
2. *Data and reporting.* A more accurate picture of the prevalence and extent of computer crime will come with advances in data recording, reporting, collection, and analysis.
3. *Uniform training and certification courses.* Professional skills essential for addressing electronic crimes must be cultivated among law enforcement officers to complement and augment their traditional duties. For example, first-responding patrol officers to the scene of a crime should be well trained on electronic evidence collection techniques, and prosecutors and judges must be kept on the cutting edge of new developments related to information technology and crime.

4. *Management assistance for onsite electronic crime task forces.* County or regional task forces consisting of highly specialized staff devoted specifically to investigating and combating computer crime are urgently required. These will provide the personnel and the organizational and technical resources in a centralized location to best assist constituent agencies in their efforts.

5. *Updated laws.* The development and application of legislation must keep pace with the perpetually changing domain of electronic crime to most aptly promote apprehension and prosecution.

6. *Cooperation with the high-tech industry.* Partnership with corporations involved in high technology is essential for sponsorship and funding, expert assistance, and the sharing of equipment, and presumably will facilitate a greater incidence of electronic crime reporting by private sector victims.

7. *Special research and publications.* A repository of informational resources must be created and compiled to provide those who deal with computer crime with the insight and guidance necessary to address it, as well as a directory of experts, practitioners, investigators, and prosecutors who specialize in the various domains of high-tech wrongdoing.

8. *Management and awareness support.* Those in the upper echelon of public sector agencies must be cognizant of the gravity of the computer crime phenomenon, and be motivated to develop strategies to counter it.

9. *Investigative and forensic tools.* Technological resources to deal with electronic crime must be up-to-date and made available to law enforcement, despite their seemingly prohibitive cost.

10. *Structuring a computer crime unit.* Questions related to the place of such a specialized force within a department and the coordination of investigative and forensic duties must be answered. Specifically, it is suggested that "the experience of successful existing units . . . be thoroughly documented" and that "results of such research . . . be widely distributed and used as part of direct technical assistance to state and local agencies" (Borrowman et al., 2001, p. 36).

Two summary imperatives were also identified: the need for speedy action in accomplishing the aforementioned strategies, and the need to do so in a centralized and coordinated manner (Borrowman et al., 2001).

The current research analyzing the computer crime needs of agencies in Michigan and the MSP's goals to serve their constituents with a specialized computer crimes unit seeks to build on the knowledge retrieved from the NIJ inventory. Survey data collected will ideally clarify the pressing concerns and requirements of local departments in the state, and the findings detailing the experiences of one task force should provide guidance for others in current or incipient existence.

Historical Background

In November 1998, the MSP established a computer crimes project team after recognizing the toll that high-tech crimes were taking, in step with their commitment to improving public safety through innovative practices. This

137

*Perceptions of Local
and State Law
Enforcement
Concerning the Role
of Computer Crime
Investigative Teams*

team was assigned the task of reviewing the scope and prevalence of these crimes, identifying issues related to training law enforcement personnel, and determining the possibility of developing a computer forensic center for the proper analysis of collected evidence. Six months later (May 1999), a final report was issued to the state legislature petitioning for support in the form of legislation, funding, and training. The legislature responded with a request for a comprehensive feasibility study, subsequently developed during the latter half of 1999. Informative sessions were also organized and held in cooperation with Eastern Michigan University to equip and train 70 local and 23 state police officers with necessary investigative techniques to address computer crime. Also, in December of 1999 a $300,000 Internet Crimes Against Children (ICAC) federal grant was awarded to the MSP and the Michigan Office of Attorney General by the Department of Justice. With this allocation, a multifaceted attack on the sexual exploitation of children was put forth in the form of a specialized online investigative team, a forensic and computer crime training initiative for ten officers, and an extensive public awareness and prevention campaign. This third component included the implementation of a cyber-tip telephone line, the development and display of 32 billboards across the state, extensive radio and television public service announcements, and the dissemination of creatively designed mousepads and bookmarks calling attention to online crime and the aforementioned tip line. The goal of such an endeavor was to educate parents, children, and business owners of the dangers of victimization resulting from unwitting or incautious Internet use.

The comprehensive feasibility study was completed in January 2000 and was submitted to the State Legislature. As a result, the MSP received a $1.2 million appropriation for the fiscal year 2001 to establish 12 full-time employees at two locations—five persons assigned to the Southeast Criminal Investigation Division (S/E CID) based in Livonia, and seven persons assigned to the CID in Lansing, the state capital. The former post investigates computer-related offenses in 10 counties, while the latter has jurisdiction over the remaining 73 counties. To note, the S/E CID is responsible for a more densely populated area, while the CID covers a much larger geographical region.

The S/E CID Computer Crimes Unit (CCU) is a multi-jurisdictional task force comprised of members from the MSP, Ann Arbor Police Department, Livingston County Sheriff Department, Troy Police Department, Detroit Police Department, Attorney General's Office, U.S. Postal Service, U.S. Secret Service, U.S. Customs, Drug Enforcement Administration, and Social Security Administration. The Lansing CCU is not currently a multi-jurisdictional task force, but efforts are underway towards the realization of this in the near future. A primary intent of the CCU is to provide investigative and forensic assistance to aid agencies in the identification, investigation, arrest, and prosecution of cyber-criminals. Another major function is to pursue civil and criminal remedies for computer wrongdoing and to promote protective measures among the citizenry. It must be mentioned that while the current work concentrates on the MSP's role, the computer crime initiative is a joint effort with each entity duly committed to attaining the overall objectives.

The crimes that Michigan—and, because of the distributed and boundless architecture of the Internet, the rest of the nation—must contend with range from the theft of computer hardware and software, to network security contravention, to cyberterrorism and hate group agenda propagation, to the dissemination of child pornography. These are only a small sampling of the types of high-tech deviance that have achieved notoriety and which compete for the resources and attention of law enforcement across the country. Both crimes unique to the "virtual" environment in which it occurs, and crimes traditionally handled by law enforcement, have been burgeoning as a result of the union between telecommunications and computer systems. Ancillary issues which also must be addressed include problems associated with jurisdiction; the acquisition, preservation, and admissibility of evidence; and how the courts will apply current laws to cybercrime. Finally, the relative anonymity and the transcendence of geographical and physical limitations afforded by the Internet render difficult the detection of criminals who are able to take advantage of practically any person among a virtually limitless pool of victims.

Since mid-February 2001 to the end of October 2001, the Lansing CID CCU has officially investigated 158 cases, and no lull in the flow of incoming computer crime cases appears imminent. In addition, the department has taken a leadership role in constructing a strategic plan of action, and has developed mutually beneficial working relationships with other agencies to integrate resources and collectively further such efforts. The present study continues this leadership trend by empirically assessing the needs of law enforcement across the state resulting from the commission of these offenses.

Methodology

In May 2001, a comprehensive survey was mailed out to the head of law enforcement agencies in the 73 counties that the Lansing CID covers in an effort to understand the role and function that the CCU might best strive to fulfill. The sampling frame was a comprehensive list of every law enforcement office in the State of Michigan—a total of 490 offices. A breakdown of the number of surveys sent to agencies in each of the six primary districts of the MSP is illustrated in Table 1. A map that details the counties that compose each MSP district is provided in Figure 1. It should be noted that the Lansing CID does not cover district 2, and the areas that previously comprised district 4 were assimilated into other districts in 1995 (personal correspondence, August 6, 2003).

This research was deemed essential to identify the specific needs of the population that the Lansing CID covered, because of the vast size and diversity associated with the region for which they are responsible. Primarily, the hope was to ascertain which computer crimes each responding agency was dealing with, and how the unit could most appropriately and effectively be of service. In the following text, an explication of the research results is presented. Ideally, this will not only sharpen the efforts of the MSP in optimally utilizing resources to address high-technology miscreance across the state, but will also serve as an educational tool from which other departments can learn,

139

*Perceptions of Local
and State Law
Enforcement
Concerning the Role
of Computer Crime
Investigative Teams*

TABLE 1. Distribution of Surveys Sent

Michigan State Police District	Count
1	49
3	116
5	92
6	91
7	63
8	79
Total	490

FIGURE 1. Michigan State Police Districts

TABLE 2. Distribution of Surveys Received

Michigan State Police District	Count	Percent of Agencies in Each District
Unknown	3	–
1	28	57.1
3	64	55.2
5	62	67.4
6	48	52.7
7	31	49.2
8	40	50.6
Total	276	56.3

benefit, and construct efficacious policy towards dealing with computer crime.

Prior to distributing the questionnaire to the Michigan law enforcement community, the instrument was pretested among five professional academic colleagues at Michigan State University for comments and suggestions. Minor modifications were made based on the responses received to prevent inconsistencies from flawing the research before its commencement, and to improve the clarity of each survey item. Suggestions were accordingly incorporated to increase the reliability and validity of the instrument.

A cover letter from the commanding officer of the MSP CID was then mailed out with each survey, introducing recipients to the intention and objective of the research and asking them to take the time to respond to, and return, the voluntary questionnaire in the accompanying self-addressed stamped envelope within two weeks of its receipt. An informational brochure was also included, and detailed the mission statement of the CCU, the investigative and forensic services it could provide, and a list of relevant Michigan laws applicable to computer crimes. Of the 490 surveys sent out, 275 were returned—a response rate of 56.1%. The distribution of responses by MSP district is presented in Table 2.

Instrument

With regard to the instrument, questions were straightforward with predominantly closed-ended questions, and took no more than a few minutes for the respondent to fill out. The survey commenced by asking the county (and/ or city) of the responding agency, the name of the agency (optional), and the name and telephone number of a contact person (also optional). It was determined that if participants could choose whether to provide contact information, candid and forthright responses would be more probable. Next presented were two items inquiring whether the respondent was aware of the existence of the CCU and of the services it can provide. A list of 18 specific computer-related crimes was subsequently listed [1], along with the request to specify which types of crime were must commonly investigated. Two questions were then posed to determine the frequency of both primary and secondary [2] computer crime investigations.

The following section sought to determine the amount and types of training previously received by agency personnel to specifically combat computer crime, and particulars as to the perceived utility of services the CCU could offer to the responding department. The questionnaire culminated with inquiries as to whether training, personnel, or equipment would be the most advantageous provision, along with the specific types of training most desired (among a list of 13 options) [3]. An open-ended response area was presented in conclusion to provide an opportunity for the respondent to share any additional comments, concerns, or ideas about the role of the CCU.

Findings

Descriptive statistics allow researchers to summarize data in an easily interpretable format, and to identify basic and important measures of distribution. Concerning the location of respondents among the MSP jurisdictional areas, most were located in district 3 (23.4%), district 5 (22.7%), and district 6 (17.6%). Over two-thirds (78.3%) were aware that the CCU was functional, but a lesser proportion (65.2%) had knowledge of the services and support the unit was designed to offer. Almost two-thirds (65.2%) of agencies surveyed reported that they had dealt with a computer- or Internet-related crime in the past 12 months, testifying to its somewhat extensive incidence throughout the state. When presented with a question soliciting the most prevalent type of incident investigated, a sizable 39.5% (109 of 276 agencies) specified "harassment/stalking" via the use of a computer and/or the Internet. Other crimes which Michigan law enforcement personnel are most regularly dealing with include "child pornography" (31.9%), "solicitation of minors" (15.2%), "identity theft" (17.4%), "e-commerce fraud" (16.3%), and "forgery or counterfeiting" (19.2%). Some of the agency responses did not fit into the categories specified in the survey instrument, and included solicitation of prostitutes, the fencing of stolen property (including computers themselves), suicide notes posted on message boards, the defacement of web sites, spam (unsolicited junk e-mail), and a host of episodes involving threats of violence (including bombs). These particular crimes did not occur often, but even singular instances point out that they warrant the attention of police. The complete results are depicted in Table 3, while Table 4 shows the percent of agencies in each district that stated a particular computer crime was most prevalent.

A large percentage of agencies (66.3%, or 183 of 276) declared that they investigated between 1 and 10 computer crimes during the year 2000, which supports NIJ's assertion that the onus of responsibility in addressing these novel forms of wrongdoing will predominantly fall on the shoulders of law enforcement (Borrowman et al., 2001). Slightly over 25% of agencies (76) had not experienced any, and only one department had dealt with over 30 incidents. While 72.1% stated that all of their cases were initially reported to them, almost one-quarter (22.8%) revealed that between 1–20% of computer crime investigations they assumed were based on referrals from other agencies (who presumably did not have the resources to adequately address the matter). Five respondents asserted that between 81–100% of computer crimes they examined were first reported to another agency. Also corroborating the trends identified by NIJ, there appeared to be a severe lack of trained personnel on staff to respond competently to computer-related wrongdoing in Michigan, as

TABLE 3. Computer Crimes Dealt with among Law Enforcement Agencies

Most Prevalent Computer Crime	Count	Percent
Harassment or stalking	109	39.5
Child pornography	88	31.9
Forgery or counterfeiting	53	19.2
Identity theft	48	17.4
E-commerce fraud	45	16.3
Solicitation of minors	42	15.2
Hacking	29	10.5
Inflammatory material posted online	24	8.7
Online auction fraud	20	7.2
Privacy invasions	17	6.2
Computer viruses	16	5.8
Other	16	5.8
Miscellaneous intellectual property theft	10	3.6
Theft of telecommunication services	9	3.3
Information warfare	3	1.1
Trafficking of proprietary information	2	0.7
Software piracy	1	0.4
Cryptography used to mask illegal activity	0	0.0

Note: Agencies could indicate multiple computer crimes as "most prevalent"

TABLE 4. Percent of Agencies by District Where a Specific Crime Was Most Prevalent

Most Prevalent Computer Crime	District						
	1	3	5	6	7	8	Total
Number of agencies	28	64	62	48	31	40	273
Child pornography	32.1	25.0	27.4	45.8	41.9	25.0	31.9
Computer viruses	0.0	9.4	8.1	0.0	3.2	10.0	5.9
Cryptography used to mask illegal activity	0.0	0.0	0.0	0.0	0.0	0.0	0.0
E-commerce fraud	14.3	15.6	22.6	8.3	9.7	25.0	16.5
Forgery or counterfeiting	21.4	10.9	25.8	20.8	22.6	12.5	18.7
Hacking	17.9	15.6	6.5	6.3	12.9	5.0	10.3
Harassment or stalking	42.9	39.1	38.7	31.3	29.0	57.5	39.6
Identity theft	21.4	20.3	16.1	16.7	9.7	17.5	17.2
Inflammatory material posted	10.7	15.6	4.8	4.2	3.2	12.5	8.8
Online information warfare	0.0	1.6	1.6	0.0	3.2	0.0	1.1
Miscellaneous intellectual property theft	3.6	0.0	3.2	6.3	3.2	5.0	3.3
Online auction fraud	7.1	10.9	9.7	2.1	6.5	5.0	7.3
Other	3.6	6.3	4.8	4.2	3.2	12.5	5.9
Privacy invasions	7.1	12.5	4.8	2.1	0.0	5.0	5.9
Software piracy	0.0	1.6	0.0	0.0	0.0	0.0	0.4
Solicitation of minors	21.4	17.2	11.3	14.6	19.4	12.5	15.4
Theft of telecommunication services	0.0	1.6	4.8	2.1	6.5	5.0	3.3
Trafficking of proprietary information	0.0	0.0	1.6	0.0	3.2	0.0	0.7

Note: Three agencies did not indicate a district

demonstrated by the statistic that only 18.8% (52) of agencies attested to the presence of one or more individuals so skilled. Only 34.4% (95) responded in the affirmative that they did have someone who had received specific training, and a nominal 12.3% (34) acknowledged that a member of their team was capable of conducting forensic examinations of a computer.

To note, it was not possible to perform bivariate analyses in the form of cross-tabulations to determine if the amount of computer crime cases investigated was correlated with the presence of skilled personnel. This was because the distribution of such incidents was extremely positively skewed (as expected); it could not be statistically proven that those departments with professionally trained individuals were able to tackle more incidents simply because only 17 out of 276 investigated more than 10 such cases. Further, as illustrated in the aforementioned statistics, formal education in computer crimes was lacking to a disproportionate degree overall. An examination of the extent of this training among the sample of respondents now follows.

Law enforcement agencies across the state of Michigan have received training from a wide assortment of institutions, and the substance of such training has varied in its content, scope, and intensity. Some department personnel have obtained a substantial amount of training from programs conducted under the auspices of the U.S. Department of Justice and the Department of Defense, as well as from academic establishments (such as the Cybercrime Investigation School of Eastern Michigan University (EMU)) and leader organizations in this particular field. Others have been privy to perhaps only one or two seminars lasting no more than a few hours in duration, and a large majority have not received any type of formal skill enhancement. A primary determinant concerns the fact that some classes incur a substantial cost to the department, while others are provided for free by various institutions. This imbalance is one of the areas that the CCU seeks to rectify by providing educational opportunities—as well as specialized personnel—to assist smaller agencies who have not yet had the benefit of purposive instruction.

Before detailing the formal education received by Michigan law enforcement, it is important to present the reader with a cumulative roster of training available from national entities. SEARCH, the National Consortium for Justice Information and Statistics, has organized Internet crime curricula for investigators covering the subject matter of online child exploitation, crime scene investigation and evidence procurement, and specific lawbreaking engendered by computer networks. Members of ICAC Task Force Units are invited each year to attend the National ICAC Training Conference, where informational and educational seminars are held to increase the competence of those responsible for combating the exploitation of children. The National White Collar Crime Center puts on Basic and Advanced Data Recovery and Analysis (BDRA and ADRA) courses to better prepare personnel for the forensic analysis of computer storage media. The Federal Bureau of Investigation (FBI) Academy, the Middle Atlantic-Great Lakes Organized Crime Law Enforcement Network (MAGLOCLEN), the High Technology Crime Investigation Association (HTCIA), and the International Association of Computer Investigative Specialists (IACIS) are all additional renowned organizations that provide training to law enforcement. Finally, Guidance Software, the producer of the forensic tool ENCASE, has also held sessions to sufficiently train personnel in data evidence acquisition, analysis, and presentation. The MSP and the Attorney General's office have offered basic classes and seminars to familiarize agency members with the nuances of high-technology crime, and plan to do so on an increased basis now that a more thorough appraisal of training needs has been conducted.

A sizable number of respondents who had received cybercrime training (68.4% (65 of 95)) characterized it as "basic," "general," or "introductory"; such seminars were administered predominantly by the MSP and the Attorney General's office. At least four departments had participated in EMU's program, and at least nine had the opportunity to attend the White Collar Crime Center's BDRA and/or ADRA classes. Additionally, at least five obtained substantive training in using the ENCASE hard drive forensic analysis tool through the software company's proprietary learning sessions, seven attended panels and seminars through MAGLOCLEN, and three did so through the Justice Department's SEARCH consortium.

A few questions posited in the survey instrument were intended to more thoroughly understand the strain on fiscal and temporal resources associated with addressing high-tech illegalities. For example, 36.3% (95) of the 276 responding agencies revealed that computer crimes detract from officers' attention to traditional crimes—which generally make up the vast majority of criminal incidents. Moreover, 62.7% (165) indicated that budgetary constraints are unquestionably a significant detriment to the agency's ability to prevent or oppose computer crimes. These statistics again speak to the tensions involved in managing the resources of departments to best address this novel form of lawbreaking without compromising the execution and success of their conventional duties. They also illustrate the need for funding and sponsorship by the private sector, and the requirement for up-to-date tools and equipment in order to be successful in investigations; both of these issues were deemed priority needs in the NIJ study.

A primary impetus in the creation and development of the CCU was to meet the requirements of smaller departments with the provision of personnel, equipment, training, and advice. This will ideally equip other agencies with the ability to combat such crimes in their jurisdiction—which may serve a deterrent effect to would-be perpetrators. Accordingly, a substantial 92.7% of agencies anticipate taking advantage of the investigative services, and 93.4% of the forensic services that the unit was constructed to provide. In many instances, contact information was provided by the responding agency, which will allow the CCU to develop a symbiotic working relationship with those who require the resources and assistance it makes available.

An interesting finding stemmed from a question seeking to determine the biggest need of the responding agency—training, personnel, or equipment. An overwhelming amount (74.9%) stated that training was the primary requirement that would enable them to more effectively handle the computer crime complaints received (see Table 5). Almost one-fifth (19.2%) felt that personnel were the most important resource necessary for successful response measures. By extension, it may be concluded that there are individuals in most law enforcement agencies who would gladly undertake training requisite to

TABLE 5. The Biggest Needs of Law Enforcement Agencies

	Training		Personnel		Equipment	
	n	%	n		n	%
Biggest need	191	74.9	49	19.2	31	12.2
Second biggest need	44	17.3	75	29.4	101	39.6
Third biggest need	20	7.8	131	51.4	123	48.2

increase their proficiency in this area. Equipment was viewed as the greatest need by only 12.2% of those queried—once again illustrating a call for developing competence in addressing computer crime through training.

To delve deeper into this facet, respondents were provided with a list of specific training topics and asked to identify which would most substantially benefit the efforts of their department. The greatest demands were in the areas of search and seizure training and evidence collection and processing training, at 61.4% and 69.5% respectively. This depicts an important need for applied investigative knowledge as to how computer crime differs from traditional crime, rather than what might have been intuitively considered by some as most imperative—technical knowledge associated with hardware, software, and digital communications. That aspect, however, is not neglected nor underestimated as 43.4% of agencies identified a need for operating systems and network training.

More advanced skills usually possessed by only the Internet "elite" appear to be necessary for law enforcement as well. For instance, 28.3% believed that training in hacking, cracking, and profiling was essential to their crime prevention mission, and 32% felt that it was important to be well-versed in areas of password protection and encryption. Without a doubt, the networking facet has taken on increased import as dedicated broadband connections are becoming available to a larger multitude of computer users. As a consequence, 30% of departments are calling for specialized training in that area, and 29% seek specific guidance concerning security vulnerabilities in server and workstation software. Over one-fifth (21%) of agencies desire training for prosecutors so that they develop techniques to effectively construct and close computer crime cases. Finally, 50% desire training for front-line officers, so that they are equipped with the basic skill set essential for the proper management of interrogations, crime scenes, computer evidence, and the attendant paperwork involved. The importance of prosecutorial and front-line officer training was emphasized in the national study and is supported by the current work. The full distribution of training desired by agencies is depicted in Table 6, and Table 7 displays the breakdown by MSP district.

An overwhelming amount of respondents left helpful comments in the final open response area concerning their conception of the CCU's role. An interesting parallel was made between a computer technical support department and the CCU, as many considered imperative the facility to call in and receive advice, guidance, and instruction when investigating a computer crime (both offsite and onsite). Respondents also felt that the CCU should increase training opportunities to departments with personnel available to learn, and should take over investigations that exceed the limited resource base of smaller agencies.

TABLE 6. Training Viewed as Necessary and Beneficial by Law Enforcement Agencies

Specific Types	Count	Percent
Evidence collection and processing training	189	69.5
Search and seizure training	167	61.4
Front-line officer training	136	50.0
Operating systems and network training	118	43.4
Forensic tools training	116	42.6
Password and encryption training	87	32.0
Systems analysis training	82	30.1
Network expertise training	82	30.1
Intrusions and security training	79	29.0
Hacks, cracks, and profiling training	77	28.3
Undercover investigations and training	72	26.5
Prosecutor training	57	21.0
Politician and supervisor training	46	16.9

Note: Agencies could indicate multiple types of training as necessary and beneficial

Meeting this need would include the provision of training, forensic analysis, specialized hardware and software equipment, technical support, advice, and general availability (ideally 24 hours a day, seven days a week) as experts in the subject area. A call was made for quicker response times when help is requested or when cases are referred to the CCU. Furthermore, it was suggested that the CCU allocate team members to each district to better enable an expansive statewide support network.

TABLE 7. Percent of Agencies by District That Desired Specific Training

| Specific Types of Training | District | | | | | | |
	1	3	5	6	7	8	Total
Number of agencies	27	64	62	46	31	39	269
Evidence collection and processing training	77.8	53.1	72.6	71.7	71.0	84.6	69.9
Forensic tools training	40.7	37.5	48.4	45.7	35.5	46.2	42.8
Front-line officer training	55.6	48.4	54.8	50.0	35.5	53.8	50.2
Hacks, cracks, and profiling training	33.3	31.3	30.6	26.1	16.1	28.2	28.3
Intrusions and security training	25.9	32.8	24.2	28.3	25.8	38.5	29.4
Network expertise training	11.1	31.3	24.2	45.7	22.6	41.0	30.5
Operating systems and network training	40.7	43.8	37.1	45.7	38.7	59.0	43.9
Password and encryption training	25.9	35.9	27.4	39.1	26.2	35.9	32.7
Politician and supervisor training	11.1	21.9	12.9	19.6	12.9	17.9	16.7
Prosecutor training	11.1	29.7	14.5	19.6	16.1	30.8	21.2
Search and seizure training	70.4	53.1	61.3	63.0	54.8	74.4	61.7
Systems analysis training	22.2	23.4	37.1	26.1	35.5	38.5	30.5
Undercover investigations and training	22.2	25.0	27.4	21.7	22.6	38.5	26.4

Note: Three agencies did not indicate a district, and four did not indicate that they desired any types of training

Also recommended was the mass distribution of salient information concerning computer crimes to all law enforcement departments in the state. One example given was a weekly or monthly newsletter updating the community on relevant cases, precedents, and technologies. Another was the development of an e-mail listserv where law enforcement personnel can post general questions and comments concerning their investigative efforts, and can subsequently receive feedback from others across the state who may have dealt with a similar problem or know of a potential solution. A third was the construction of a basic but thorough training manual—a procedural roadmap, perhaps—detailing: the fundamentals of computer crime; investigations and prosecutions; evidence recovery, preservation, and analysis; technology terms and definitions; World Wide Web links for more information; cautionary tales from other departments to preclude the same mistakes; and other relevant content. A training video depicting the proper procurement of computer evidence in the field would be of great value as well, according to respondents. Towards this end, the CCU can and should also serve as a centralized information clearinghouse for all matters related to law enforcement's battle with computer crime. These recommendations attest to the critical necessity of information sharing and record keeping, and substantiate the national findings.

One respondent pointed out that many complaints could be handled by a person who can accurately distinguish exactly what constitutes a computer crime. Some method of consistent interaction must be developed between the MSP and other departments to provide this service. Some final suggestions included the need for the unit to coordinate collaboration among agencies, to take the initiative in leading multijurisdictional cases, and to aid local departments in the federal grant application process for monies that can be used towards addressing such lawbreaking.

Discussion and Implications

Overall, these data support the critical priority needs expressed by the NIJ inventory of 114 agencies across the USA. Furthermore, they build upon the national research by delineating the specific types of computer crime most prevalent to Michigan law enforcement and the specific types of training most desired to combat high-tech wrongdoing. The results of the analysis underscore the potential for victimization online and offline through the use of computers and the Internet, and emphasize the new antisocial and criminogenic repercussions that have stemmed from advances in IT. The future augurs additional instances of these types of crime as more individuals become "wired" and computer-savvy, and as the price of personal workstations and Internet connections decrease. Such trends necessitate continued vigilance and active response by law enforcement, as well as proactive measures undertaken by the governmental sector, private corporations, and the general public. Incidentally, monies have not been identified in the fiscal year 2002–2003 budget for the expansion of the CCU. It is hoped that future allowances will be made for this general purpose, and specifically to increase skill sets internally, to provide opportunities for training external departments, and to engage in quantitative and qualitative research to determine the extent of computer and Internet-related crime in the state. The numbers retrieved from the present study demonstrate that continued financial assistance is merited.

In conjunction with the collaborative efforts of the other public organizations involved, the CCU aims to continue to promote and coordinate efforts in developing practical response protocols, to acquire the requisite know-how to outsmart offenders, and to increase computer literacy among the law enforcement community through training and assistance. Because the FBI will not open up a computer crime case unless the fiscal loss exceeds $10,000, a great proportion of this criminal activity will be delegated to, and investigated, by local and state agencies—emphasizing the need for competence and preparedness among administrators and officers (Reames, 2000). Furthermore, the CCU seeks to augment outreach efforts to inform the community of potential online dangers, promote prevention initiatives, and facilitate open and candid communication between the citizens, organizations, and law enforcement whenever an instance of computer crime occurs, a need similarly emphasized by the national research.

This present study makes several useful contributions to the areas of criminal justice and applied computer crime research. First, the examination accurately assesses the distribution and (Reames, 2000) hierarchy of needs of law enforcement offices in the state of Michigan for the purposes of determining the type and amount of computer crime assistance required. Such knowledge can be used to pointedly shape and direct efforts, consequently fine-tuning the department's endeavors. Second, it is hoped that this work will in part effect the development of policy to curtail the salience of this wrongdoing, and to instruct similar units around the country how to best allocate resources to meet needs. The useful feedback from agencies reinforces the importance of developing and executing a professional needs-based assessment of how to efficiently and effectively utilize a specialized task force to aid local and state law enforcement's efforts against the criminal exploitation of computer technology. Finally, a latent objective has been to spark additional interest in, and subsequent research of, the criminal justice system's efforts to deal with these increasingly injurious offenses.

Future research aims to determine the perceived role that the CCU should fulfill in order to meet the needs of two distinct populations—the general public and the private sector. How do these groups differ in their victimizations of computer crime? How can the CCU most adequately prepare for, prevent, and react towards high-tech miscreance committed against individuals and businesses? Which computer crimes are most frequent and what resources would be most valuable to each? Finally, how can each collective entity work synergistically to address the problem and develop potential solutions? Additionally, it would be interesting to determine the extent to which local and state agencies in Michigan have taken advantage of the services provided by the MSP CCU since this research was conducted, and to document the experience of the unit in meeting the requirements of their constituency. These issues should be addressed in future works; it is hoped that the current study has shed light on the needs of Michigan law enforcement and availed towards a deeper understanding of the cogency and reality of computer crime on a state and local level.

Conclusion

149

*Perceptions of Local
and State Law
Enforcement
Concerning the Role
of Computer Crime
Investigative Teams*

Until recently, computer-related crime was concentrated in the economic environment. The law enforcement community responded by training existing commercial crime or economic crime experts in tactics to address the issue. Within the last few years, however, the Internet has become the catalyst of many other forms of deviance. Emerging computer-related crime will require practically all law enforcement departments to participate in the Internet in some form; members of the policing community must stretch beyond the narrow crime-response paradigm and embrace the positive aspects of this global communication network (Manning, 1997). It is essential that law enforcement personnel develop additional skills to capably respond to and address computer crimes, and also obtain an understanding of their etiology. Instruction and knowledge dissemination to individuals in all sectors of the justice system will promote an appreciation of the complexities that have arisen in this new area of enforcement, and will foster consistency in the application of criminal sanctions and procedures (United Nations, 1994). It has been said that it is easier and more beneficial to educate law enforcement officers about computer crime than to instruct computer programmers and system administrators about law enforcement (Leibowitz, 1999). This is apparently because there is an instinct among police personnel that impels them towards securing justice and going after the "bad guy" in order to uphold the law of the land and protect against infringement on the rights and liberties of others.

As of June 2003, the estimated number of individuals in U.S. households that have Internet access is 177,547,277 (NetRatings, 2003). Worldwide, the number of people online is predicted to reach 940 million by 2004 (Global Reach, 2003). Most of these individuals will use the Internet for legitimate purposes, but many will exploit its vulnerabilities and weaknesses, and violate the rights of others through criminal activity. Law enforcement must do away with their predominant mentality of a police officer's traditional role of crime control and order maintenance, and equip personnel with knowledge and training to form specialized units to focus specifically on high-tech offenses. The outlook for the future is not bleak. Law enforcement must summon the resources, intelligence, and manpower to effectively weed out a sizable proportion of the troublemakers from the rest of the online community, and must no longer underestimate or downplay the true destructive nature of this novel form of criminality, or procrastinate in initiating policy solutions. They must seek ways to preclude computer crime from outweighing the benefits associated with the growth in IT.

Notes

1. These included: child pornography; computer viruses; cryptography used to mask illegal activity; e-commerce fraud; forgery/counterfeiting; hacking; harassment or stalking; identity theft; inflammatory material posted online; information warfare; miscellaneous intellectual property theft; online auction fraud; privacy invasions; software piracy; solicitation of minors; theft of telecommunication services; trafficking of proprietary information; other.

2. "Secondary" investigations concern those referred to the CCU by other agencies.
3. These included evidence collection and processing; forensic tools; front-line officer training; hacks, cracks, and profiling; intrusions and security training; network expertise; operating systems and network training; password and encryption training; politician and supervisor training; prosecutor training; search and seizure training; systems analysis training; undercover investigations training.

References

Appelman, D. L. (1996). "Policing the 'net's red light district", *National Law Review Journal*, March 25.

Borrowman, S. et al. (2001). *Electronic Crime Needs Assessment for State and Local Law Enforcement*, research report, National Institute of Justice, U.S. Department of Justice. Office of Justice Programs, National Institute of Justice, Washington, DC.

Carter, D. L. and Katz, A. J. (1996). "Computer crime: an emerging challenge for law enforcement," *FBI Law Enforcement Bulletin, 65*, pp. 1–8.

Denning, D. (1996). "Protection and defense of intrusion," paper presented at the National Security in the Information Age Conference, U.S. Air Force Academy, Colorado Springs, CO, February 28–March 1.

Global Reach (2003). *Global Internet Statistics,* available at http://global-reach.biz/globstats/index.php3 (accessed August 6, 2003).

Jefferson, J. (1997). "Deleting cybercrooks: prosecutors want tough laws to put hackers, scam artists, and pedophiles on permanent log off," *ABA Journal, 83,* October, pp. 68–74.

Kabay, M. E. (2000). "Studies and surveys of computer crime," available at www.securityportal.com/cover/coverstory20001211.html (accessed December 12, 2002).

Leibowitz, W. R. (1999). "How law enforcement cracks cybercrimes," *New York Law Journal,* p. 5.

Manning, W. W. (1997). "Should you be on the net?," *FBI Law Enforcement Bulletin, 66,* no. 1, p. 18.

NetRatings (2003). "Average Web usage, month of July 2002, U.S.", available at: http://pm.netratings.com/nnpm/owa/NRpublicreports.usagemonthly (accessed August 6, 2003).

Reames, J. E. (2000). "Computer crimes, hacking, and cybernetic warfare," *Journal of California Law Enforcement, 34,* no. 1, pp. 17–26.

Royal Canadian Mounted Police (2000). "Computer crime, can it affect you?" available at http://www3.sk.sympatico.ca/rcmpccs/cpu-crim

United Nations (1994). *International Review of Criminal Policy—United Nations Manual on the Prevention and Control of Computer-Related Crime,* available at www.ifs.univie.ac.at/~pr2gql/rev4344.html (accessed June 20, 1999).

Wise, D. (1997). "Local agencies get tough on cybercrime," *New York Law Journal,* October.

Wittes, B. (1994). "Perils of policing the Internet: law enforcement lacks the tools needed to go after a new breed of online criminal," *The Recorder,* October 11.

AN AD HOC REVIEW OF DIGITAL FORENSIC MODELS

MARK M. POLLITT   *University of Central Florida*

1. Introduction

The field of digital forensics is undergoing a rapid metamorphosis: it is changing from skilled craftsmanship into a true forensic science. Part of this change is expressed by the interest in this field as an academic study. Ironically, the teaching portion of academe has led the way and research is tying to catch up.

Research usually starts with a literature review. That is particularly difficult in this field for a number of reasons. Some of the work predates the Internet and therefore is only available in paper form, in largely obscure or unavailable documents. Much discussion and learning has not been published at all. And few are familiar with the work that has been published.

My own experience bears this out. I often have to rely on my fading memory or that of colleagues to locate a reference for something that I know was published. As a reviewer and editor, I have found that many researchers are going over plowed ground, innocent of the work already done. This seems to be true in virtually all of the digital forensic space, but especially with respect to modeling the digital forensic process.

In discussions with the program committee for this conference, I offered to try to and provide some background. And so, on very short notice, I decided to try and use my feeble flashlight to illuminate some of the work already done. I must do so with some significant caveats.

First, this research was done in a very short time frame utilizing sources with which I am familiar. As a result, it does not represent an exhaustive search or explanation of the state of digital forensic models. It is an arbitrary and not unbiased selection. But it is my hope that it will provide a starting point for future inquiry.

Second, I did not choose to evaluate or otherwise catalog all of the issues described in the various papers. The reader must seek these for themselves.

And lastly, this may not represent the true state of digital forensic models. These are merely data points whose value will change with insight and analysis.

The descriptions of the papers follow their citation and are in approximate chronological order.

2. Pollitt 1995

Pollitt, M. "Computer Forensics: An Approach to Evidence in Cyberspace," *Proceedings II*, pp. 487–491, of the National Information Systems Security Conference, Baltimore, MD 1995. http://www.digitalevidencepro.com/Resources/Approach.pdf

In this very early paper, the computer forensic process is compared and mapped to the admission of documentary evidence in a court of law. Four distinct steps are identified precedent to the admission of any evidence into court. The steps were depicted as follows:

The paper further described the admissibility in knowledge management terms:

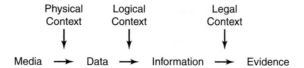

3. Noblett, et al. 2000

Noblett, M., Pollitt, M., Presley, L. "Recovering and Examining Computer Forensic Evidence," *Forensic Science Communications* 2, no. 4, 2000. http://www.fbi.gov/hq/lab/fsc/backissu/oct2000/computer.htm

In another early article, the authors try to integrate the investigative motives for digital forensic examinations with the traditional requirements of forensic science. The rapid evolution of both technology and the criminal use of same suggested that a rigorous, yet flexible form of standards might be more useful than the rigid protocols usually found in traditional forensic laboratories. The following model was suggested:

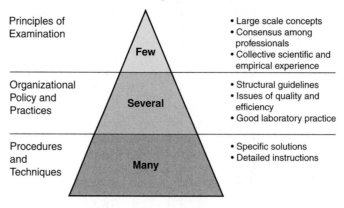

A Three–Level Hierarchical Model for Developing Guidelines for Computer Forensic Evidence

4. Digital Forensic Research Workshop 2001

Digital Forensic Research Workshop (DFRWS). *Research Road Map*, Utica, NY. (2001) http://www.dfrws.org/archive.html

At the first Digital Forensic Research Workshop held in Utica, New York, in 2001, the group created a consensus document that outlined the state of digital forensics at that time. Among their conclusions was that digital forensics was a process with some reasonably agreed upon steps. The grey boxes at the top of their matrix (reproduced below) were identified by the attendees as core processes, although many would debate the "forensic" nature of each step of the process.[1]

Identification	Preservation	Collection	Examination	Analysis	Presentation	Decision
Event/Crime Detection	Case Management	Preservation	Preservation	Preservation	Documentation	
Resolve Signture	Imaging Technologies	Approved Methods	Traceability	Traceability	Expert Testimony	
Profile Detection	Chain of Custody	Approved Software	Validation Techniques	Statistical	Clarification	
Anomalous Detection		Approved Hardware	Filtering Techniques	Protocols	Mission Impact Statement	
Complaints	Time Synch.	Legal Authority	Pattern Matching	Data Mining	Recommended Countermeasure	
System Monitoring		Lossless Compression	Hidden Data Discovery	Timeline	Statistical Interpretation	
Audit Analysis		Sampling	Hidden Data Extraction	Link		
Etc.		Data Reduction		Spacial		
		Recovery Techniques				

5. Reith, Carr, and Gunsch 2002

Reith, M., Carr, C., and Gunsch, G. "An Examination of Digital Forensic Models," *International Journal of Digital Evidence 1*, no. 3 (Fall 2002). http://www.utica.edu/academic/institutes/ecii/ijde/articles.cfm?action=article&id=A04A40DC-A6F6-F2C1-98F94F16AF57232D

In an article published in the International Journal of Digital Evidence, these authors review a number of published models/frameworks for digital forensics. They offer a model comprised of nine steps: Identification, Preparation, Approach Strategy, Preservation, Collection, Examination, Analysis, Presentation, and Returning Evidence. They suggest that this model tracks the traditional forensic evidence collection strategy as practiced by law enforcement.

[1]http://www.dfrws.org/2001/dfrws-rm-final.pdf

6. Carrier and Spafford 2003

Carrier, B., and Spafford, E. "Getting Physical with the Digital Investigation Process," *International Journal of Digital Evidence 2,* no. 2 (Fall 2003). http://www.utica.edu/academic/institutes/ecii/publications/articles/A0AC5A7A-FB6C-325D-BF515A44FDEE7459.pdf

In this major work, Carrier and Spafford provide a useful review of previous work and then map the digital investigative process to the physical investigative process. Their product is called the Integrated Digital Investigation Process and defines 17 phases organized into five groups: Readiness, Deployment, Physical Crime Scene Investigation, Digital Crime Scene Investigation, and Review Phases.

7. Stephenson 2003

Stephenson, P. "Modeling of Post-Incident Root Cause Analysis," *International Journal of Digital Evidence 2,* no. 2 (Fall 2003). http://www.utica.edu/academic/institutes/ecii/publications/articles/A0AE98D6-E1F6-1C9D-481CEE8C29401BFE.pdf

Stephenson begins with the Digital Forensic Research Workshop framework. He views each of the processes as a "class" and each of the actions taken as "elements" of the class. He then states that the six classes define the investigative process. He extends the processes into nine steps which he calls the End-to-End Digital Investigation Process, or EDDI. He then develops a formal representation of this process using Colored Petri Net Modeling.

8. Carrier 2003

Carrier, B. "Defining Digital Forensic Examination and Analysis Tools Using Abstraction Layers," *International Journal of Digital Evidence 1,* no. 4 (Winter 2003). http://www.utica.edu/academic/institutes/ecii/publications/articles/A04C3F91-AFBB-FC13-4A2E0F13203BA980.pdf

In Carrier's paper, he outlines the layers of abstraction that constitute forensic examination. For example, the content of a Word document is extracted via an operating system, a file system, and an application. Carrier identifies an abstraction layer as having two inputs and two outputs:

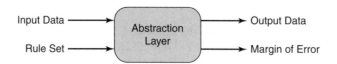

He further identifies that forensic tools can be classified into translation tools and presentation tools. The former reads the data, applies a set of rules, and passes it to the presentation tool, which then displays the information in a meaningful way. He uses these principles to suggest analysis tool requirements.

9. Mocas 2003

Mocas, S. "Building Theoretical Underpinnings for Digital Forensics," DFRWS 2003, Cleveland, OH. http://www.dfrws.org/2003/presentations/Brief-Mocas.pdf

In her presentation at the Digital Forensic Research Workshop in Cleveland, Ohio, Mocas recognized that there were multiple contexts for digital forensics. She identified a law enforcement context, a military context and a business system security context. But for each of the contexts she identified a common process whereby one or more precipitating events initiated an examination that was constrained by external forces and that specific outcomes could be defined with a specific subset the desired outcome. In each context the participating events, constraints, and outcomes could be different.

10. Baryamueeba and Tushabe 2004

Baryamureeba V. and Tushabe, F. "The Enhanced Digital Investigation Process Model," DFRWS 2004, Baltimore, MD. http://www.dfrws.org/2004/bios/day1/Tushabe_EIDIP.pdf

Tushabe suggested a modification to Carrier and Spafford's Integrated Digital Investigation Model of 2003. In her paper she describes two additional phases—*trace back* and *dynamite*—which seek to separate the investigation into primary crime scene (the computer) and the secondary crime scene (the physical crime scene). The goal is to reconstruct the two crime scenes concurrently to avoid inconsistencies.

11. Beebe and Clark 2004

Beebe, N., and Clark, J. "A Hierarchical, Objectives-Based Framework for the Digital Investigations Process," DFRWS 2004 Baltimore, MD. http://www.dfrws.org/2004/bios/day1/Beebe_Obj_Framework_for_DI.pdf

Beebe provides an excellent review of previously proposed digital forensic models and thereafter proposes that while most of the previous models were single tier, in fact the process tends to be multitiered. They specifically propose several subtasks for the data analysis phase using the SEE approach: Survey, Extract, and Examine. They introduce the concept of objectives-based tasks wherein the investigative goals are used to select the analysis tasks.

12. Carrier and Spafford 2004

Carrier, B., and Spafford, E. "An Event-Based Digital Forensic Investigation Framework," DFRWS 2004, Baltimore, MD. http://www.dfrws.org/2004/bios/day1/Beebe_Obj_Framework_for_DI.pdf

In their 2004 paper and briefing, Carrier and Spafford add several new elements to the digital forensic framework: events and event reconstruction. In examining security incidents and sometimes in traditional media examinations, it is necessary to be able to reconstruct one or more events. Events are defined in this paper as follows:

> A digital event is an occurrence that changes the state of one or more digital objects. If the state of an object changes as a result of an event, then it is an effect of the event. Some types of objects have the ability to cause events and they are called causes.[2]

13. Pollitt 2004

> Pollitt, M. "Six Blind Men from Indostan," DFRWS, 2004, Baltimore, MD. http://www.dfrws.org/2004/bios/day1/D1-Pollitt-Keynote.ppt

In this presentation the author reviews the NIST Incident Response model and the DFRWS Framework. These models are then overlaid on a Zachman Framework. The similarities are striking. He then takes up the issue that many models cannot agree on a precise order and that time is a critical element in all models. The Zachman Framework is further modified to represent Investigative Roles as the Y axis and steps of the forensic process as the Y axis measured by time. The paper concludes with the following:

> Forensics is not a single process, but is a set of tasks that can be grouped into functions that are selected based upon the purpose for which the process is being applied (role) and are bound by constraints that are defined by either internal or external requirements.

14. Ruibin, Yun, and Gaertner 2005

> Ruibin, G., Yun, C., and Gaertner, M. "Case-Relevance Information Investigation: Binding Computer Intelligence to the Current Computer Forensic Framework," *International Journal of Digital Evidence 4*, no. 1 (Spring 2005). http://www.utica.edu/academic/institutes/ecii/publications/articles/B4A6A102-A93D-85B1-96C575D5E35F3764.pdf

This paper reviews the previous work of Carrier and Beebe and introduces several new concepts. First is the notion of *seek knowledge*. These are defined as being the investigative clues that drive the analysis of data. The authors recognize this as tacit knowledge by the analyst. Further, the authors identify the need for knowledge reuse within cases and across multiple cases. Another concept described in the paper is the notion of case-relevance, which they define as follows:

> Case-Relevance: the property of any piece of information, which is used to measure its ability to answer the investigative "who, what, where, when, why and how" questions in a criminal investigation.

The authors use this notion to describe the distinctions between computer security and forensics even defining degrees of case-relevance:

---

[2]http://www.dfrws.org/2004/bios/day1/Carrier-event.pdf

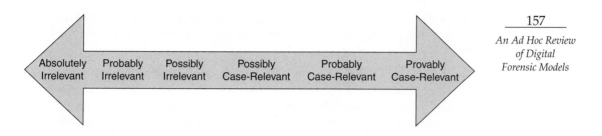

| Absolutely Irrelevant | Probably Irrelevant | Possibly Irrelevant | Possibly Case-Relevant | Probably Case-Relevant | Provably Case-Relevant |

15. Erbacher, Christensen, and Sundberg

Erbacher, Robert F., Christensen, Kim, and Sundberg, Amanda. "Visual Forensic Techniques and Processes," Proceedings of the 9th Annual NYS Cyber Security Conference Symposium on Information Assurance, Albany, NY, June 2006, pp. 72–80. http://www.cs.usu.edu/~erbacher/publications/NetworkForensicProcesses.pdf

In this paper, Erbacher et al. propose a network forensic process that models a number of critical issues. It recognizes that network forensics is not a linear process and must have multiple feedback loops to integrate both text and visual analysis. This process is mapped as follows:

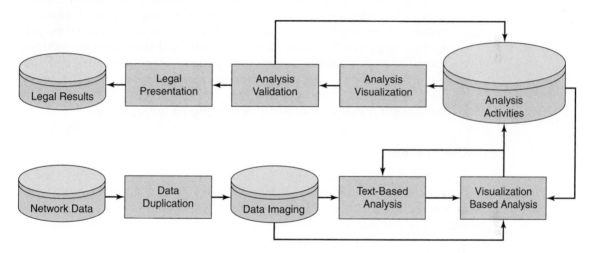

They further describe a number of problems involved in the visualization of data in both intrusion and network forensic situations. They posit that different visualization techniques will be required for different aspects of the analysis but that these, in turn, must be integrated.

16. Kent, Chevalier, Grance, and Dang 2006

Kent, K., Chevalier, S., Grance, T., and Dang, H. *Guide to Integrating Forensics into Incident Response*, Special Publication 800-86, Computer Security Division Information Technology Laboratory, National Institute of Standards and Technology, Gaithersburg, MD August 2006. http://csrc.nist.gov/publications/nistpubs/800-86/SP800-86.pdf

The National Institute of Standards and Technology (NIST), has published the *Guide to Integrating Forensics into Incident Response*. In it they define the basic forensic process:

- Regardless of the situation, the forensic process comprises the following basic phases:
- *Collection.* The first phase in the process is to identify, label, record, and acquire data from the possible sources of relevant data, while following guidelines and procedures that preserve the integrity of the data. Collection is typically performed in a timely manner because of the likelihood of losing dynamic data such as current network connections, as well as losing data from battery-powered devices (e.g., cell phones, PDAs).
- *Examination.* Examinations involve forensically processing large amounts of collected data using a combination of automated and manual methods to assess and extract data of particular interest, while preserving the integrity of the data.
- *Analysis.* The next phase of the process is to analyze the results of the examination, using legally justifiable methods and techniques, to derive useful information that addresses the questions that were the impetus for performing the collection and examination.
- *Reporting.* The final phase is reporting the results of the analysis, which may include describing the actions used, explaining how tools and procedures were selected, determining what other actions need to be performed (e.g., forensic examination of additional data sources, securing identified vulnerabilities, improving existing security controls), and providing recommendations for improvement to policies, guidelines, procedures, tools, and other aspects of the forensic process. The formality of the reporting step varies greatly depending on the situation.

Conclusion

It has been over a decade since the publication of the first paper reviewed in this article. But even the casual observer will note that the work in this area in accelerating and becoming more robust. This paper is dedicated to those who will carry this work forward and allow this budding area to bloom.

Conclusion

The ability of the criminal justice system to control and combat cybercrime is paramount to reduce instances of the different behaviors. As training improves and personnel become more fluent with equipment, the control and combating of cybercrime will improve. To date, a number of opportunities for criminal justice to use to control and combat cybercrime have emerged, but these activities have hurdles that need to be overcome.

Discussion Questions

1. What are the major issues in understanding cybercrime for law enforcement?
2. Why is it necessary for criminal justice to be involved in the Internet environment?
3. What is digital forensics?
4. Explain the differences among three of the digital forensic models.

8

Future Issues

The future of cybercrime is unpredictable and vast. However, one issue that is of particular interest is privacy. Privacy, in this context, refers to the anonymity and confidentiality of an individual's data. Hinduja's article outlines the importance of this issue and the probability that this will be a major concern in the future.

THEORY AND POLICY IN ONLINE PRIVACY

SAMEER HINDUJA   *Florida Atlantic University*

> *Civilization is the progress toward a society of privacy. The savage's whole existence is public, ruled by the laws of his tribe. Civilization is the process of setting man free from men.*
>
> —AYN RAND

Privacy on the Internet has become an increasingly important issue as we progress into an information-based economy and society. As citizens in a democracy, we have become accustomed to various privileges and rights that allow us to protect and defend against invasions into our private lives. Social control in real space—the offline, physical environment—affords us this ability, as government and the private sector have been regulated through law and normative cultural standards. In an online environment, however, many infringements on our entitlement to anonymity and privacy occur with impunity. This, to some extent, seems to be due to the lack of social control constraining the behaviors of web sites and their owning entities.

159

Another interesting dynamic concerning privacy revolves around adherence to socially prescribed behavior. In real space, anonymity is generally ensured if one abides by the dictates and mores in place and follows the accepted conventions of activity. That is, only deviations from the norm elicit inquiry and consequent invasion by regulative institutions. Conversely, in cyberspace that same observance of mainstream and conventional behavior actually increases the likelihood that one's privacy will be invaded. To avoid this, then, individuals who seek to prevent their demographic and personal preference data from being culled and harvested for targeted advertising purposes or other ends must operate on the fringes of standard practice. They must engage in atypical behaviors such as the employment of anonymizers, proxies, infomediaries, encryption, and other mechanisms to disable the infrastructure that by default is set up to violate privacy for exploitative purposes.

In the following text, first, general statistics depicting the value of privacy to Internet users are provided to introduce the issue and attest to its merit for study. An explication of cookies—the dominant instrument used by online corporations to breach privacy rights—is also supplied, along with significant case studies that evidence the gravity of online privacy and present the reader with tangible examples of possible harms. Next follows a summary of notable legislation within which the protection of personal information on the Internet is a prevailing theme. The crux of the paper then ensues: two theories are proffered as paradigms from which to view and explain the major issues surrounding online privacy. Specifically, the role of social control and the dialectical relationship of routine activities regarding privacy are expounded upon, and will ideally provide a novel framework for future examination. An ancillary objective of this paper is to stimulate further thought into how functional policy can be constructed to resolve this particular issue. Some suggestions for testing the theoretical models in any forthcoming research will be made in conclusion, along with a call for increased national legislative intervention and the personal utilization of technical mechanisms by privacy-conscious individuals.

General Statistics

The significance of privacy as a public concern is illustrated through the findings of Georgia Tech University's World Wide Web Surveying team, which has studied the growth and relevant trends in Internet use by Americans since 1994. It must be noted that these results are based on the input of self-selected (and therefore more Internet-savvy) individuals, but the research does provide useful information on privacy perceptions. Some of the topics specifically analyzed include individual and technological demographics, electronic commerce participation, beliefs toward privacy and security, habits of particular online activities, and attitudes towards commercial uses of the Internet. In the most recent results, the researchers found that 71.5% of 1,482 respondents believe that Internet privacy laws should be developed and implemented ("Graphs and Tables," 1999). Moreover, a sizable 77.5% of 1,482 respondents chose "privacy" over "convenience" when asked which is most important to them. These introductory numbers testify to the salience of this issue, and

illustrate the need for pronounced inquiry and policy development by scholars, practitioners, and the IT industry.

Another interesting finding concerned the amount of transactional data or
"mouse droppings"—information that individuals presumed was recorded
when visiting a web page. The feedback received varied markedly, illustrative
of a lack of consensus and accurate knowledge about possible threats to privacy incurred through the simple practice of web browsing. For instance, over
half (54.5%) of respondents believed that one's e-mail address was recorded
(viewed by only 10.1% as appropriate), and 47.1% believed that one's geographical location was revealed (viewed by only 14.1% as appropriate) when
visiting a web page. Exactly what is, and can be, recorded by web site owners
will be enumerated in the following text.

Most respondents asserted the sentiment that they would voluntarily provide demographic information on the Web if certain statements are provided
outlining exactly what is being collected (56.5%), the uses of the compiled data
(73.1%), and if it would be used in an aggregate form only (56.1%). Accordingly, when queried regarding their disinclination to fill out online registration
forms, the primary reasons provided were lack of information concerning how
the data is to be employed (75.2%), a belief that it was "not worth the risk"
(73.1%), and an overall distrust of the collecting entity (67.3%). An overwhelming number of individuals either strongly or somewhat agreed that the user
should have control over what information is granted to a visited web site
(90.5%), and indicated that they value the anonymous nature of the Internet
(88.1%). Most tellingly, the highest proportion of respondents perceived privacy as the primary Internet issue requiring resolution. It is unquestionable,
therefore, that the vast majority of Internet users are generally wary of providing personal information to web sites. But information that users do not provide
is nevertheless garnered by Web entities *sub rosa*, and is still very valuable in
accomplishing marketing and profit-making ends. This practice, as discussed
below, is the linchpin of the current work.

Cookies

Most discussions of privacy on the Internet are dotted with the mention
of "cookies." Unfortunately, a complete understanding of their use and potential for misuse is often lacking among online users, despite the necessity of
such comprehension in accurately addressing the issue. Cookies[1] were developed because the traditional logs created on web servers provided extraneous
and nondemographic information about visitors, information that could not be
employed to hone marketing tactics. Therefore, there was a need for some way
to generally identify a visitor and, moreover, to historically indicate a repeat
visit. The technology of the cookie was consequently developed, and its aforementioned use as a user identifier is inherently benign and unproblematic.

Controversy arises, however, when the cookie is utilized as a reference or
pointer to a database of information created about an individual. This database could contain the number of times one has accessed particular web pages
within a site (indicative of one's interests and preferences), past behavior or
activity at that web site, what information requests have been made, what site
or specific page one has been referred from (again revealing specific online

activities and destinations), and even other personal information voluntarily given when registering for a contest or promotion, or for specialized content, or to simply avail oneself of an offered service. To note, some may argue that a web site has a right to track their visitors, who stop by on their own accord and without any compulsion. While this appears decidedly true, soon there may come a time when all web sites engage in such undisclosed practices of collecting, processing, and tracking personal data. Then, web-browsing individuals may be compelled against their will to relinquish private information if they want to enjoy the content and functionality of the Internet at all.

Netscape Corporation defines a cookie as "a general mechanism which server-side connections (such as CGI scripts) can use to both store and retrieve information on the client side of the connection. The addition of a simple, persistent, client-side state significantly extends the capabilities of Web-based client/server applications." ("Persistent Client State," 1999). This loaded definition fails to capture the dubious uses of the technology—to record and track the online activities of the Internet user. There are two types of cookies: transient and persistent. The former are stored in the temporary memory of the computer rather than on the hard drive, and are erased when a user logs out of the current system or closes his or her web browsing session. The current analysis focuses on persistent cookies.

Mayer-Schonberger (1997) outlines two stages of cookie usage that compromise privacy. In the first stage, the cookie is stored on the web page visitor's hard drive without his or her consent or knowledge (most users are unaware that web browsing involves the storage of temporary files, cookies, and the creation of logs in order to assist the client application in rendering pages and to facilitate interaction between the two players). Second, the cookie is transferred in a secretive or clandestine manner to the web server, allowing for the acquisition of data specific to the person who has established the HTTP connection. To note, if cookies are not enabled in the client's web browser software, many web-based e-mail sites and some sections of other web sites that merely provide content and information are unusable.

Cookies are initially transferred from the server to the client within the HTML code that makes up a requested web page. When a user visits a web site for a second time (or third, etc.), the web browser uploads the cookie obtained during the initial visit. Its value can also be changed based on current behavior at that site, so that it remains up-to-date on one's habits and actions. This, of course, is ostensibly to provide goods, services, content, and aesthetic and auditory preferences specifically tailored to the likes and interests of that person (Wacks, 1998). Some examples include a particular preferred layout of a web site, the ability to shop online without consistently re-entering one's login and password, and the delivery of information which meets the requirements of the person.

When patrons register for a customized service at a web site and provide only a few, seemingly meaningless morsels of private information, they are easily able to convince themselves that no self-harm will result from their actions. Discarding as digressive or extraneous their answers to the web site's personal queries, they fail to realize that such a provision is sometimes inexpedient. Furthermore, while some might enjoy the convenience and personalization afforded by customized content, the amount of extraneous data collected by the corporation or web site owner can be harmful to the maintenance of one's personal privacy. As Berman and Mulligan (1999) state, "While a certain web site or product registration card may only ask for a few minor pieces of personal information, together they constitute a fairly complete profile or one's associations, habits, health condition and personal interests, combining credit card transactions with magazine subscriptions, telephone numbers, real estate records, car registrations and fishing licenses." Whether this occurs on an occasional or regular basis is not relevant for the purposes of this paper—what's relevant is that it can, and has, taken place.

Some of the data that can be collected by Internet sites include IP (Internet Provider) address, network adapter address, general geographical location of one's Internet connection, time of the request, the requested page, browser type, OS (operating system) type, screen resolution, specific search queries for products and services previously conducted at the current web site, the referring site, counts of repeat visitations, and even some contents of the individual's hard drive (such as OS registry entries). Undoubtedly, some information is essential for network communications, such as the IP address. Others pieces of information are superfluous, however, and important only for the purposes of constructing a blueprint of an individual's habits and practices, or even for his or her identity. For instance, if a person is on a corporate or university LAN (local area network), the IP address often resolves to a computer hostname that is based on his or her last name, or login name, or some permutation of a personal designation. If one's NetBios port (139) is open, that information is revealed to any web site or individual who is scanning for potential vulnerabilities. A blatant example is contained in my university network. My username in my office is "hindujas"—an eight character ID that is comprised by the first seven letters of my last name and then the initial letter of my first name. This is the protocol by which login IDs are assigned to individuals on the campuswide LAN. If one's last name is longer than seven characters, it is truncated. With common last names, such as "Smith" or "Jones," consecutive numbers are appended to the username to ensure uniqueness for each person. Nevertheless, with more rare last names (such as "Hinduja"), the specific identity of an individual is easily discernable. When a mischievous or malicious individual is port scanning the network for vulnerabilities, and discovers my machine name is "hindujas," he or she can deduce some of or all of my last name, then run a search query through the University's contact database, and ultimately obtain my real space address and telephone number. To an emphatic and severe degree, my privacy has been compromised.

To further underscore the potential for privacy contravention: in increasing proportions, individuals are using the Internet through dedicated connections. For example, recent statistics from Nielsen NetRatings (2003) indicate that in just one year, from May 2002 to May 2003, broadband connectivity among Americans increased from 26.1 million to almost 39 million—a rise of 49.2%. Internet addresses are primarily static when these broadband technologies are used, providing a concrete and unique identifier that can accurately associate an individual with personal data previously gathered. The web site can thus always be aware when that person is visiting, what he or she is doing currently, and what he or she has done formerly.

Case Studies

Detailed profiles of activity can be (and have been) generated by certain companies online, validating consumer fears of personal privacy infringement and pointing to the possibility for greater and more grievous misuse by Internet businesses engaged in similar practices. In one prominent case, a leading Internet advertising company doing business as DoubleClick, Inc. was charged with using computer software to compile personally identifiable information about individuals into a nationally marketable database, which enabled the company to track users' movements, patterns, and activities across the web (Stone, 2000). This capability involved over a thousand web site partners of the company, each of which agreed to display a banner ad and deliver cookies to visitors. Consequently, DoubleClick could track each visit on a networkwide level. More important, based on unique numbers in each cookie, DoubleClick's technology could determine individual browsing, reading, and shopping patterns, along with other technical information retrieved across a tremendously broad and inclusive range of popular web sites—sites frequented by tens of thousands of users daily.

The upshot was that DoubleClick's behavioral data could be coupled with other, personally identifying data—such as the name and address of individuals, plus their offline and online purchasing history—as well as with demographic data available from the extensive databases of Abacus Direct Corporation, a sizable marketing company (Sobel, 2000). This convergence would no longer maintain anonymity among those who visited sites serving DoubleClick advertisements and cookies, and hence it constituted a major invasion of privacy. A breakdown of the social and economic factors involved in such a practice is provided in a speculative examination below.

A few other notable instances of online privacy violations are worth mentioning before discussing their potential theoretical implications. In 1996, Lexis-Nexis was compelled by public outcry to close P-Trak, an online database containing the Social Security numbers of millions of individuals—accessible by anyone at any time ("Where Is Our Data?," 1997). Also in that year, Yahoo came under intense attack because of its People Search service, a reverse telephone directory allowing users with just a phone number to obtain the names and personal addresses of some 175 million Americans gleaned from telephone books, CD-ROMs, and commercial mailing lists ("Yahoo," 1997). Then in 1997, AOL planned to disclose the telephone numbers of its subscribers to commercial advertisers. But following loud protests, the company jettisoned that idea out of fear of losing its customer base (Kornblum, 1997).

Among private credit and insurance agencies in real space, the practice of computer matching to detect disparities and wrongdoing by individuals has occurred frequently. For instance, records in the databases of automobile registrations and tax filings might be matched in order to discern the identity of those who own expensive cars, but who are not officially making enough money to warrant such profligate purchases (Kling, 1995). Also, many public records are available to profit-making companies, as evidenced by Image Data, LLC's endeavor to purchase drivers' license photo records[2] from Florida and South Carolina without public permission or support, and other divulgences of personal information to marketers, charities, political campaigns, and even individuals ("Image Data," 1999; "Secret Service," 1999). Image Data, LLC, interestingly enough, was financially supported in their photo database purchases by the United States Secret Service. The government agency provided $1.46 million to assist the corporation, which had sought only to use the database to prevent check and credit-card fraud. The intentions of the Secret Service were to employ the database to combat terrorism, immigration abuses, and identity crimes ("Secret Service," 1999). In sum, this particular example demonstrates that even photographs are being matched up with personal data and used by private corporations and the federal government without the express consent of those affected.

Legislation

An enumeration of important and relevant legislation is vital to privacy discourse. Remarkably, the Constitution does not include even one instance of the word "privacy," but the implicit presence of a right to privacy in the First, Third, Fourth, Fifth, Ninth, and Fourteenth Amendments has been upheld by the Supreme Court—thereby making it a "penumbral right" ("Information Security," 1994; Walton, 1999). The Fourth Amendment specifically provides protection against unreasonable searches and seizures in a place where the individual has a legitimate expectation of privacy. It does not restrict the type or amount of personal information that the government can collect, but does qualify the ways in which that data can be obtained (Singleton, 1999). Additional legislation has been passed for the purpose of protecting individuals from abuses of power committed by government, corporations, and big business. In a seminal *Harvard Law Review* piece, Warren and Brandeis (1890) wrote about the "right to be left alone," but they were concerned primarily with privacy and the press. Article 12 of the Universal Declaration of Human Rights (1948), put forth by the United Nations, explicitly states: "No one shall be subjected to arbitrary interference with his privacy, family, home or correspondence, nor to attacks upon his honour and reputation. Everyone has the right to the protection of the law against such interference or attacks." These laws cumulatively enunciate the crucial importance of countering invasions and misappropriations of personal data, and champion such protection as an inalienable right. Generally, the legal system has recognized a right to privacy and anonymity, and some significant pieces of legislation have been passed in the effort to curb abuses of the rights of individuals to control the terms of acquisition and usage of their personal information.

In the early 1970s, following increased governmental surveillance of communication lines as well as tax, bank, and telephone records during protests against the Vietnam War, the public's rallying cry resulted in the Privacy Act of 1974. In this significant piece of legislation, federal agencies are permitted to keep personal records only if they are "relevant and necessary," and they are required to allow individuals to access the files kept on them. In addition, agencies are expected to inform persons as to what is being compiled. Information is to be used only according to the purpose for which it is collected, and any other intent requires explicit authorization (Kling, 1995). Finally, the act requires individual consent prior to the disclosure of personal records to any other entity, except with judicial approval, or for the purposes of law enforcement, or for "routine use" (Singleton, 1999). Incidentally, this "routine use" clause undermined the legitimacy of the law and generally allowed for all intra-agency purposes, as any activity promoting the efficiency of the organization could fall under such an exception (Clarke, 1994).

The Electronic Communications Privacy Act of 1986 prevents the government's unauthorized interception of private electronic communications. While communications companies collect transactional data on the activities of persons related to the services provided, the government must obtain a subpoena before it can access such subscriber information ("Wire and Electronic Communications," 2000). Also, providers cannot disclose the content of communications unless one party consents, the disclosure is necessary for service provision, or the transmission is related to evidence in a criminal investigation. Unfortunately, the Digital Telephony Act, signed into law in 1994, hindered this progressive move by requiring all telecommunications companies to configure their systems to allow federal wiretapping for the purposes of combating criminal activity ("Communications Assistance," 1994).

The Computer Matching and Privacy Protection Act of 1988 ("Records Maintained," 2000) concerns the compilation of data, and detection of patterns in that aggregation, for the purposes of comparing and extracting cases of particular interest. With computer matching, individuals are monitored by their data, rather than by their person, and this is primarily used in real space to compare records from multiple sources in an effort to discern discrepancies (Clarke, 1994). While conducted mainly to cross-check questionable behavior by certain individuals and to discover organizational and administrative errors, it can also be used to detect unscrupulous activity such as fraud by those in a large and widespread population who have done nothing to warrant such inquiry—thereby presuming guilt and compromising their right to privacy. The Act provides for procedural uniformity, due process, and protections for individuals subject to computer matching, and oversight through a proprietary regulatory agency in each organization. With the explosion of the Internet, computer matching has been adopted by Web companies to develop profiles of individuals for the purposes of targeted advertising of goods and services and, arguably, to keep tabs on visitors. Undoubtedly, the law has not had a pronounced effect on activities of data culling and tracking by the private sector in a networked environment. With this inability of federal legislation to effectuate behavior change among the corporate sector online and to protect the privacy rights of the nation's constituents, individuals concerned about the use of their personal information seem to be left to protect themselves.

Social Control

Social control refers to the formal and informal mechanisms in society that influence and regulate behavior to promote obedience to the dominant normative standards in place. Most of these mechanisms are institutional, and include the family, school, government, religion, and culture. Other more individualistic factors that constrain and guide behavior include personal values, morals, and ethics that are inculcated from varying sources. Institutional and individual factors often interact with each other to bring about conformity. According to social control theory, such forces cumulatively shape one's belief system and dictate to a large degree what activities and actions will be allowed and encouraged, and what will be frowned upon and dissuaded. This particular analysis will concentrate on how formal social control is lacking in an online setting, allowing corporate behavior to be conducted unrestrainedly in an effort to attain an esteemed end—the maximization of profit and the minimization of overhead. Social control of corporations establishes and defines the boundaries for the practices in which they engage. The efficacy of such behavioral constraints is largely related to privacy concerns. The freer companies feel to appropriate and utilize the personal data of the consumer base, the greater the risk for violation and infringement.

To begin, though, it must be noted that anonymity on the Internet is oftentimes sought to escape the confining pressures of social control. There is no denying this. When an individual's identity is known, that individual is generally compelled to adhere to societal norms for fear of sullying his or her reputation and experiencing a backlash of communal repercussions (both formal and informal). In effect, that person is induced to "do the right thing" because of the fact that he or she is known in some capacity, and has stakes in conformity that must be maintained and cannot be jeopardized (Toby, 1957; Hirschi, 1969). A compromise of one's good name is not easily and readily made if others are likely to find out about such a transgression. The anonymous nature of the Internet, however, allows many to engage in behaviors and activities they would not publicize—essentially skirting social control mechanisms. But anonymity and privacy, though, are fundamental rights that should be sustained for the general public, irrespective of the proportion who use it to facilitate the commission of crime and deviance. In addition, the individual is not the level of analysis in this work; the corporate entity is—along with the ramifications of its actions on an individual's privacy. With that stated, we can now begin to develop several arguments, including the concept of privacy as afforded to persons online, how Internet businesses are posing a threat to that personal value, and what can be done in response.

In the United States, human rights protections are plentiful in the offline realm, mainly due to centuries of effort by the citizenry to voice concerns and demands for the right to control personal information. Concomitant with freedom, liberty, and equality—the cornerstones on which this country was built—is the right to defend against unlawful or unethical intrusions into the private worlds of individuals. We have become conditioned to expect that only information we choose to reveal about ourselves can and should be available to another person or entity; if any breach of privacy is committed in real space, civil and criminal recourse usually ensues. Specific legislation developed to support this concept has been outlined in the preceding text, demonstrating that the position of the citizenry on this issue—that privacy is fundamental and requires preservation—has been backed by (and to a large degree substantiated by) the law and the public sector in real space.

The subject matter of privacy has made its effect known in all areas of society, such as government, healthcare, and financial institutions. Essentially, many individuals have come to believe that they are afforded an unconditional guarantee of privacy as long as their behavior does not adversely affect the rights or well being of others. This conviction has been reflexively extended to the Internet, and users have assumed that corporations will not misappropriate and misuse personal information provided during engagement in typical online activities such as World Wide Web browsing or electronic commerce. A genuine sense of trust and the expectation of an even-handed, cooperative exchange has been carried over from real space, and it is this naïve and misguided assurance that has perceivably made it easier for corporations to impinge on the rights of the unsuspecting.

Perhaps this sentiment is an offshoot of the fact that we are usually ensconced in the private environment of our home or office when making online purchases, or when simply "surfing the Net." Nevertheless, individuals must recognize that they are visiting places and engaging in interactive business transactions, albeit in a virtual setting. Specifically, a paradigm shift in thinking must occur, wherein these practices are perceived as decidedly public activities, because their associative or equivalent tasks in real space are, of course, conducted in public. It is this author's contention that what is appropriate in business ethics offline should be seamlessly transferable to the online milieu, and persons should not need to reassess their perception of the practices of corporations simply because of the change in context. Regardless, this complacency by consumers has allowed for improper dealings by the corporate sector, which holds the notion that personal data of others not relevant to the transaction are free to be used in any legal manner, regardless of the provider's perceptions or input. In fact, many consider user information to be their annexed property—to be utilized as the business sees fit and without acquiring approval from the providing person.

This occurs in real space, as well, perhaps with the same or greater frequency. Nonetheless, individuals in real space choose to give up certain private data when executing a transaction, and they are able to keep private the data they do not want to give—or at least they are aware of what private data they are forced to abandon. Thus in real space, nothing occurs behind the scenes.

By contrast, in cyberspace many users are not aware that their browsing and shopping activities are being tracked and matched with personal information that they have provided—some consciously and some unknowingly. Furthermore, the effect seems much more pronounced and exploitive when it is done online, ostensibly because of the perceived anonymity associated with the Internet. Marc Rotenberg, director of the Washington-based Electronic Privacy Information Center (EPIC), summarizes the greatest fear as being the creation of a "digital dossier" on everyone who uses the Internet: "The big, long-term concern about privacy is the surreptitious compilation of every site you click, every page you download, and every product you order, into a single database" (Hansell, 1998).

Undisputedly, more protections are afforded to the individual in the form of legislation (see above) and a general consensus on what is "acceptable" to compile during a traditional, offline business dealing. In cyberspace, only some web sites make the visitor aware (to varying degrees) of what is being collected. Most employ "opt-out" policies requiring users to explicitly disallow the collecting and tracking of their information, rather than amassing data from only those who specifically agreed to it (Novak and Hoffman, 1998). This puts a tremendous burden on the patron to be responsible for the privacy of their personal information, and to police the behavior of corporations.

Incidentally, opt-out policies in real space have proven to be problematic because of a difficulty to understand and process them. Recently making headlines and worthy of acknowledgement is the Gramm-Leach-Bliley Financial Modernization Act of 1999, which allows banks, credit lenders and insurance companies to share personal financial data on their clients with each other beginning 1 July 2001, unless individuals specifically prohibit it (Martin, 2001; Quinn, 2001). Fundamentally, financial institutions with which a person has a relationship are able to share all information they have about that person (what you own, whom and how you pay, what you buy, etc.) with any entity they are affiliated or associated with, as long as it is necessary for "business purposes." The point of this is that the very concept of "opt-out" is egregious, and that companies entrusted with the personal information of individuals should guard and protect that data, rather than sharing it if no explicit dissent is given. If real space organizations are unable to maintain privacy-conscious standards of practice, it bodes poorly for the largely unregulated and amorphous environment of cyberspace.

Privacy concerns have been at the forefront of consumers' minds for decades, and are not a recent phenomenon initiated by information technology. In 1994, the credit bureau of Equifax, Inc. commissioned a survey of a cross-section of adults in the contiguous United States, and garnered a sample of 1,005 responses proportionate to the demographic makeup (age, gender, race, and education) of the coterminous nation. Testifying to the salience of the issue, 84% of individuals reported that they were either "very" (51%) or "somewhat" (33%) concerned about threats to their privacy ("Equifax/Harris," 1994). To note, this organization has been conducting yearly privacy surveys among a sample of adults 18 years of age and older, proportionate to the age, race, sex, and education distribution of the entire population of adults in the contiguous United States.

Issues related to abuses of privacy rights were prevalent in the world before computers existed. With computers, though, an increased threat of invasion has come because of the capability to retrieve, process, analyze, and store gigabytes of data very quickly and easily. The Internet and networks in general have multiplied risks of data culling and harvesting by facilitating information gathering on a spatially broad scale, and by greatly reducing the legwork involved in accessing data about an individual or group. That which was previously stored in hard-copy format is now available in electronic format, further simplifying the process of retrieval, aggregation, and analysis. Interestingly, the Internet was used solely for noncommercial matters until 1994, but as federal funding ended, the private sector quickly saw the potential of a global audience and a low-cost method of advertising and product or service promotion, and accordingly capitalized on such benefits through intense commercialization (Goldhamer, 2000). Internet users were reticent about paying for information and services provided through this new medium, however, akin to the reluctance to pay for enjoying a song on the radio or a television show on a network TV channel. Commercial entities discovered this disinclination, and the Internet moved into an advertising-based model for revenue generation (Goldhamer, 2000). Here, customers do not directly pay for the furnished content—advertisers do.

Along with this emphasis on advertising necessarily follows a desire to maximize sales by marketing a product or service specifically to those who would be most interested, willing, and capable of purchasing it. Therein lays the need for the accumulation, sorting, and management of detailed information (as previously specified) about potential patrons, both voluntarily and unwittingly supplied. The focus on specifying and directing marketing to those most likely to purchase has always been in place, even in real space, but computers and the Internet have increased the amount of data being culled and processed from unsuspecting users expecting relative anonymity in their transactions. There is money to be made in creating a "profile" of individuals in the interests of targeted advertising, and many corporations believe this practice is vital to succeeding in the competitive environment of the "dot.com" world. In many cases, economic gain is the motivation, regardless of the attendant commodification and disrespect of personal and private data.

The value of detailed information about a population compels many corporations to view data culling as an integral and acceptable part of the Internet experience. Indeed, it is unarguably beneficial to making a sale—but at what expense to privacy? When an individual engages in a transaction and provides personal data, there is an unstated expectation of proper use of that information (Laufer and Wolfe, 1977; Lind and Tyler, 1988). When an individual does not actively disclose personally sensitive data, it is expected that complete anonymity and privacy is maintained, and that no data is being acquired invisibly or "behind the scenes." Based on what has transpired during the growth of the Internet, there is no reasonable expectation of privacy provided to patrons by the companies with which they interact. Corporations are not compelled by societal or legislative forces to furnish the same amount of privacy in a virtual realm as is supplied in the offline realm. Since users are not intrinsically afforded such protections when using the Internet, it can be contended that they should have the right to decide for themselves what personal information is or is not given—which essentially requires having accurate knowledge as to what is collected and how it will be used. Analogous to business interaction in real space, the interests of protecting individual privacy have unfortunately taken a back seat to the interests of profitmaking by online corporations. Many commercial entities have no incentive to comply with this notion, believing it would be detrimental to the fiscal objectives of the organization. A new set of goals is thus introduced, based on the economic value extractable from the commodity of historically private information. As such, this questionable practice allows businesses to capitalize on the benefits that information technology is able to provide. Data collection now occurs by default—transparently and without any burden to the user (Lessig, 1998). That which was previously impossible or extremely difficult now becomes inordinately facile, and results in a desired end to the corporation collecting it.

There are two, nonexclusive, methods by which society seeks to ensure propriety among businesses in their everyday dealings: legislation, and self-regulation. Self-regulation has been historically and predominantly trumpeted as the most effective controlling mechanism. That is, the practices of corporations bent on obtaining a competitive advantage, or driven to succeed at any cost, are assumedly tempered by their own desire to perpetuate a harmonious relationship with the consumer base, and when that fails, by legislation. The patronage of the customer—the other requisite player in the dichotomous interface that comprises business dealing—is crucial to maintain (Culnan and Milberg, 1999; Osterhus, 1997). The customer's cooperation and support is integral for continued revenue generation in America's capitalistic economy, and it has been proven unwise to risk alienating a customer through shady or unscrupulous business practices. Despite instances of infringement by, and consequent backlashes towards business and government in the real world, no pronounced deterrent effect seems to have resulted. The trend has not attenuated: both well-established corporate entities and entrepreneurial "dot.com" startups have been accused of misappropriating data from Internet users in a surreptitious effort to profit. Social control stemming from law in real space and the general public appears to be ineffective in curtailing some privacy-invading practices of online businesses. Additionally, regulatory social control among Internet businesses themselves is not facilitated, as so many deem these practices to be justified and appropriate to organizational intentions.

Primarily, these endeavors involve collecting personal information about individuals in an effort to develop a profile that can be used generally to identify certain aspects of one's life (Culnan and Milberg, 1999). Advertising corporations are able to profit by promising companies seeking promotion that their banners will be placed in front of a specific group of consumers. This audience consists of those most likely to purchase a product or service from that company, and lends itself to a lucrative enterprise. In essence, a profile is developed on each person and groups of similar persons are then used as a potentially rewarding customer base to which companies can pitch their wares (Hansell, 1998). These profiles are stored in databases, and can be harvested for the purposes of unsolicited or unwanted targeted advertising by both the collecting entity and its partners in marketing. In real space, these decisions to infringe are made ostensibly with the logic that more informed decisions will be possible with regard to giving a loan, renting out an apartment, hiring an employee, and approaching a potential consumer base. The profitability of this practice is demonstrated by the fact that advertisers can increase the effectiveness of their ads (by eliciting click-throughs and subsequent purchases) by as much as five times when data about a visitor's habits, interests, and general demographics are known (Hansell, 1998). Likewise, Internet companies assert that they collect data so that they may serve the customer best. It is unlikely that this practice benefits the client solely, serving instead organizational pursuits of profit. Self-regulation of these activities is not enforceable and has proven to be an ineffective strategy, as evidenced by the frequent news reports of Internet privacy breaches and concerns (Hansell, 1998;[3] Yahoo, 1997;[4] "Carnivore," 2001;[5] "Echelon," 2001[6]). Taken cumulatively, these reported breaches reinforce the need for legislation to govern behavior.

Interestingly, targeted advertising is likely to be the most innocuous use of personal information. Many databases are being constructed and utilized specifically for duplicitous means—to garner as much knowledge as possible about the habits, interests, customs, geographic locations, and demographics of Internet users and to sell this knowledge to the highest bidder in either the public or private sector. Anyone can obtain specific personal profiles of individuals, irrespective of their intended plan of use and regardless of the reasons for which those private data were initially disclosed. Activities, interests, habits, and preferences online can be coupled with offline record-sets of one's address, phone number, or other confidential information, essentially allowing that person to be tracked and followed as he or she uses the Internet—the ultimate Orwellian realization. The "information super-highway" was developed for the contained and private use of the national defense and universities for the purposes of wartime communication and research collaboration and dissemination, rather than for the pervasive and public use of everyone. As such, the Internet has been slow to adapt to and accommodate the possibility of deviant and antisocial behavior, and is striving intensely to catch up (as evidenced by recent federal, state, and local law enforcement policy initiatives). Put succinctly, effective formal social control instruments seeking to enforce corporate propriety are not yet in place in the virtual realm.

Moreover, because of the Internet's still embryonic state of existence, and its globally distributed nature, Internet users have yet to organize a concerted effort to authoritatively declare a demand for the implementation of privacy protection mechanisms. Some organizations, such as the Electronic Frontier Foundation (EFF), the Electronic Privacy Information Center (EPIC), and the Center for Democracy and Technology (CDT), have arisen to lead the way in articulating the importance of defending against unwarranted intrusions into the personal space of Internet users. Unfortunately, their collective voice—while resulting in societal attention to such breaches—has not been completely effective in generating long-term and enduring change in the information-gathering practices of online corporations. As mentioned earlier, self-regulation stemming from the incentive of corporations to prevent estrangement of the consumer population has not substantively materialized. This leads one to believe that governmental legislation is the only solution to personal privacy infringements by the Internet business sector, as a good proportion are seemingly neither motivated nor conscientious enough to regulate their practices voluntarily.

Routine Activities

Another dynamic that warrants analysis concerns the issue of conventional behavior by the general public and the attendant consequences of privacy encroachments. Most individuals in real space go about their own business and generally abide by the directives prescribed by society, law, and culture in their pursuit of commonly valued goals. By and large, these persons are not subject to the unsolicited violation of their personal privacy and are not forced to relinquish the right to choose what information to provide to another party unless they feel comfortable that the supplied data will be used in an appropriate manner. Furthermore, by following normative behavioral dictates in the course of their routine life activities, they give no reason for additional attention or inquiry by the public (regulative) or private (commercial) sector. By conducting oneself in the same way as the majority of people in a society, an individual's behavior and manner is deemed suitable and is allowed or encouraged to continue. By straying from orthodox definitions of acceptable activity, though, one brings upon himself or herself additional notice and consideration by others. That person is subsequently labeled as a deviant who has chosen to disrespect and transgress certain commonly held and institutionalized beliefs, in place presumably to facilitate a stable, productive, symbiotic society. In sum, an individual who aligns with socially established precepts of good living and who "does what everyone else does" has little to worry about with respect to personal privacy contravention. Conversely, those who engage in questionable activity—for whatever reason (to pursue self-interest, to stand up for a cause, or even to attempt to garner some additional semblance of privacy which one feels is lacking through a nonconformist channel)—are considered deviants whose behavior should be curbed or corrected in the interests of communal harmony. The topical principle to be extracted from the real world environment is this: privacy is virtually ensured when one walks in step with the majority; privacy is threatened when one deviates from the norm. Alignment and allegiance encourage personal information security; anomaly encumbers it.

Remarkably, this trend is turned on its head in a networked world. Mainstream behavior of Internet users involves some amalgamation of the following: visiting web sites without reservation or care; registering for specific visual and content-related preferences at these sites; assuming proper use of cookies by Internet entities, and perceiving as irrelevant any contemporaneous data siphoning by corporations; trusting that these entities will not take unfair or unauthorized advantage of a panoptic consumer community at their disposal; and holding the notion that encryption and tools used to facilitate anonymity are for the Internet "elite." These practices unfortunately conduce to privacy intrusions online by companies seeking to enhance capital gains and attain other commercially valued ends.

As stated earlier, the IT-based economy is tremendously competitive and cutthroat. Internet businesses are born, shimmer for a moment, and then fade away into oblivion in mere months. Transience is the norm rather than the exception when it comes to these types of organizations, as it is becoming more difficult to compete successfully in such an aggressive, "take-no-prisoners" market environment. As such, corporations are pressured to participate in socially injurious methods of profit-making in an attempt to stay afloat. Moreover, many companies discount the dubious nature of their actions as a "cost of doing business," or a harmless effect resulting from voluntary participation, submission, and agreement by the web site visitor. It is this author's contention that through the misuse and manipulation of an Internet user's inexperience and trust in an already nascent and uniquely mediated environment, harm is done. This includes the gleaning and harvesting of personal data unreservedly and with impunity, compromising the sense of security individuals traditionally anticipate and associate with transactions.

The chief question remains: what can online users do to reclaim pure and comprehensive anonymity that by default was annexed from them through mere interaction on the Internet terrain? If they continue to engage in normative behavior—which inherently assumes flawless propriety by corporations—they can be sure that the personal information not generally disclosed will continue to be expropriated. Therefore, those individuals who seek to take a stand against this unethical practice must join a deviant group of sorts—a cadre or faction that utilizes available technologies to safeguard their privacy. The mechanisms available to the Internet user to rail against the commodification of personal data range from simple cookie-blocking and filtering applications, to software products that serve as a liaison between one's computer and the rest of the Internet to separate communication networks and novel message-routing protocols yet to be implemented on a wide scale.

Noted speaker D. L. Moody asserts that "character is what you do in the dark," and such sentiments are commonly held by the majority of people. So, the greatly esteemed attribute of character is called into question on many levels when one is not completely forthright and open about his or her behavior, and chooses to veil or mask it with anonymizing methods. These technologies are considered marginal by the mainstream and are believed to be only necessary for employment by "cloak-and-dagger" individuals. In addition, these technologies and the behaviors they afford are often viewed (mistakenly) as too protective, too restrictive, and indicative of needless, paranoid, and conspiracy-minded suspicion.

An imputation of a deviant identity is ascribed to these behaviors because they fall on the fringes of standard practice, despite their meritorious worth and the beneficial ends they promote concerning the defense of privacy. As a consequence, those who partake in such anomalous activities are subject to the same delinquent label, despite sensing the real necessity to do so because of privacy violations committed by online business entities. This problematic incongruence must be resolved and, when coupled with increased awareness of privacy threats and instances of invasions, will ideally lead to increased government interference in such online practices, and to more users proactively shielding themselves against (sometimes) unscrupulous behavior by corporations. This is the primary objective of this paper—to develop these themes and spark change on both macro and micro levels to preserve personal privacy for constituents in the online domain.

Suggestions for Theory Testing

What future inquiries can be performed to accurately assess the value of these theoretical models? Concerning social control, perhaps a qualitative survey could be made to ascertain why businesses and organizations online feel less compelled to honor privacy concerns of the consumer base than in real space. Such feedback can then ideally be used to develop policy which increases the collective respect of individuals and their personal information. Also, if more persons are aware of possible negative ramifications stemming from privacy contravention, a demand for propriety in all transactions will be fostered, and the standard for upright dealings will be raised. Sadly, it sometimes appears that for online users to take a stand and vociferously denounce shady practices of covert data culling, analyzing, tracking, and sharing, a blatant and severe—and perhaps even life-threatening—privacy violation is going to have to make the news. It is this author's hope that as more attention is given to the phenomenon, more persons will see the value in championing personal privacy protections on the Internet.

With regard to routine activities, it would be interesting to determine what makes some individuals more apt to employ technological methods to prevent breaches of their privacy online. Is it because they are more technically savvy and inclined to experiment with new software? Is it because they are paranoid and overcautious? Or is it because they sense a real danger for exploitation and data misuse with the current state of affairs? How can the impetus for the protective measure they take be shared with, and spread to, the rest of the Internet community? What will it take for all users—automatically and by default—to be wary of the unnecessary disclosure of private information? The majority of us would not recklessly supply our demographics, interests, penchants, preferences, and address and location to a stranger, and yet that is exactly what happens all too often when "surfing the Net." Some of it is unarguably essential for the processing of a transaction; much more, however, is extraneous and detrimental to the interests of private citizens who would prefer more anonymity. In sum, qualitative research would best retrieve a rich conception of why businesses and privacy-conscious Internet users behave the way they do, and should clarify what needs to be done to decrease the chances of contravention and increase the trust endemic to networked exchanges and dealings.

Conclusion

Laurence Tribe, Tyler Professor of Constitutional Law at the Harvard University Law School, has proposed a Twenty-Seventh Amendment to the United States Constitution which would do for cyberspace what the Ninth Amendment did for protecting rights and espousing values not expressly stated in its text. That is, it would render applicable to the new technological terrain the constitutional protections developed during its construction— thereby acknowledging the reality of originally unspecified rights held by individuals. As proposed, it would state: "This Constitution's protections for the freedoms of speech, press, petition, and assembly, and its protections against unreasonable searches and seizures and the deprivation of life, liberty, or property without due process of law, shall be construed as fully applicable without regard to the technological method or medium through which information content is generated, stored, altered, transmitted, or controlled"(Tribe, 1991). While it is unknown how much legitimacy such a proposal is given, its contents speak volumes about what is apparently imperative to constrain unethical and infringing behavior by corporations and organizations online.

Other legal precedents have proven groundbreaking by impacting society and attenuating privacy concerns of the citizenry. For example, *Katz v. United States* (1967) specified that the content of telephone conversations—regardless of the location or owner of the telephone being used—should be private and not subject to wiretapping or interception. Moreover, the Video Privacy Act of 1988 made video rental records private information when Supreme Court nominee Robert Bork's records were published. The Cable Communications Policy Act of 1984 also privatized individual subscriber records. The Right to Financial Privacy Act of 1978 and the Fair Credit Reporting Act of 1992 each endorsed protections against the unhindered disclosure of financial information of bank customers to a government agency or other entities. The Driver's Privacy Protection Act—part of the Violent Crime Control and Law Enforcement Act of 1994—made driver licenses private records, privy only to state agencies ("DMV Access,"1998). All of these instances demonstrate how privacy laws have championed the rights of individuals to control their personal information, and have prevented the use of such data in ways other than their original purpose. They were deemed as necessary to maintaining fundamental national ideals when supported by the public and ratified by the legislature, and the corresponding current demands for privacy protections online warrant a similar response. In June of 1995, the National Information Infrastructure Task Force (NIITF) Privacy Working Group specified that individuals on the Internet should be assured of their reasonable expectation of privacy, and that personal data should be used solely for relevant purposes germane to its provision. In addition, businesses collecting such information online should enumerate what data is being collected and for what uses, along with specifying guidelines to assure its confidentiality, security, and proper use, and avenues of recourse in the case of wrongdoing by the company ("Privacy," 1995). This plan of action merited complete implementation before the extraordinary burgeoning of the Internet, and an extensive application of its tenets has still not been realized. It seems to be time for appropriate legislation to be constructed and upheld online so that the practice of data culling is rendered unlawful, reestablishing the veracity of the information's definitive descriptive term—"personal." How we interact necessitates a reassessment and revision in practice so that personal privacy is guarded and not appropriated by others without explicit consent. In our thriving networked world and with the consequent decrease in physical boundaries where individuals can generally control what is revealed to others, proper legal guidelines need to be established governing the acquisition and use of personally sensitive information. The collection of data and its exploitation for commercial gain, its unauthorized distribution to third parties, and the archival and storage of that data for interminable periods of time weakens the civil protections of freedom of association and privacy. Self-regulation is ineffective, and legislation appears to be the only way to best serve the citizenry of the United States, and to prevent American companies from taking advantage of the online consumer. Without such governmental initiatives, Internet users are left to their own devices—to obtain privacy through employing technological tools such as anonymizers, proxies, infomediaries, encryption, and other related mechanisms. Privacy is a fundamental human right; it makes us who we are. Provided to all, it maintains similarities in that it allows others to know only what we choose to divulge, affords us control over the social context of relationships and interactions with others, and grants dignity and respect to the Internet user—who should be able to maintain command over the use of personal information. Provided to all, it also perpetuates valuable differences, because we are able to preserve the individuality inherent in each of us.

Notes

1. According to the writer of the cookies specification for Netscape Navigator 1.0, the first web browser to use the technology, "A cookie is a well-known computer science term that is used when describing an opaque piece of data held by an intermediary" (Whalen, 2001).
2. Underscoring the possible severe repercussions of unwarranted disclosure of personal data, an actress was stalked and murdered by an individual who obtained private information from her driver's license file (Berman and Mulligan, 1999).
3. Some of the largest commercial web sites have agreed to partner with a Massachusetts company to cooperatively build a database of online customer interests, habits, and general demographics for the purposes of targeted advertising (Hansell, 1998). When a user visits one of the participating network sites, a cookie is written to his or her hard drive, which is then tracked across the Internet.
4. In 1997, Yahoo, Inc. was forced to dispose a popular reverse telephone directory from its site. It had allowed individuals to discover the names and addresses of others with only their telephone number.
5. The Carnivore system was developed by the FBI and, when installed on the network of an Internet Service Provider, gives the agency access to all of the traffic and email of anyone communicating across their lines. This facility is to be used only for the purposes of aiding criminal investigations, but there are no guarantees or checks in place to prevent the unrestricted ferreting, filtering, and analysis of any and all communications by the FBI (Steinhardt, 2000).
6. ECHELON is a covert global electronic surveillance system that, according to reports, captures, processes, and analyzes enormous amounts of communications traffic in order to gather intelligence about persons and their activities. Pundits have suggested that the system may intercept as many as 3 billion communications each day (some even estimate up to 90% of all Internet traffic), and filter out relevant data with artificial intelligence software (Poulsen, 1999; Lindsay, 1999).

References

Berman, J. and Mulligan, D. (1999). "Privacy in the Digital Age: Work in Progress," *Nova Law Review,* 23 (2), http://www.cdt.org/publications/lawreview/1999nova.shtml

Cable Communications Policy Act of 1984, 47 U.S.C. § 551 (1996).

"Carnivore: FBI Surveillance Software." (2001). *Computer World, Inc.,*<http://www.computerworld.com/resources/carnivore>.

Clarke. R. (1994). "The Technique of Computer Matching." *Information Technology and People,* 7(2): 46–85.

"Communications Assistance for Law Enforcement Act." (1994). Electronic Privacy Information Center, <http://www.epic.org/privacy/wiretap/calea/calea_law.html>.

Culnan, M. J. and Milberg, S. J. (1999). Consumer Privacy. In M. J. Culnan, R. J. Beis, and M. B. Levy (Eds), Information Privacy: Looking Forward, Looking Back. Washington, D.C.: Georgetown University Press.

"DMV Access." (1998). *Cohn and Marks,* Washington, D.C., <http://www.cohnmarks. com/WhatsNews/dmvacces.htm>.

"Echelon watch." (2001). American Civil Liberties Union, <http://www.echelonwatch.org>.

"Email Encryption Made Simple." (1999). Information and Privacy Commissioner, Toronto, Ontario, <http://www.ipc.on.ca/english/pubpres/papers/cncryp-e.htm>.

"Equifax/Harris Consumer Privacy Survey: Executive Summary." (1994). Equifax, Inc. and Louis Harris & Associates, <http://www.privacyexchange.org/iss/surveys/ eqfx.execsum.1994.html>.

Fair Credit Reporting Act of 1970, 15 U.S.C. § 1681 et seq.

Goldhamer, D. (2004). "Privacy concerns." *SHARE,* Boston. MA, 24 July, <http://home. uchicago.edu/~dhgo/privacy-intro/>.

"Graphs and Tables of the Results." (1999). GVU's 10th WWW User Survey. Graphics, Visualization, & Usability Center. Georgia Tech Research Corporation, <http:// www.gvu.gatech.edu/user_surveys/survey–1998–10/graphs/graphs. html#general>.

Hansell, S. (1998). "Big Web Sites to Track Steps of Their Users." *New York Times,* 16 August.

Hirschi, T. (1969). *Causes of Delinquency.* Berkeley: University of California Press.

Hong, T. (2001). "Freenet: A Distributed Anonymous Information Storage and Retrieval System." in *Designing Privacy Enhancing Technologies: International Workshop on Design Issues in Anonymity and Unobservability,* LNCS 2009. Federrath, H. (ed.). New York: Springer.

"How PGP Works." (1999). Introduction to Cryptography. PGP 6.5.1 documentation. *Network Associates. Inc.,* <http://www.pgpi.org/doc/pgpintro/>.

"Image Data Contracted by Secret Service." (1999). *Cipherwar,* 7 December <http:// cipherwar.com/news/99/imagedata.htm>.

Information Security and Privacy in Network Environments. (1994). United States Office of Technology Assessment. OTA-TCT–606 (September). Washington, D.C.: U.S. Government Printing Office.

Katz v. United States 389 U.S. 347. (1967). Legal Information Institute. Cornell Law School. <http://supct.law.cornell.edu:8080/supct/historic_idx/389_347.htm>.

Kling, R. (1995). Information Technologies and the Shifting Balance between Privacy and Social Control." Part VI, Article A of *Computerization and Controversy: Value Conflicts and Social Choices,* 2nd ed. San Diego, Academic Press, <http://www.slis. indiana.edu/kling/cc/6-CNTR4.html>.

Kornblum. J. (1997). "AOL to Give Out Phone Numbers." *CNET News.com,* 22 July, <http://news.cnet.com/news/0–1005–200–320749.html>.

Laufer, R. S. and Wolfe, M. (1977), "Privacy as a Concept and a Social Issue: A Multi-dimensional Developmental Theory." *Journal of Social Issues,* 33(3): 22–42.

Lessig, L. (1998). "The Architecture of Privacy." (Draft 2). *Taiwan Net '98,* Taipei, Taiwan, <http://cyber.law.harvard.edu/works/lessig/architecture_priv.pdf>.

Lind, E. A. and Tyler, T. R. (1988). *The Social Psychology of Procedural Justice.* New York, NY: Plenum Press.

Lindsay, G. (1999). "The Government Is Reading Your E-Mail." *Infowar.com, LLC,* 24 June, <http://www.infowar.com/class_1/99/class1_063099b_j.shtml>.

Martin, J. (2001). "Opting Out or Not: Financial Privacy Forms Criticized for Length, Complexity." *ABC News.com,* 21 June, <http://abcnews.go.com/sections/wnt/DailyNews/ privacy_notices_010621.html>.

Mayer-Schonberger, V. (1997). The Internet and Privacy Legislation: Cookies for a Treat? *West Virginia Journal of Law and Technology,* 1(1).

"Nearly 40 Million Internet Users Connect Via Broadband, Growing 49%." (2003). *Nielsen Net Ratings,* <http://www.nielsen-netratings.com/news.jsp>.

Novak, T. P. and Hoffman, D. L. (1999). "Building Consumer Trust in Online Environments: The Case for Information Privacy." *Communications of the ACM,* <http://www2000.ogsm.vanderbilt.edu/papers/CACM.privacy98/CACM.privacy.htm>.

Oram, A. (2000). "The Value of Gnutella and Freenet." *Web Review—Cross Training for Web Teams,* 12 May, <http://www.webreview.com/pi/2000/05_12_00.shtml>.

Osterhus, T. L. (1997). Pro-Social Consumer Influence Strategies: When and How Do They Work? *Journal of Marketing 61*: 16–29.

"Persistent Client State—HTTP Cookies." (1999). *Netscape Corporation,* <http://home.netscape.com/newsref/std/cookie_spec.html>.

Poulsen, K. (1999). "Echelon Revealed." *TechTV, LLC,* 9 June, <http://www.techtv.com/cybercrime/chaostheory/story/0,23008,2120457,00.html>.

"Privacy and the National Information Infrastructure: Principles for Providing and Using Personal Information." (1995). Privacy Working Group. Information Policy Committee, Information Infrastructure Task Force, 6 June, <http://www.iitf.doc.gov/documents/committee/infopol/niiprivprin_final.html>.

Quinn, J. B. (2001). "New Privacy Law Gives Consumers 'Opt Out' Rights." *Washington Post* 15 May, <http://washingtonpost.com/wpsrv/business/longterm/quinn/columns/051501.htm>.

"Records maintained on individuals." (2000). U.S. Code, Title 5, Section 552a. The Legal Information Institute. Cornell Law School. <http://www4.law.cornell.edu/uscode/5/552a.html>.

Right to Financial Privacy Act of 1978, 12 U.S.C. § 3401–34 (1996).

"Secret Service Aided License Photo Database."(1999). *Associated Press,* Cable News Network, 18 February, <http://www.cnn.com/US/9902/18/license.photos/>.

Singleton, S. (1999). "Privacy and Human Rights: Comparing the United States to Europe." *CATO Institute,* 1 December, <http://www.cato.org/pubs/wtpapers/991201paper.html>.

Sobel, D. (2000). "EPIC Complaint Against DoubleClick Inc." Electronic Privacy Information Center, <http://www.epic.org/privacy/internet/DCLK_complaint.pdf>.

Steinhardt, B. (2000). "Carnivore Needs to be Caged." *Computerworld,* 9 August <http://www.computerworld.com/cwi/story/0,1199,NAV47_STO48349,00.html>.

Stone, M. (2000). "DoubleClick Accused of Double-Dealing Double-Cross." Newsbytes. *E-Commerce Times,* 2 February, <http://www.ecommercetimes.com/news/articles2000/000202-nb3.shtml>.

Syverson, P. F., Reed, M. G., and Goldschlag, D. M. (2000). "Onion Routing Access Configurations." *DISCEX 2000: Proceedings of the DARPA Information Survivability Conference and Exposition,* Volume I, Hilton Head, SC, IEEE CS Press, 34–40, <http://www.onion-router.net/Publications/DISCEX–2000.pdf>.

Toby, J. (1957). "Social Disorganization and Stake in Conformity: Complementary Factors in the Predatory Behavior of Hoodlums." *Journal of Criminal Law, Criminology, and Police Science,* 48, 12–17.

Tribe, L. H. (1991). "The Constitution in Cyberspace: Law and Liberty beyond the Electronic Frontier." Keynote address at the first conference on Computers, Freedom & Privacy.

"Universal Declaration of Human Rights." (1948). The Office of the High Commissioner for Human Rights. *United Nations Department of Public Information,* Geneva, Switzerland, <http://www.unhchr.ch/udhr/lang/eng.htm>.

Video Privacy Protection Act of 1988, 18 U.S.C. § 2710.

Wacks, R. (1998). "The Death of Online Privacy?" 13th Annual BILETA Conference: "The Changing Jurisdiction," Trinity College, Dublin, <http://www.bileta.ac.uk/98papers/wacks.html>.

Warren, S. and Brandeis, L. (1890). "The Right to Privacy," *Harvard Law Review 4* (193).

Walton, T. J. (1999). "Internet Privacy Law." *Internet Attorney,* <http://www.netatty.com/privacy/privacy.html>.

Whalen, D. (2001). "The Unofficial Cookie FAQ," Section 1.2, Version 2.53, <http://cookiecentral.com/faq>.

"Where Is Our Data?" (1997). *Secure Computing: The Magazine for the Protection of Information,* 18–22, August.

Wire and Electronic Communications Interception and Interception of Oral Communications. (2000). U.S. Code, Title 18, Chapter 19. The Legal Information Institute. Cornell Law School. <http://www4.law.cornell.edu/uscode/18/ch119.html>.

"Yahoo Pulls Phone Search." (1997). *CNET News.com,* 3 January, <http://news.cnet.com/news/0–1005–200–315556.html>.

Conclusion

This chapter raises the issue of privacy. Hinduja suggests frameworks for understanding how to interpret this issue. In addition, his frameworks are important for the interpretation of the issues and testing.

Discussion Questions

1. What's Hinduja's definition of privacy?
2. Why does Hinduja focus on privacy?
3. How does technology produce an opportunity to compromise privacy?

Text Credits

Chapter 2. Cyberharassment/Cyberstalking

Barak, A. (2005). Sexual harassment on the Internet. *Social Science Computer Review, 23,* 1, 77–92.

Ybarra, M. L., & Mitchell, K. J. (2004). Online aggressor/targets, aggressors, and targets: A comparison of associated youth characteristics. *Journal of Child Psychology and Psychiatry and Allied Disciplines, 45,* 1308–1316.

Chapter 3. Cyberpornography

Buzell, T. (2005). Demographic characteristics of persons using pornography in three technological contexts. *Sexuality and Culture, 9,* 1, 28–48.

Stack, S., Wasserman, I., & Kern, R. (2004). Adult social bonds and use of Internet pornography. *Social Science Quarterly, 85,* 1, 75–88. Reproduced with permission of Blackwell Publishing Ltd.

With kind permission from Springer Science+Business Media: *Sexuality & Culture,* Demographic characteristics of persons using pornography in three technological contexts, *9,* 2005, 28–48, Buzell, T.

Chapter 5. Intellectual Property Theft

With kind permission from Springer Science+Business Media: *Trends in organized Crime, Causes and Prevention of Intellectual Property Crime Trends in Organized Crime, 8,* (4), 2005, 40–61, Piquero, N. L.

Higgins, G. E., Fell, B. D., & Wilson, A. L. (2006). Digital piracy: Assessing the contributions of an integrated self-control theory and social learning theory. *Criminal Justice Studies: A Critical Journal of Crime, Law, and Society 19,* (1), 3–22. Reprinted by permission of Taylor and Francis.

Piquero, N. L. (2005). Causes and prevention of intellectual property crime. *Trends in Organized Crime, 8,* 4, 40–61.

Chapter 6. Hackers, Crackers, and Phone Phreaks

Wark, M., *Theory, Culture, & Society, Hackers, 23,* (2-3), pp. 320–322. (2004). Reprinted by permission of SAGE.

Chapter 7. Criminal Justice and Cyberspace

Hinduja, S. (2004). Perceptions of local and state law enforcement concerning the role of computer crime investigative teams. *Policing: An International Journal of Police Strategies & Management, 27,* 341–357.

Chapter 8. Future Issues

With kind permission from Springer Science+Business Media: *Knowledge, Technology, Theory and policy in online privacy & Policy, 17,* 2004, 38–58, Hiduja, S.

Hinduja, S. (2004). Theory and policy in online privacy. *Knowledge, Technology & Policy, 17,* 1, 38–58.

Index

Abacus Direct Corporation, 164
Active graphic gender harassment, 8
Active verbal sexual harassment, 7
Akers, R. L., 100–101, 112–113
Anonymity, and online behavior, 11–12, 33, 167
AOL, 164
Archer, Norm, 74–86
Assets, 85

Barak, Azy, 5–17
Behavior online
 disinhibition effect, 11–12
 gendered, 13
 identity and, 11–12, 33, 167
 Penta-A Engine, 11
 ways of affecting, 16, 36
Biometrics, 81, 86
Bork, Robert, 176
Bullying. *See* Online bullying
Business Software Alliance, 2, 91
Buzzell, Timothy, 40–53

Cable Communications Policy Act, 176
CCU. *See* Computer Crimes Unit
Center for Democracy and Technology
 (CDT), 172
Child pornography, 10, 64
Classical School of Criminology, 95
Computer crimes
 categories of, 1–2
 defined, 1–2, 134
 issues associated with, 138
 See also Cybercrimes
Computer Crimes Unit (CCU), 137–138, 141,
 143–145, 147–148
Computer Matching and Privacy Protection
 Act, 166
Conditioning of behavior, 101
Confidentiality, 71

Conservatism, 57–58
Consumer Privacy Protection Act, 70
Consumer Sentinel, 79
Cookies, 161–164
Copyleft, 89
Copyright Act, 110
Copyright Felony Act, 110
Copyrights, 89–90
Crackers, 130
Creative Commons Movement, 131
Criminal justice, 4
 digital forensics, 151–158
 law enforcement, 133–149
 See also Law enforcement
Culture, intellectual property theft and, 99.
 See also Cyberspace culture
Cybercrimes
 characteristics of, 138
 defined, 2
 extent of, 2–3
 forms of, 2
 law enforcement training in, 143–145, 146t, 147
 reporting of, 134
Cyberfraud. *See* Identity theft
Cyberharassment, 3
 bullying, 24–37
 sexual harassment, 5–17
Cyberpornography, 3
 analysis and discussion, 61–64
 deviant sexual lifestyles and, 58, 60, 63
 factors in use of, 55–64, 61t
 gender and, 63
 growth of, 55
 opportunity factors, 59, 60
 participant characteristics, 60–61, 63
 prevalence of, 52
 research methods, 59–61
 research on, 43, 53, 56–59
 sex-drivenness and, 58, 60

social bonds protecting against, 63
viewer characteristics, 49t, 50
See also Pornography
Cyberspace culture
characteristics of, 12–13
masculine emphasis in, 11–13, 15
ways of affecting, 16
Cyberstalking, 9

Deterrence theory, 95–96, 102
Deviant behavior
adult bonds protecting against, 57–58
privacy and, 172–174
sexual lifestyles, 58, 60, 63
social control theory and, 114–115
social learning theory and, 100–101, 113–115
Differential association, 99, 113, 117
Differential reinforcement, 113
Digital certificates, 82
Digital Forensic Research Workshop, 153
Digital forensics, 151–158
Digital piracy, 93–94, 109–121
enabling factors, 109
growth of, 109–110
legislation concerning, 110
research methods, 115–117, 126–127
research on, 110
research results and discussion, 117–121
self-control theory and, 111–112, 114–121
social learning theory and, 112–115
Digital Telephony Act, 166
DoubleClick, 164
Driver's Privacy Protection Act, 176

Eastern Michigan University (EMU), 143, 144
Economic Espionage Act, 103
Education
identity theft protection, 80–81
intellectual property theft, 102–103
of Michigan public, 137
online behaviors, 16, 36
Elbirt, A. J., 67–73
Electronic Communications Privacy Act, 166
Electronic Frontier Foundation (EFF), 172
Electronic Privacy Information Center
(EPIC), 172
ENCASE (forensic tool), 144
Equifax, 79, 169
Equity theory, 96–98
Ethical decision-making process, 98–99
Experian, 79

Fair and Accurate Credit Transactions Act, 70
Fair Credit Reporting Act, 176
Federal Bureau of Investigation (FBI), 79,
134, 143
Federal Trade Commission, 3

Fell, Brian D., 109–121
Flaming, 8
Forensic science. *See* Digital forensics
Fourth Amendment, 165
Free Software Movement, 131

Galactic Network, 2
Gender
cyberpornography and, 63
harassment, 7–8
intellectual property theft and, 94, 98–99
online behavior and, 13
See also Masculinity; Women
General Social Survey (GSS), 43–44
Georgia Tech University, 160
Gottfredson, M. R., 111–112, 114
Gramm-Leach-Blily Act, 69–70, 169
Graphic gender harassment, 8
Grasmick et al. scale, 116, 118
Guidance Software, 143–144

Hackers, 4, 129–131
Harassment. *See* Cyberharassment
Hardt, Michael, 130
Health Insurance Portability and Accountability
Act (HIPPA), 69
Higgins, George E., 109–121
High Technology Crime Investigation
Association (HTCIA), 143
Hinduja, Sameer, 133–149, 159–177
Hirschi, T., 111–112, 114
Hypersexualism. *See* Sex-drivenness

Identity, online behavior and, 11–12, 33, 167
Identity certificates, 75–76, 82
Identity checkers, 78–79
Identity issuers, 78
Identity owners, 78
Identity protectors, 79
Identity theft, 4, 67–86
contextual framework, 76–79, 77f
cost-benefit analysis of countermeasures,
85–86
current problems, 84t
defined, 67
detection of, 82–83
effects of, 68
future research, 84–86
growth of, 67–68, 74
legislation regarding, 69–70, 83–84
perpetrators of, 75
prevention technologies, 81–82
protection against, 70–73, 79–84, 80t
recovering from, 72–73
risk management, 84–85
stakeholders in, 78–79, 80t
tactics of, 68–69, 75–76

Identity Theft and Assumption Deterrence Act, 69, 79, 83
Identity thieves, 75
Image Data, 165
Imitation, 113
Information security
 confidentiality, 71
 disposal, 72
 importance of, 68
 methods of, 74
 storage, 71–72
 tracking, 71
 See also Identity theft
Intellectual property
 characteristics of, 90–91
 defined, 88–89
 hackers and, 131
 importance of, 89
 protections concerning, 89
 types, 89–90
 See also Intellectual property theft
Intellectual property theft, 4
 causes of, 93–102, 104–105
 costs of, 91–92
 deterrence of, 95–96, 102
 digital piracy, 109–121
 equity theory and, 96–98
 ethical decision-making process and, 98–99
 extent of, 91
 future research, 104–106
 law enforcement effects, 105
 legislation concerning, 96, 103, 110
 opportunity factors, 93–94
 participant characteristics, 94–95
 prevalence of, 104
 prevention technologies, 102
 protections against, 92–93, 102–105
 social learning theory and, 100–102, 112–115
 theory of reasoned action and, 99–100
International Association of Computer Investigative Specialists (IACIS), 143
International Federation of Phonographic Industries, 110
Internet
 access to, 149
 beneficial and harmful uses of, 6, 17, 134, 149
 development of, 2
 security on, 2
 user access and capabilities, 59
Internet Crimes Against Children (ICAC), 137
Internet harassment. *See* Cyberharassment; Online bullying

Johnson Commission, 46

Katz v. United States (1967), 176
Kern, Roger, 55–64

Lane, F. S., III, 41–42
Law enforcement, 15, 133–149
 cybercrime needs in, 149
 cybercrime training, 143–145, 146t, 147
 future research, 148
 history of MSP, 136–138
 intellectual property theft, 105
 research findings and discussion, 141–148
 research methods, 138–141
 state and local needs, 135–136, 144–145, 145t
 types of crimes handled, 141, 142t
Learning theory. *See* Social learning theory
Legal issues
 enforcement, 15
 identity theft, 69–70, 83–84
 lack of boundaries, 12
 sexual harassment, 12, 15
 See also Legislation
Legislation
 digital piracy, 110
 identity theft, 69–70, 83–84
 intellectual property theft, 96, 103, 110
 privacy, 165–166, 176
 sexual harassment, 15
Lexis-Nexis, 164
Liberty Alliance, 82
Licklider, J. C. R., 2

Marriage, 57
Masculinity
 and flaming, 8
 of online environment, 11–13, 15
 See also Gender
Massachusetts Institute of Technology (MIT), 129
Meese Commission, 41, 42, 44, 52
Michigan Office of Attorney General, 137, 144
Michigan State Police (MSP), 135–148, 139t, 140t
Microsoft Passport, 82
Middle Atlantic-Great Lakes Organized Crime Law Enforcement Network (MAGLOCLEN), 143, 144
Miller v. California (1973), 46
Mitchell, Kimberly J., 24–37
Motion Picture Association of America (MPAA), 2, 91, 103
MSP. *See* Michigan State Police (MSP)

Napster, 102
National Information Infrastructure Task Force (NIITF) Privacy Working Group, 176
National Institute of Justice, 106, 135, 147
National Institute of Standards and Technology (NIST), 158
Negri, Antonio, 130
Netscape Corporation, 152
Networks, computer, 2
No Electronic Theft Act, 110

Office of the U.S. Trade Representative, 92
Online behavior. *See* Behavior online
Online bullying, 24–37
    compared to offline, 25–26, 32–33
    effects of, 32
    measures of, 27–29, 34
    participant characteristics, 25–26, 30,
        31t, 32–35
    prevention of, 35–36
    psychosocial challenge and, 35
    research methods, 26–30
    research results and discussion, 30–36
Online disinhibition effect, 11–12
Online stalking, 9
Open Source Movement, 131
Opportunity theory, 59, 62, 63
Opt-out policies, 169

Passive graphic gender harassment, 8
Passive verbal sexual harassment, 8
Patents, 89
Penta-A Engine, 11
Pentagon. *See* U.S. Department of Defense
Personal Information Protection and Electronic
        Documents Act (PIPEDA) (Canada), 83–84
Phishing, 75
PhoneBusters, 79
Piquero, Nicole Leeper, 88–106
Piracy, 93–94. *See also* Digital piracy
Piracy and Counterfeiting Amendments
        Act, 110
Pollitt, Mark M., 151–158
Pornography
    attitudes toward, 64
    effects of, 64
    interpretations of, 52
    prevalence of, 55
    research findings and discussion, 45–51
    research methods, 44–45
    research on technology and, 42–51
    social control theory and, 57–58
    technological influences on, 40–53
    viewer characteristics, 46, 47–49t, 50–52
    See also Cyberpornography
Privacy, 159–177
    attitudes and knowledge concerning,
        160–161, 168–169
    case studies, 164–165
    data collection and use, 161–164,
        168–172, 176
    identity theft and, 86
    legislation concerning, 165–166, 176
    offline protections for, 159, 167–168
    routine activities and, 160, 172–175
    social control and, 159, 166–172, 174–175
Privacy Act, 165–166
Punishment, 101

Rand, Ayn, 159
Reciprocation, 97
Recording Industry Association of America, 91
Reinforcement, 101, 113
Religion, as factor in pornography use,
        57, 59, 62, 63
Right to Financial Privacy Act, 176
Risk management, 84–85
Rotenberg, Marc, 168
Routine activities, privacy and, 160, 172–175
Royal Canadian Mounted Police (RCMP), 79

SEARCH (National Consortium for Justice
        Information and Statistics), 143
Self-control theory, 111–112, 114–121
Self-regulation, of corporate information
        gathering, 171–172
Senate Bill 893, 103
Sex-drivenness, 58, 60
Sexual coercion, 7, 9–10
Sexual harassment on the Internet, 5–17
    categories of, 7
    compared to offline, 6–7
    dynamics of, 11–14
    effects of, 14–15
    gender harassment, 7–8
    prevalence of, 10
    prevention of, 15–16
    scope of, 10
    sexual coercion, 9–10
    unwanted sexual attention, 9
SIDE (Social Identity explanation of
        Deindividuation Effects), 11–12
Smart cards, 82
Social control, privacy and, 159, 166–172, 174–175
Social control theory, 56–57, 62–63, 167
Social Identity explanation of Deindividuation
        Effects (SIDE), 11–12
Social learning theory, 100–102, 112–115
Social Security Misuse Prevention Act, 70
Social security numbers, 70, 71
Socioeconomic bonds, 58, 60
Software piracy. *See* Digital piracy
Spoofing, 75
Stack, Steven, 55–64
Stalking, online, 9
Stallman, Richard, 130
Structural equation modeling (SEM), 117–118
Subcultures, 129–131

Technology crime, 1
Theory of reasoned action, 99–100
Threats, 85
Trademark Counterfeiting Act, 103
Trademarks, 89–90
Trade-Related Aspects of Intellectual Property
        Rights (TRIPS), 92

Trade secrets, 90
Transactional data, 161–164, 168–172, 176
TransUnion, 79
Tribe, Laurence, 175
Twenty-Seventh Amendment, proposed, 175

Universal Declaration of Human Rights, 165
Unwanted sexual attention, 7, 9
USA PATRIOT Act, 70
U.S. Constitution, 165
U.S. Department of Defense (Pentagon), 130, 143
U.S. Department of Justice, 106, 137, 143
U.S. Secret Service, 134, 165
U.S. Visitor and Immigrant Status Indicator
    (US-VISIT) Technology, 86

Verbal sexual harassment, 7–8
Video Privacy Act, 176
Violent Crime Control and Law Enforcement
    Act, 176
Vulnerabilities, 85

Wang, Wenjie, 74–86
Wark, McKenzie, 129–131
Wasserman, Ira, 55–64
White Collar Crime Center, 143, 144
Williams, L., 41–42, 52
Wilson, Abby L., 109–121
Women
    and flaming, 8
    online environment hostile to, 8, 13, 15
    See also Gender; Sexual harassment on
        the Internet
World Trade Organization (WTO), 92

Yahoo, 164
Ybarra, Michele L., 24–37
Yuan, Yufei, 74–86